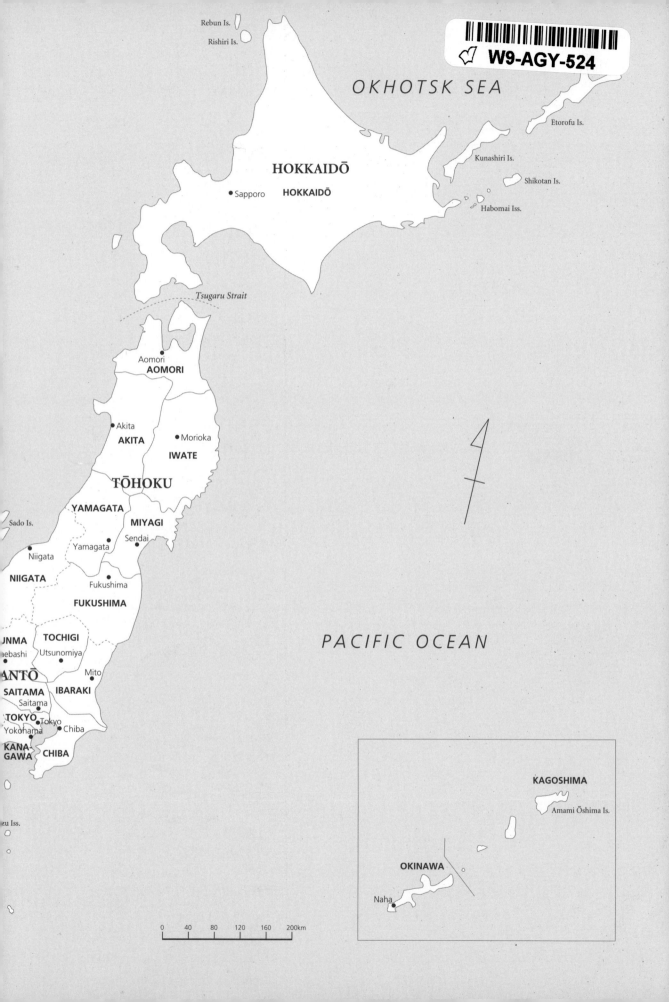

JAPANESE FOR BUSY PEOPLE I

JAPANESE FOR BUSY PEOPLE

Revised 3rd Edition

I

Romanized Version

Association for Japanese-Language Teaching
AjALT

KODANSHA INTERNATIONAL
Tokyo • New York • London

The Association for Japanese-Language Teaching (AJALT) was recognized as a nonprofit organization by the Ministry of Education in 1977. It was established to meet the practical needs of people who are not necessarily specialists on Japan but who wish to communicate effectively in Japanese. In 1992 AJALT was awarded the Japan Foundation Special Prize. AJALT maintains a website at www.ajalt.org, through which they can be contacted with questions regarding this book or any of their other publications.

Illustrations by Shinsaku Sumi.

CD narration by Yuki Minatsuki, Aya Ogawa, Yuri Haruta, Koji Yoshida, Tatsuo Endo, Sosei Shinbori, and Howard Colefield.

CD recording and editing by the English Language Education Council, Inc.

PHOTO CREDITS: © Sachiyo Yasuda, 1, 19, 47, 87, 159 (timetable only), 177, 203, 221. © Sebun Photo, 67. © JTB Photo Communications, Inc., 69 (top). © Orion Press, 109. © Ben Simmons, 139. © iStockphoto. com/Lawrence Karn, 159. Tokyo National Museum (Image: TNM Image Archives; Source: http://TnmArchives.jp/), 188.

Distributed in the United States by Kodansha America, LLC, and in the United Kingdom and continental Europe by Kodansha Europe Ltd.

Published by Kodansha International Ltd., 17–14 Otowa 1-chome, Bunkyo-ku, Tokyo 112–8652.

First published 1984
Second edition 1994
Third edition 2006
18 17 16 15 14 13 12 11 10 09 08   15 14 13 12 11 10 9 8 7 6 5

Library of Congress Cataloging-in-Publication Data

Japanese for busy people. I, Romanized version / Association for
  Japanese-Language Teaching.—Rev. 3rd ed.
        p. cm.
  Includes index.
  ISBN 978-4–7700–3008–5
  1. Japanese language—Textbooks for foreign speakers—English. I.
Kokusai Nihongo Fukyu Kyokai (Japan)

PL539.5.J3 J359 2006
495.6'82421—dc22

2006040889

CONTENTS

UNIT 1   MEETING PEOPLE   1

GRAMMAR   2

| LESSON 1   3 | ■ Talk about nationalities and occupations |
| INTRODUCTIONS | ■ Introduce yourself and others, at your workplace or at a party |

| LESSON 2   9 | ■ Talk about a nearby object and its owner |
| EXCHANGING BUSINESS CARDS | ■ Ask for telephone numbers |

UNIT 2   SHOPPING   19

GRAMMAR   20

| LESSON 3   21 | ■ Talk about the times of meetings and parties |
| ASKING ABOUT BUSINESS HOURS | ■ Ask the hours of services in stores and hotels |

| LESSON 4   28 | ■ Ask the prices of items in a store and make a purchase |
| SHOPPING, PART I | |

| LESSON 5   37 | ■ Ask what the size, color, and country of origin of an item is, and buy the item |
| SHOPPING, PART II | ■ Buy one or more of an item, telling the clerk how many you need |

QUIZ 1 (UNITS 1–2)   45

UNIT 3   GETTING AROUND   47

GRAMMAR   48

| LESSON 6   49 | ■ Talk about where you will go, when, and with whom |
| CONFIRMING SCHEDULES | |

| LESSON 7   59 | ■ Talk about travel destinations, places and people to visit, dates and times, and means of transportation |
| VISITING ANOTHER COMPANY | |

PREFACE
TO THE REVISED 3RD EDITION

The new *Japanese for Busy People* is made up of three volumes: Book I (available in both romanized and *kana* editions), Book II, and Book III. *Japanese for Busy People I* was first published in 1984. It was based on materials used by AJALT teachers with more than ten years of experience teaching Japanese at every level from beginning to advanced.

The series was first revised in 1994, when *Japanese for Busy People II* was divided into two volumes, Book II and Book III. Only a minimum number of modifications were made to Book I at that time. This 3rd Edition, then, constitutes the first major revision of Book I. It involves a wide variety of changes, including the adoption of a unit-based structure, notes about Japanese culture, new and expanded exercises, and updated dialogues. The authors have made every effort to apply the results of the most recent research in Japanese-language education to ensure that learners acquire a clearer understanding of the situations in which Japanese is actually used, and gain increased confidence in their communicative abilities.

It is our fervent hope that this book will inspire people to learn more about Japan and the Japanese language.

Acknowledgments for *Japanese for Busy people I* (1st edition, 1984)
Compilation of this textbook has been a cooperative endeavor, and we deeply appreciate the collective efforts and individual contributions of Mss. Sachiko Adachi, Nori Ando, Haruko Matsui, Shigeko Miyazaki, Sachiko Okaniwa, Terumi Sawada, and Yuriko Yobuko. For English translations and editorial assistance, we wish to thank Ms. Dorothy Britton.

Acknowledgments for *Japanese for Busy People I, Revised Edition* (1994)
We would like to express our gratitude to the following people: Mss. Haruko Matsui, Junko Shinada, Keiko Ito, Mikiko Ochiai, and Satoko Mizoguchi.

Acknowledgments for *Japanese for Busy People I, Revised 3rd Edition*
Six AJALT teachers have written this textbook. They are Mss. Yoko Hattori, Sakae Tanabe, Izumi Sawa, Motoko Iwamoto, Shigeyo Tsutsui, and Takako Kobayashi. They were assisted by Ms. Reiko Sawane.

INTRODUCTION

Aims

This first volume of *Japanese for Busy People, Revised 3rd Edition* has been developed to meet the needs of busy beginning learners seeking an effective method of acquiring a natural command of spoken Japanese in a limited amount of time. The book is suitable for both those studying with a teacher and those studying on their own. In order to minimize the burden on busy learners, the vocabulary and grammar items presented have been narrowed down to about a third of those introduced in a typical first-year course. However, the textbook is set up so that learners can use the material they have learned right away in conversations with speakers of Japanese. In other words, *Japanese for Busy People I* is a textbook for learning "survival Japanese."

Despite this, *Japanese for Busy People I* does not present simple, childish Japanese. That is, we do not focus on mere grammatical correctness. Instead, we place our emphasis on conversational patterns that actually occur. Thus, by studying with this book, learners will acquire the most essential language patterns for everyday life, and be able to express their intentions in uncomplicated adult-level Japanese. They will also start to build a basis for favorable relations with the people around them by talking about themselves and their surroundings and circumstances, and asking about those of others.

This book is intended for beginners, but it can also provide a firm foundation for more advanced study. Learners can acquire a general idea of the nature of the Japanese language as they study the dialogues and notes in it. For this reason, *Japanese for Busy People I* is suitable as a review text for those who already know a certain amount of Japanese but want to confirm that they are using the language correctly.

Major features of *Japanese for Busy People I, Revised 3rd Edition*

In this newly revised version of *Japanese for Busy People I*, we have made the following modifications to ensure that those studying Japanese for the first time will have an enjoyable and effective learning experience.

Adoption of a unit structure. The content of the thirty lessons that made up the previous editions of *Japanese for Busy People I* has been reedited into eleven units, each consisting of two or three lessons linked by a single theme. The reason for this new design is that we believe learning sociocultural information, linguistic information, and communication strategies in an interrelated way is important for producing natural and appropriate Japanese.

Culture notes. We have placed culture notes at the beginning of each unit. These notes describe Japanese customs and events, as well as features of Japan itself. Here our intention is to get learners interested in the lives and customs of the Japanese people, in order to increase their desire to learn Japanese and deepen their understanding of it. We hope that as readers come into contact with the social and cultural information presented in these notes, they will gain an awareness of cultural diversity and acquire specific mental images of the themes introduced in the units.

Practice. In this section we have drawn on our classroom experience as well as recent thinking in Japanese-language education to reconstruct and revise the exercises to emphasize both language production and comprehension. Recognizing the importance of vocabulary acquisition at the beginning stages, for example, we have added a "Word Power" subsection that presents the major vocabulary that forms the basis for learning in the lesson. Here we have taken great pains with the presentation of the vocabulary, grouping similar items together to make them easier for learners to memorize. In addition, we have stated and highlighted in italics the intention of each exercise so that learners can understand it at a glance. The exercises themselves incorporate drawings, charts, tables, and other illustrations that we hope will make for a stimulating learning experience. Finally, we have added brief listening exercises to each lesson.

Other features. A 70-minute CD containing the Target Dialogues, Word Power sections, listening exercises, and Short Dialogues is attached to the inside back cover of this book. Additional features of this textbook include profiles of the characters who appear in it and an expanded contents page that lets learners see at a glance the goals to be achieved in each unit. We have also added quizzes every few units, so that learners can consolidate their understanding of recently introduced language.

The structure of the unit

A unit is made up of a culture note, a page on grammar, and two or three lessons. The culture notes are designed to stimulate interest in the themes of each unit and help learners construct a mental image of what they are going to learn. The grammar page, appearing right after the culture note, provides simple explanations of the basic grammatical items introduced in the unit. To the extent possible, the explanations here do not cover knowledge or information beyond that which pertains to the usage of the grammatical items in the unit.

The twenty-five lessons in Book I are each composed of the following four elements:

Target Dialogue. The Target Dialogues, which appear at the beginning of each lesson, indicate specifically what kinds of things the learner will be able to talk about after studying the lesson. We have limited these dialogues to practical expressions and grammatical items necessary for everyday conversation. Vocabulary lists, as well as notes that explain particularly difficult expressions, accompany the dialogues.

Practice. The Practice section consists of Word Power, Key Sentences, and Exercises. Word Power introduces basic vocabulary that learners should memorize before moving on to the other exercises. The words in this section are introduced with the aid of illustrations and charts, and all are available on the CD. The Key Sentences demonstrate the grammatical items from the lesson by using them in simple sentences. Finally, the Exercises consist of five different types of practice activities:

(1) Exercises that consist of repeating vocabulary or the conjugations of verbs or adjectives.

(2) Basic sentence-pattern exercises that aim to help learners comprehend the sentence structures of Japanese and gain an idea of their meanings.

(3) Substitution drills and drills in the form of dialogues that lead to conversation practice.

(4) Conversation practice created with an awareness of the situations and circumstances in which Japanese is actually used.

(5) 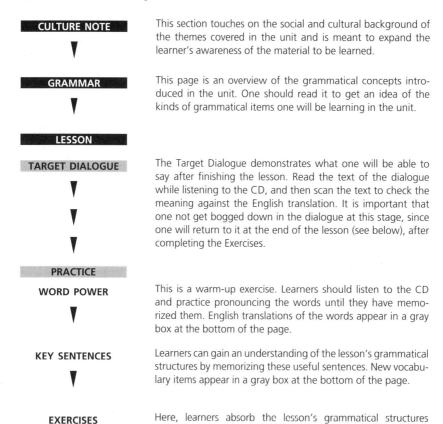 Listening exercises in which learners listen to the CD and answer questions about what they hear.

Practicing exercise types (1), (2), and (3) allows learners to make a smooth transition to type (4), the conversation practice, and finally to move on to the Target Dialogue.

Short Dialogue(s). These are relatively short conversations that demonstrate helpful expressions, ways of getting people's attention, and ways of acknowledging what people have said. Like the Target Dialogues, they are often accompanied by notes that explain points to be aware of when using certain phrases and expressions.

Active Communication. This section, coming at the very end of the lesson, presents one or two tasks for which the learners themselves select the vocabulary, grammar, and expressions they need from the material in the lesson and use them in actual situations or classroom-based communication activities.

Using *Japanese for Busy People I*

We recommend the following methods of use, both for those who use *Japanese for Busy People I* as teachers and for self-taught learners. Materials should be adapted flexibly, depending on the learner's circumstances, but as a rule it should take about sixty hours to finish *Japanese for Busy People I.* We suggest learners proceed through the lessons as follows, with each lesson taking about two hours.

CULTURE NOTE

This section touches on the social and cultural background of the themes covered in the unit and is meant to expand the learner's awareness of the material to be learned.

GRAMMAR

This page is an overview of the grammatical concepts introduced in the unit. One should read it to get an idea of the kinds of grammatical items one will be learning in the unit.

LESSON

TARGET DIALOGUE

The Target Dialogue demonstrates what one will be able to say after finishing the lesson. Read the text of the dialogue while listening to the CD, and then scan the text to check the meaning against the English translation. It is important that one not get bogged down in the dialogue at this stage, since one will return to it at the end of the lesson (see below), after completing the Exercises.

PRACTICE

WORD POWER

This is a warm-up exercise. Learners should listen to the CD and practice pronouncing the words until they have memorized them. English translations of the words appear in a gray box at the bottom of the page.

KEY SENTENCES

Learners can gain an understanding of the lesson's grammatical structures by memorizing these useful sentences. New vocabulary items appear in a gray box at the bottom of the page.

EXERCISES

Here, learners absorb the lesson's grammatical structures through exercises that ask one to apply them. The exercises usually begin with vocabulary repetition or conjugation practice, then move on to tasks in which one is asked to make up sentences or dialogues and, finally, to full-fledged conversation reenactment. The last exercise, recorded on the CD, is intended to help learners hone their listening skills.

SHORT DIALOGUE(S)	One should thoroughly practice these short dialogues that contain handy, frequently used expressions. If one practices them so thoroughly that they begin to come naturally, one will be able to use them in a variety of situations.
▼ ▼	
TARGET DIALOGUE	The Target Dialogue is the culmination of one's study of the lesson. After learners have finished the exercises, they should return to the Target Dialogue and practice it.
▼ ▼	
ACTIVE COMMUNICATION	If the learner is in an environment that allows him or her to perform linguistic tasks, he or she should test himself or herself with the challenges presented here.

Introducing the characters

The following characters feature in this textbook. Since they often appear in the exercises, it is a good idea to remember their names, faces, and relationships.

Sumisu

Mike Smith (32 years old), an American, is an attorney for ABC Foods. He is single.

Chan

Mei Chan (30 years old) is from Hong Kong. She works in ABC Foods' sales department. She is single.

Gurīn

Frank Green (56 years old), an American, is the president of the Tokyo branch of ABC Foods. He lives in Tokyo with his wife.

Sasaki

Keiko Sasaki (53 years old), a Japanese, is the department manager of ABC Foods' sales department. She is married.

Katō

Akira Kato (46 years old), a Japanese, is the section chief of ABC Foods' sales department. He is married.

Nakamura

Mayumi Nakamura (26 years old), a Japanese, works as a secretary to Ms. Sasaki. She is single.

Suzuki

Daisuke Suzuki (24 years old), a Japanese, is a member of ABC Foods' sales staff. He is single.

Takahashi

Shingo Takahashi (48 years old), a Japanese, works for Nozomi Department Store, where he is the division chief of the sales department. His wife's name is Junko.

Yamamoto

Ichiro Yamamoto (45 years old), a Japanese, is the president of the Kyoto branch of ABC Foods.

In addition to the above, the following people also appear in this book: Hideo Ogawa (male, 49 years old, a friend of Mr. Green), Taro Yamada (male, a banker and a friend of Mr. Smith), and Ayako Matsui (female, the Greens' next-door neighbor).

WRITING AND PRONUNCIATION

There are three writing systems in Japanese:

1. *Kanji*: Chinese characters as used to represent words of both Chinese and native-Japanese origin, most of which have at least two readings.
2. *Hiragana*: A phonetic syllabary. The symbols are curvilinear in style.
3. *Katakana*: Another syllabary used primarily for foreign names and words of foreign origin. The symbols are made up of straight lines.

Written Japanese normally makes use of all three of these systems, as in the following example:

"I am going to Canada."　私　は カ ナ ダ に 行 きます。

Watashi wa　Kanada　ni　i　kimasu.

kanji	私			行	
hiragana		は		に	きます
katakana			カナダ		

Besides these three systems, Japanese is sometimes written in *romaji* (roman letters), particularly for the convenience of foreigners. *Romaji* is generally used in teaching conversational Japanese when time is limited. There are various ways of romanizing Japanese, but in this book we use the modified Hepburn system.

Hiragana, katakana and romaji

The *kana* to the left are *hiragana*; *katakana* are in parentheses.

I. Basic syllables: vowel, consonant plus vowel, and **n**

c＼v	a	i	u	e	o
	a あ (ア)	i い (イ)	u う (ウ)	e え (エ)	o お (オ)
k	ka か (カ)	ki き (キ)	ku く (ク)	ke け (ケ)	ko こ (コ)
s	sa さ (サ)	shi し (シ)	su す (ス)	se せ (セ)	so そ (ソ)
t	ta た (タ)	chi ち (チ)	tsu つ (ツ)	te て (テ)	to と (ト)
n	na な (ナ)	ni に (ニ)	nu ぬ (ヌ)	ne ね (ネ)	no の (ノ)
h	ha は (ハ)	hi ひ (ヒ)	fu ふ (フ)	he へ (ヘ)	ho ほ (ホ)
m	ma ま (マ)	mi み (ミ)	mu む (ム)	me め (メ)	mo も (モ)
y	ya や (ヤ)	[i い (イ)]	yu ゆ (ユ)	[e え (エ)]	yo よ (ヨ)
r	ra ら (ラ)	ri り (リ)	ru る (ル)	re れ (レ)	ro ろ (ロ)
w	wa わ (ワ)	[i い (イ)]	[u う (ウ)]	[e え (エ)]	o を (ヲ)
n	— ん (ン)				

NOTE: The syllables **yi**, **ye**, **wi**, **wu**, and **we** do not occur in modern Japanese.

II. Modified syllables: consonant plus basic vowel

g	ga が（ガ）	gi ぎ（ギ）	gu ぐ（グ）	ge げ（ゲ）	go ご（ゴ）
z	za ざ（ザ）	ji じ（ジ）	zu ず（ズ）	ze ぜ（ゼ）	zo ぞ（ゾ）
d	da だ（ダ）	ji ぢ（ヂ）	zu づ（ヅ）	de で（デ）	do ど（ド）
b	ba ば（バ）	bi び（ビ）	bu ぶ（ブ）	be べ（ベ）	bo ぼ（ボ）
p	pa ぱ（パ）	pi ぴ（ピ）	pu ぷ（プ）	pe ぺ（ペ）	po ぽ（ポ）

III. Modified syllables: consonant plus **ya**, **yu**, **yo**

kya きゃ（キャ）	kyu きゅ（キュ）	kyo きょ（キョ）
sha しゃ（シャ）	shu しゅ（シュ）	sho しょ（ショ）
cha ちゃ（チャ）	chu ちゅ（チュ）	cho ちょ（チョ）
nya にゃ（ニャ）	nyu にゅ（ニュ）	nyo にょ（ニョ）
hya ひゃ（ヒャ）	hyu ひゅ（ヒュ）	hyo ひょ（ヒョ）
mya みゃ（ミャ）	myu みゅ（ミュ）	myo みょ（ミョ）
rya りゃ（リャ）	ryu りゅ（リュ）	ryo りょ（リョ）
gya ぎゃ（ギャ）	gyu ぎゅ（ギュ）	gyo ぎょ（ギョ）
ja じゃ（シャ）	ju じゅ（ジュ）	jo じょ（ジョ）
bya びゃ（ビャ）	byu びゅ（ビュ）	byo びょ（ビョ）
pya ぴゃ（ピャ）	pyu ぴゅ（ピュ）	pyo ぴょ（ピョ）

IV. Double consonants (See note 6 on next page.)

kk, pp, ss, tt	っ（ッ）

V. Long vowels

ā	ああ	（アー）
ii, ī	いい	（イー）
ū	うう	（ウー）
ē, ei	ええ、えい	（エー）
ō	おう、おお	（オー）

(handwritten notes in right margin:)
Otó san - father
"-" say it longer
kiku - to listen
kite - to come
massugu - straight

Points to note

1. The top line of the Japanese syllabary (chart I) consists of the five vowels **a**, **i**, **u**, **e**, and **o**. They are short vowels, pronounced clearly and crisply. If you pronounce the vowels in the following English sentence, making them all short, you will have their approximate sounds. The **u** is pronounced without rounding the lips.

   Ah,   we   soon   get   old.
   a   **i**   **u**   **e**   **o**

2. Long vowels are written as shown in chart V. Both **ē** and **ei** are used for an elongated **e**, which in Japanese is either ええ or えい. Long vowels are a doubling of a single vowel, so care should be taken to pronounce them as a continuous sound, equal in value to two identical short vowels.

3. The rest of the syllabary from the second line down in chart I are syllables formed by a consonant and a vowel.

4. Japanese consonants more or less resemble those in English. Listen to the Japanese recorded on the attached CD, or to a native speaker, for the exact sounds. Especially note the following: *t* in the **ta** row, *f* in the syllable **fu**, and *r* in the **ra** row. The *g* in the syllables **ga**, **gi**, **gu**, **ge**, and **go** at the beginning of a word is hard (like the [g] in *garden*), but when it occurs in the middle or last syllable of a word (as in **eiga**, "movie"), it takes on a nasal sound, like the [g] in *thing*. The particle **ga**, too, is usually nasal, although many Japanese today use a [g] sound that is not nasal.

   N is the only independent consonant not combined with a vowel. When it is at the end of a word, it is pronounced somewhat nasally. Otherwise it is usually pronounced like the English [n]. But if **n** is followed by syllables beginning with *b*, *m*, or *p*, it is pronounced more like [m] and accordingly spelled with an *m* in this textbook (except for when it appears before a hyphen, e.g., **nan-ban** not **nam-ban**). Special care is necessary when **n** is followed by a vowel, as in the word **kin'en** (**ki-n-en**, "nonsmoking"); note that this is different in syllable division from **kinen** (**ki-ne-n**, "anniversary").

5. *Hiragana* and *katakana* are phonetic symbols, and each symbol is one syllable in length. The syllables in chart III that consist of two characters—the second written smaller—are also only one syllable in length, although if elongated by the addition of a vowel (i.e., きゃあ **kyā**, きゅう **kyū**, きょう **kyō**) they become two syllables.

6. What are written in roman letters as the double consonants **kk**, **pp**, **ss**, and **tt** in chart IV are expressed in *kana* (*hiragana* and *katakana*) with a small っ (ッ) in place of the first consonant, i.e., けっこん **kekkon** ("marriage"), きっぷ **kippu** ("ticket"), まっすぐ **massugu** ("straight"), and きって **kitte** ("stamp"). This small っ is one syllable in length, and there is the slightest pause after it is pronounced (as between the *k*'s in *bookkeeping*). In the case of the **chi** syllable, the **tsu** is represented by a *t* in roman letters, i.e., マッチ **matchi** ("match").

7. In *hiragana*, the syllables **ji** and **zu** are written じ and ず as a general rule. In a few rare cases they are traditionally written ぢ and づ.

8. *Hiragana* follows a tradition in which the following three particles are written a special way:

   o when used as a particle is written を, not お.
   e when used as a particle is written へ, not え.
   wa when used as a particle is written は, not わ.

CHARACTERISTICS OF JAPANESE GRAMMAR

The grammar in this text is derived from a natural analysis of the Japanese language, rather than being an interpretation adapted to the syntax of Western languages. We have given as few technical terms as possible, choosing ones that will make for a smooth transition from the basic level to more advanced study.

The following points are basic and in most cases reflect differences between the grammars of Japanese and English.

1. Japanese nouns have neither gender nor number. But plurals of certain words can be expressed by the use of suffixes.

2. The verb (or the copula **desu**) comes at the end of the sentence or clause.

    ex. **Watashi wa Nihon-jin desu.** "I am a Japanese."
    Watashi wa Kyōto ni ikimasu. "I go (or *will go*) to Kyoto."

3. The gender, number, or person of the subject does not affect the other parts of the sentence.

4. Verb conjugation shows only two tenses, the "present form" and the "past form." Whether use of the "present form" refers to habitual action or the future, and whether the "past form" is equivalent to the English past tense, present perfect, or past perfect can usually be determined from the context.

5. Japanese adjectives, unlike English ones, inflect for tense (present and past) and mood (for example, to show whether the word is negative).

6. The grammatical function of nouns is indicated by particles. Their role is similar to English prepositions, but since they always come after the word, they are sometimes referred to as *postpositions*.

    ex. **Tōkyō de**, "at Tokyo"
    15-nichi ni, "on the 15th (of the month)"

7. Many degrees of politeness are expressible in Japanese. In this book the style is one that anyone may use without being rude.

NOTE: The following abbreviations are used in this book:

aff.	affirmative
neg.	negative
A*a*:	answer, affirmative
A*n*:	answer, negative
ex.	example
-i adj.	**-i** adjective
-na adj.	**-na** adjective

USEFUL DAILY EXPRESSIONS

1. おはようございます。**Ohayō gozaimasu.** "Good morning." Used until about 10:00 a.m.

2. こんにちは。**Konnichiwa.** "Hello." A rather informal greeting used from about 10:00 a.m. until sundown.

3. こんばんは。**Kombanwa.** "Good evening."

4. おやすみなさい。**Oyasuminasai.** "Good night." Said at night before going to bed and when parting at night during late hours outside the home.

5. さようなら。**Sayōnara.** "Good-bye." On more formal occasions one uses **shitsureishimasu**.

6. では／じゃ　また。**Dewa/Ja mata.** "Well then . . ." Said informally when parting from relatives or friends.

7. おさきに　しつれいします。**O-sakini shitsureishimasu.** Said when leaving the office or a meeting before other people.

8. いってらっしゃい。**Itterasshai.** "So long." (*lit.*, "Go and come back.") Said to members of a household as they leave the house. Occasionally it is used at work.

9. いってきます。**Ittekimasu.** "So long." (*lit.*, "[I'm] going and coming back.") This expression forms a pair with **itterasshai**. (See 8 above.) Occasionally it is used at work. A politer form is **ittemairimasu**.

10. ただいま。**Tadaima.** "I'm back." (*lit.*, "[I have returned] just now.") Said by a person on returning home. Occasionally it is used at work.

11. おかえりなさい。**Okaerinasai.** "Welcome home." This expression forms a pair with **tadaima**. (See 10 above.) Occasionally it is used at work.

12. いただきます。**Itadakimasu.** Said before eating a meal.

13. ごちそうさまでした。**Gochisōsamadeshita.** Said after eating a meal.

14. おめでとうございます。**Omedetō gozaimasu.** "Congratulations."

15. どうも　ありがとうございます。**Dōmo arigatō gozaimasu.** "Thank you very much."

16. どういたしまして。**Dō itashimashite.** "You're welcome."

17. すみません。**Sumimasen.** "Excuse me," "I'm sorry."

18. ちょっと　まってください。**Chotto matte kudasai.** "Wait just a moment, please."

19. もう　いちど　おねがいします。**Mō ichi-do onegaishimasu.** "Once more, please."

20. どうぞ　おさきに。**Dōzo o-sakini.** "Please, go ahead."

21. きをつけて。**Ki o tsukete.** "Take care," "Be careful."

22. おだいじに。**O-daijini.** "Take care of yourself." Used toward an ill or injured person.

MEETING PEOPLE

In Japan, people bow rather than shake hands, hug, or kiss, when they meet for the first time. A typical bow is performed with both feet together, the hands flat on the thighs (for men) or crossed in front (for women), and the torso inclined at a 15- to 45-degree angle. The eyes remain open during the bow, and the bowing person's line of sight moves with his or her torso rather than staying fixed on the other person. Generally, the deeper and slower the bow, the politer it is. Bowing properly is essential to making a good first impression, so we recommend practicing it until you become comfortable with it.

1 GRAMMAR

Identifying People and Things

noun 1 **wa** noun 2 **desu**

> *ex.* **Gurei-san wa bengoshi desu.** "Mr. Grey is an attorney."

■ The particle **wa**—the topic marker

Wa ("as for . . .") follows noun 1, singling it out as the "topic" of the sentence. Noun 2 is then identified, and the phrase is concluded with **desu**. The topic is the person or thing that the sentence is about. The topic is often the same as the subject but not necessarily.

noun 1 **wa** noun 2 **desu ka**
Hai, (noun 1 **wa**) noun 2 **desu**
Iie, (noun 1 **wa**) noun 2 **dewa/ja arimasen**

> *ex.* **Gurei-san wa bengoshi desu ka.** "Is Mr. Grey an attorney?"
> **Hai, bengoshi desu.** "Yes, (he) is an attorney."
> **Iie, bengoshi dewa arimasen.** "No, (he) isn't an attorney."

■ The particle **ka**—the question marker

It is easy to make questions in Japanese. Simply place the particle **ka** at the end of the sentence. No change in word order is required even when the question contains interrogatives like "who," "what," "when," etc.

NOTE: Intonation normally rises on **ka**, i.e., **. . . desu ka**. ↗

■ **Hai/Iie**

Hai is virtually the same as "yes," and **iie** is virtually the same as "no."

■ Omission of the topic (noun 1)

When it is obvious to the other person what the topic is, it is generally omitted.

> *ex.* **(Watashi wa) Gurei desu.** "(As for me) I'm Grey."

But when it is necessary to make clear what the topic is, it is not omitted.

> *ex.* **Kochira wa Gurei-san desu.** "This is Mr. Grey."

Often the topic is omitted in answers to questions.

> *ex.* **Gurei-san wa bengoshi desu ka.** "Is Mr. Grey an attorney?"
> **Hai, bengoshi desu.** "Yes, (he) is an attorney."
> **Iie, bengoshi dewa arimasen.** "No, (he) isn't an attorney."

■ **Dewa/Ja arimasen**

Dewa arimasen or **ja arimasen** is the negative form of **desu**. **Ja** is more informal than **dewa**; otherwise they are the same. The chart below summarizes the forms of **desu**.

PRESENT FORM		PAST FORM	
aff.	*neg.*	*aff.*	*neg.*
desu	**dewa arimasen**	**deshita**	**dewa arimasendeshita**
is	is not	was	was not

INTRODUCTIONS

 TARGET DIALOGUE

TRACK 1

Ms. Sasaki introduces Mr. Smith to Mr. Takahashi.

ささき：たかはしさん、こちらは　スミスさんです。

スミスさんは　ＡＢＣフーズの　べんごしです。

スミス：はじめまして。スミスです。よろしく　おねがいします。

たかはし：はじめまして。のぞみデパートの　たかはしです。

よろしく　おねがいします。

Sasaki: Takahashi-san, kochira wa Sumisu-san desu. Sumisu-san wa ABC Fūzu no bengoshi desu.
Sumisu: Hajimemashite. Sumisu desu. Yoroshiku onegaishimasu.
Takahashi: Hajimemashite. Nozomi Depāto no Takahashi desu. Yoroshiku onegaishimasu.

Sasaki: Mr. Takahashi, this is Mr. Smith. Mr. Smith is an attorney with ABC Foods.
Smith: How do you do. My name is Smith. Pleased to meet you.
Takahashi: How do you do. I'm Takahashi from Nozomi Department Store. Pleased to meet you.

VOCABULARY

～さん	**-san**	Mr., Mrs., Ms., Miss (see Note 1 below)
こちら	**kochira**	this one (polite for "this person"; see Note 2 below)
は	**wa**	(particle that denotes the topic of a sentence)
です	**desu**	be
ABCフーズ	**ABC Fūzu**	ABC Foods (fictitious company name)
の	**no**	's, of (particle indicating belonging; see Note 4 below)
べんごし	**bengoshi**	attorney, lawyer
はじめまして	**hajimemashite**	how do you do
よろしく　おねがいします	**yoroshiku onegaishimasu**	pleased to meet you (see Note 5 below)
のぞみデパート	**Nozomi Depāto**	Nozomi Department Store (fictitious company name)
デパート	**depāto**	department store

NOTES

1. Takahashi-san
 -San is a title of respect added to a person's name, so it cannot be used after one's own name. **-San** may be used with both male and female names, and with either surnames or given names.

2. Kochira wa Sumisu-san desu.
 Kochira ("this one") implies "this person here" and is a polite way of saying "this person." It is used when introducing one person to another.

3. (Watashi wa) Sumisu desu.

Especially in conversational Japanese, **watashi** ("I") is hardly ever used. **Anata** ("you") is similarly avoided, especially when addressing superiors, in which case the person's surname followed by **-san** is used.

4. Nozomi Depāto no Takahashi desu.

The particle **no** attaches to nouns, and the noun-**no** combination modifies the word that comes after it. **No** expresses belonging or affiliation. Here it shows that Mr. Takahashi belongs to, in the sense that he works for, Nozomi Department Store. Japanese customarily give their company name and position when being introduced.

5. Yoroshiku onegaishimasu.

A phrase used when being introduced, **yoroshiku onegaishimasu** is usually combined with **hajime-mashite**. It is also used when taking one's leave after having asked a favor. **Yoroshiku** means "well" and is a request for the other person's favorable consideration in the future.

PRACTICE

WORD POWER

I. Countries and nationalities:

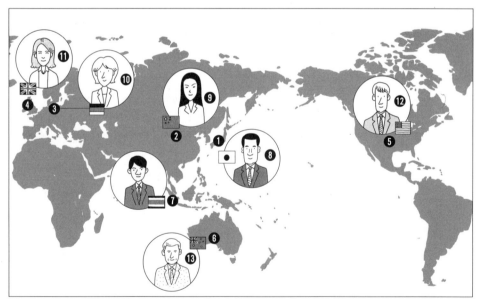

1. **Nihon**	5. **Amerika**	9. **Chūgoku-jin**	13. **Ōsutoraria-jin**
2. **Chūgoku**	6. **Ōsutoraria**	10. **Doitsu-jin**	14. **Tai-jin**
3. **Doitsu**	7. **Tai**	11. **Igirisu-jin**	
4. **Igirisu**	8. **Nihon-jin**	12. **Amerika-jin**	

Ōsutoria - australia

VOCABULARY	**Nihon**	Japan	**Amerika**	the United States
	Chūgoku	China	**Ōsutoraria**	Australia
	Doitsu	Germany	**Tai**	Thailand
	Igirisu	the United Kingdom	**-jin**	-ese, -ian (person from)

- go language

II. Occupations:

1. **bengoshi**   2. **hisho**   3. **gakusei**   4. **enjinia**

KEY SENTENCES

> 1. **(Watashi wa) Sumisu desu.**
> 2. **Sumisu-san wa ABC Fūzu no bengoshi desu.**
> 3. **Kochira wa Nozomi Depāto no Takahashi-san desu.**
>
> 1. I am Smith.
> 2. Mr. Smith is an attorney with ABC Foods.
> 3. This is Mr. Takahashi from Nozomi Department Store.

Kochira - this person

EXERCISES

 I. Make up sentences following the patterns of the examples. Substitute the underlined words with the words in parentheses.

   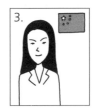 

Mr. Smith, attorney   Ms. Hoffman, engineer   Ms. Brown, secretary   Ms. Lin, student   Mr. Takahashi

A. *State someone's nationality.*

ex. **Sumisu-san** wa **Amerika-jin** desu.

1. *Hofuman-san wa Doitsu-jin desu.* (Hofuman-san, Doitsu-jin)
2. *Buraun-san wa Igirisu-jin desu.* (Buraun-san, Igirisu-jin)
3. *Rin-san wa Chūgoku-jin desu.* (Rin-san, Chūgoku-jin)
4. *Takahashi-san wa Nihon-jin desu.* (Takahashi-san, Nihon-jin)

VOCABULARY			
bengoshi	attorney, lawyer	**Hofuman**	Hoffman (surname)
hisho	secretary	**Buraun**	Brown (surname)
gakusei	student	**Rin**	Lin (surname)
enjinia	engineer		

5

B. *State someone's occupation.*

ex. **Sumisu-san** wa **bengoshi** desu.

1. Hofuman-san wa enjinia desu. .... (Hofuman-san, enjinia)
2. Buraun-san wa hisho desu. .... (Buraun-san, hisho)
3. Rin-san wa gakusei desu. .... (Rin-san, gakusei)

II. Make up dialogues following the patterns of the examples. Substitute the underlined words with the words in parentheses.

A. *Ask and answer what someone's nationality is.*

ex. **A: Sumisu-san** wa **Amerika-jin** desu ka.
    B: Hai, Amerika-jin desu.

1. A: Hofuman-san wa Doitsu-jin desu ka? ...... (Hofuman-san, Doitsu-jin)
   B: Hai, Doitsu-jin desu. .... (Doitsu-jin)
2. A: Buraun-san wa Igirisu-jin desu ka? ...... (Buraun-san, Igirisu-jin)
   B: Hai, Igirisu-jin desu. .... (Igirisu-jin)
3. A: Rin-san wa Chūgoku-jin desu ka? ...... (Rin-san, Chūgoku-jin)
   B: Hai, chūgoku-jin desu. .... (Chūgoku-jin)
4. A: Takahashi-san wa Nihon-jin desu ka? ...... (Takahashi-san, Nihon-jin)
   B: Hai, Nihon-jin desu. .... (Nihon-jin)

B. *Ask and answer what someone's occupation is.*

ex. **A: Sumisu-san** wa **enjinia** desu ka.
    B: Iie. Bengoshi desu.

1. A: Buraun-san wa hisho desu ka? .... (Buraun-san)
   B: hai, hisho desu. .... (hisho)
2. A: Rin-san wa enjinia desu ka? .... (Rin-san)
   B: Iie, Gakusei desu. .... (gakusei)

C. *Ask and answer whether someone is of one nationality/occupation or another.*

ex. **A: Sumisu-san** wa **Amerika-jin** desu ka, **Igirisu-jin** desu ka.
    B: Amerika-jin desu.

1. A: Takahashi-san wa Nihon-jin desu ka, Chūgoku desu ka? ...... (Takahashi-san, Nihon-jin, Chūgoku-jin)
   B: Nihon-jin desu. .... (Nihon-jin)

VOCABULARY	ka	(particle that denotes question)
	hai	yes
	iie	no

2. A: ~~Buraun-san wa Igirisu-jin desu ka,
Doitsu-jin desu ka?~~ .... (Buraun-san, Igirisu-jin, Doitsu-jin)

B: ~~Igirisu-jin desu.~~ .... (Igirisu-jin)

3. A: ~~Hofuman-san wa enjinia desu ka,
bengoshi desu ka?~~ .... (Hofuman-san, enjinia, bengoshi)

B: ~~enginia desu.~~ .... (enginia)

III. **Respond to a self-introduction.** Make up dialogues following the pattern of the example, assuming the roles indicated in parentheses.

> ex. **Sumisu:** Hajimemashite. ABC Fūzu no Sumisu desu. Yoroshiku onegaishimasu.
> **anata:** Hajimemashite. <u>Berurin Mōtāzu</u> no <u>Hofuman</u> desu. Yoroshiku onegaishimasu.

1. Sumisu: ~~Hajimemashite. ABC Fūzu no Sumisu desu. Yoroshiku onegaishimasu.~~

anata: ~~Hajimemashite. Rondon Ginkō no Buraun desu. Yoroshiku onegaishimasu.~~ (Rondon Ginkō, Buraun)

2. Sumisu: ~~Hajimemashite. ABC Fūzu no Sumisu desu. Yoroshiku onegaishimasu.~~

anata: ~~Hajimemashite. Nozomi Depāto no Takahashi desu.~~ (Nozomi Depāto, Takahashi) ~~yoroshiku onegaishimasu.~~

IV. **Introduce people.** Look at the illustrations and pretend you are B. Introduce A and C to each other, as in the example.

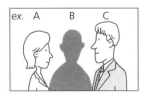  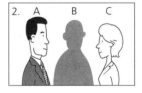

A: Berurin Mōtāzu,
Hofuman-san
C: ABC Fūzu, Sumisu-san

A: Rondon Ginkō,
Buraun-san
C: Tōkyō Daigaku, Rin-san

A: Nozomi Depāto,
Takahashi-san
C: Berurin Mōtāzu, Hofuman-san

> ex. **B: Kochira wa <u>Berurin Mōtāzu</u> no <u>Hofuman-san</u> desu. Kochira wa <u>ABC Fūzu</u> no <u>Sumisu-san</u> desu.**

1. B: ~~Kochira wa Rondon Ginkō no Buraun-san desu. Kochira wa Tōkyō Daigaku no Rin-san desu.~~

2. B: ~~Kochira wa Nozomi Depāto no Takahashi-san desu. Kochira wa Berurin Mōtāzu no Hofuman-san desu.~~

V. Listen to the CD and fill in the blank based on the information you hear.

Sumisu-san wa ...... ~~bengoshi~~ ...... desu.

VOCABULARY	**anata**	you	**Tōkyō Daigaku**	Tokyo University
	Berurin Mōtāzu	Berlin Motors (fictitious company name)	**Tōkyō**	Tokyo
	Rondon Ginkō	Bank of London (fictitious bank name)	**daigaku**	university, college
	Rondon	London		
	ginkō	bank		

SHORT DIALOGUES

I. At the reception desk of a company:

Sumisu: **ABC Fūzu no Sumisu desu. Takahashi-san o onegaishimasu.**
uketsuke: **Hai.**

Smith: I'm Smith from ABC Foods. (I'd like to see) Mr. Takahashi, please.
receptionist: All right.

VOCABULARY

o	(particle; see Note 1 below)
onegaishimasu	please (get me . . .)
uketsuke	reception desk, receptionist

II. The buzzer on a home security intercom system sounds.

Chan: **Hai. Donata desu ka.**
Nakamura: **Nakamura desu.**
Chan: **Hai, dōzo.**

Chan: Yes? Who is it?
Nakamura: It's Nakamura.
Chan: All right. Please (come in).

VOCABULARY

donata	who
hai, dōzo	please go ahead, please feel free

NOTES

1. Takahashi-san o onegaishimasu.
Use "(person) **o onegaishimasu**" when asking a receptionist to summon somebody you want to see. **Onegaishimasu** is a very convenient phrase often used in making polite requests.

2. Donata
The basic word for "who" is **dare**, but **donata** is more polite.

3. Hai, dōzo.
This expression is used when granting a visitor permission to enter a room or an office. It can also be used when handing over something that another person has asked for.

Active Communication

1. Introduce yourself to a classmate. Then introduce two classmates to each other.

2. If you're in Japan, try introducing yourself to a Japanese person. State who you are and what your occupation is.

EXCHANGING BUSINESS CARDS

TARGET DIALOGUE

Mr. Takahashi gives Mr. Smith his business card. Mr. Smith cannot read *kanji*.

たかはし：わたしの　めいしです。どうぞ。

スミス：どうも　ありがとうございます。(*flipping over Takahashi's business card to examine the other side*) これは　たかはしさんの　なまえ ですか。

たかはし：ええ、そうです。たかはし　しんごです。

スミス：これは？

たかはし：かいしゃの　なまえです。のぞみデパートです。

Takahashi: Watashi no meishi desu. Dōzo.
Sumisu: Dōmo arigatō gozaimasu. (*flipping over Takahashi's business card to examine the other side*) **Kore wa Takahashi-san no namae desu ka.**
Takahashi: Ee, sō desu. Takahashi Shingo desu.
Sumisu: Kore wa?
Takahashi: Kaisha no namae desu. Nozomi Depāto desu.

Takahashi: This is my business card. Here.
Smith: Thank you very much. Is this your name?
Takahashi: Yes that's right. It's Shingo Takahashi.
Smith: What about this?
Takahashi: It's the name of (my) company. It's "Nozomi Department Store."

VOCABULARY

わたしの	**watashi no**	my
めいし	**meishi**	business card
どうぞ	**dōzo**	please; if you please
どうも　ありがとうございます	**dōmo arigatō gozaimasu**	thank you very much
これ	**kore**	this one
なまえ	**namae**	name
ええ	**ee**	yes (less formal than **hai**)
そうです	**sō desu**	that's right
これは？	**kore wa?**	what about this?
かいしゃ	**kaisha**	company, the office

NOTES

1. (Kore wa) watashi no meishi desu.
   Watashi no meishi means "my business card." The particle **no** here expresses possession.

2. Dōmo arigatō gozaimasu.

This is an expression of gratitude. There are several levels of politeness in Japanese, and **dōmo argatō gozaimasu** is an example of the most polite level. More casual are, in descending order or politeness, **arigatō gozaimasu**, **dōmo arigatō**, and **arigatō**.

3. Kore wa Takahashi-san no namae desu ka.

Note that although addressing Mr. Takahashi, Mr. Smith uses his name rather than saying **anata no**, "your." (See Note 3, p. 4.)

4. Sō desu.

When replying to questions that end with **desu ka**, **sō** can be used instead of repeating the noun.

5. Kore wa?

A rising intonation on the particle **wa** makes this informal phrase a question without using the question marker **ka**.

PRACTICE

WORD POWER

TRACK 6

I. Numbers:

0	1	2	3	4	5	6	7	8	9
zero/rei	ichi	ni	san	yon/shi	go	roku	nana/shichi	hachi	kyū/ku

II. Business vocabulary:

① のぞみデパート ② 高橋真吾 ③ 東京都港区虎ノ門 3–25–2 ④ (03) 3459-9620* ⑤ s.takahashi@nozomidpt.com	Nozomi Department Store Shingo Takahashi 3–25–2 Toranomon, Minato-ku, Tokyo (03) 3459-9620 E-MAIL: s.takahashi@nozomidpt.com

1. **meishi**   4. **denwa-bangō**
2. **namae**   5. **mēru-adoresu**
3. **jūsho**

*The area code for Tokyo is 03. When saying a phone number aloud, put **no** between the area code (e.g., 03) and the exchange, and between the exchange and the last four numbers. The phone number here is pronounced **zero-san no san-yon-go-kyū no kyū-roku-ni-zero**.
NOTE: The 0 used in telephone numbers is pronounced **zero** instead of **rei**.

VOCABULARY			
meishi	business card	**denwa-bangō**	telephone number
namae	name	**denwa**	telephone
jūsho	address	**bangō**	number
		mēru-adoresu	e-mail address

III. Personal belongings:

1. **keitai**   2. **kasa**   3. **hon**   4. **shimbun**   5. **kagi**   6. **tokei**

KEY SENTENCES

1. **Kore wa meishi desu.**
2. **Kore wa meishi dewa arimasen.**
3. **Kore wa Sasaki-san no kasa desu.**
4. **Takahashi-san no denwa-bangō wa 03-3459-9620 desu.**

1. This is a business card.
2. This is not a business card.
3. This is Ms. Sasaki's umbrella.
4. Mr. Takahashi's telephone number is 03-3459-9620.

VOCABULARY			
keitai	cell/mobile phone	**kagi**	key
kasa	umbrella	**tokei**	watch, clock
hon	book	**dewa arimasen**	is/are not
shimbun	newspaper		

EXERCISES

 I. Make up sentences following the patterns of the examples. Substitute the underlined words with the words in parentheses.

A. *State what an object is.*

ex. **Kore wa <u>hon</u> desu.**

1. kore wa kagi desu. .... (kagi)

2. kore wa tokei desu. .... (tokei)

B. *State what an object is not.*

ex. **Kore wa <u>hon</u> dewa arimasen.**

1. kore wa kagi dewa arimasen. .... (kagi)

2. kore wa tokei dewa arimasen. .... (tokei)

II. Make up dialogues following the patterns of the examples and based on the information in the illustrations.

A. *Ask and answer whether an object is what it appears to be.*

ex. **A: Kore wa <u>shimbun</u> desu ka.**
B: Hai, <u>shimbun</u> desu.

1. A: kore wa hon desu ka. ....

   B: Hai, hon desu. ....

2. A: kore wa kasa desu ka ....

   B: Hai, kasa desu. ....

3. A: kore wa tokei desu ka. ....

   B: Hai, tokei desu. ....

B. *Negate the identity of an object.*

ex. **A: Kore wa <u>hon</u> desu ka.**
B: Iie, <u>hon</u> dewa arimasen.

1. A: Kore wa kasa desu ka.

   B: Iie, kasa dewa arimasen. ....

2. A: Kore wa tokei desu ka.

   B: _Iie, tokei dewa arimasen_

3. A: Kore wa kagi desu ka.

   B: _Iie, kagi dewa arimasen._

III. *Ask and answer what an object is.* Look at the illustrations and make up dialogues following the pattern of the example.

ex. **A: Kore wa nan desu ka.**
   B: Shimbun desu.

1. A: _kore wa nan desu ka_

   B: _kagi desu._

2. A: _kore wa nan desu ka_

   B: _tokei desu._

3. A: _kore wa nan desu ka._

   B: _keitai desu._

IV. *State who the owner of an object is.* Make up sentences following the pattern of the example and based on the information in the illustrations.

ex. **Kore wa Sumisu-san no hon desu.**

1. _Kore wa Nakamura-san no kasa desu._
2. _Kore wa katō-san no tokei desu._
3. _Kore wa sasaki-san no kagi desu._

13

V. Make up dialogues following the patterns of the examples and based on the information in the illustrations.

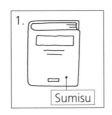
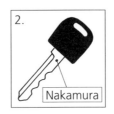

ex. Sasaki

1. Sumisu

2. Nakamura

3. Chan

A. *Ask and answer whether an object belongs to someone.*

ex. **A: Kore wa Sasaki-san no kasa desu ka.**
B: Hai, Sasaki-san no desu.

1. A: Kore wa sumisu-san no hon desu ka

   B: Hai, sumisu-san desu.

2. A: Kore wa Nakamura-san no kagi desu ka.

   B: Hai, Nakamura desu.

3. A: Kore wa chan-san no keitai desu ka.

   B: Hai, chan-san desu.

B. *Deny that an object belongs to someone.*

ex. **A: Kore wa Nakamura-san no kasa desu ka.**
B: Iie, Nakamura-san no dewa arimasen.

1. A: Kore wa Sasaki-san no hon desu ka.

   B: Iie, sasaki-san no dewa arimasen

2. A: Kore wa Chan-san no kagi desu ka.

   B: Iie, Chan-san no dewa arimasen.

3. A: Kore wa Sumisu-san no keitai desu ka.

   B: Iie, sumisu-san no dewa arimasen.

C. *Ask and answer who an object's owner is.*

ex. **A: Kore wa dare no kasa desu ka.**
B: Sasaki-san no desu.

1. A: Kore wa dare no hon desu ka.

   B: Sumisu-san no desu.

2. A: Kore wa dare no keitai desu ka.

   B: Chan-san no desu.

3. A: Kore wa dare no kagi desu ka.

B: Nakamura-san no desu.

VI. Use the information in the table to make up sentences or dialogues as in the examples.

	NAME	TELEPHONE NUMBER
ex.	Sumisu	03-3459-9660
1.	Sasaki	03-3298-7748
2.	taishikan	03-3225-1116
3.	ginkō	03-5690-3111
4.	Takahashi	03-3459-9620

A. *State someone's phone number.*

   ex. **Sumisu-san no denwa-bangō wa zero-san no san-yon-go-kyū no kyū-roku-roku-zero desu.**

1. Sasaki-san no denwa-bangō wa zero-san no san-ni-kyū-hachi no nana-nana-yon-hachi desu.
2. Taishikan-san no denwa-bangō wa zero-san no san-ni-ni-go no ichi-ichi-ichi-roku desu.
3. Ginkō-san no denwabangō wa zero-san no go-roku-kyu-zero no san-ichi-ichi-ich desu.
4. Takahashi-san no denwa-bangō wa zero-san no san-yon-go-kyū no kyu-roku-ni-zero desu.

B. *Ask for and provide someone's phone number.*

   ex. **A: Sumisu-san no denwa-bangō wa nan-ban desu ka.**
   B: Zero-san no san-yon-go-kyū no kyū-roku-roku-zero desu.

1. A: Sasaki-san no denwa-bangō wa nan-ban desu ka.

   B: Zero-san no san-ni-kyu-hachi no nana-nana-yon-hachi desu.

2. A: Taishikan-san no denwa-bangō wa nan-ban desu ka.

   B: Zero-san no san-ni-ni-go no ichi-ichi-ichi-roku desu.

3. A: Ginkō-san no denwa-bangō wa nan-ban desu ka.

   B: Zero-san no go-roku-kyu-zero no san-ichi-ichi-ichi

4. A: Takahashi-san no denwa-bangō wa nan-ban desu ka.

   B: Zero-san no san-yon-go-kyu no kyu-roku-ni-zero desu.

taishikan   embassy

nan-ban   what number

VII. *Talk about who an object's owner is.* Make up dialogues following the pattern of the example. Substitute the underlined words with the words in parentheses.

> ex. Ms. Nakamura is cleaning up the meeting room after a meeting. Mr. Smith comes into the room.
>
> **Sumisu:** **Kore wa Nakamura-san no <u>hon</u> desu ka.**
> **Nakamura:** (*looking at the book*) **Iie, watashi no dewa arimasen.**
> **Sumisu:** **Dare no <u>hon</u> desu ka.**
> **Nakamura: Chan-san no desu.**

1. Sumisu: kore wa Nakamura-san no kasa desu ka. (kasa)

   Nakamura: Iie, watashi no dewa arimasen

   Sumisu: Dare no kasa desu ka. (kasa)

   Nakamura: Chan-san no desu.

2. Sumisu: kore wa Nakamura-san no kagi desu ka (kagi)

   Nakamura: Iie, watashi no desu.

   Sumisu: Dare no kagi desu ka. (kagi)

   Nakamura: Chan-san no desu.

3. Sumisu: kore wa Nakamura-san no keitai desu ka (keitai)

   Nakamura: Iie, watashi no desu.

   Sumisu: Dare no keitai desu ka. (keitai)

   Nakamura: Chan-san no desu.

VIII. Listen to the CD and fill in the blank based on the information you hear.

Sumisu-san no denwa-bangō wa ⟨03 - 3459 - 9660⟩ desu.

SHORT DIALOGUES

I. After Mr. Takahashi leaves the room, Mr. Smith finds a datebook on the sofa.

Sumisu: **Kore wa Nakamura-san no techō desu ka.**
Nakamura: Iie, watashi no dewa arimasen.
Sumisu: **Dare no desu ka.**

Ms. Nakamura notices the name "Takahashi" on the datebook, so she runs after him.

Nakamura: Kore wa Takahashi-san no techō desu ka.
Takahashi: Ee, sō desu. Dōmo arigatō gozaimasu.

Smith: Ms. Nakamura, is this your datebook?
Nakamura: No, it's not mine.
Smith: Whose is it?

. . . .

Nakamura: Is this your datebook, Mr. Takahashi?
Takahashi: Yes, it is. Thank you very much.

VOCABULARY

techō   datebook, small notebook, planner

II. Ms. Chan meets Mrs. Matsui at a party and asks her for her telephone number.

Chan: **Matsui-san no denwa-bangō wa nan-ban desu ka.**
Matsui: 03-3459-9630 desu. Keitai wa 090-1234-5678 desu.
Chan: **Sumimasen. Mō ichi-do onegaishimasu.**

Chan: What is your phone number, Mrs. Matsui?
Matsui: It's 03-3459-9630. My mobile phone number is 090-1234-5678.
Chan: I'm sorry, could you repeat that?

VOCABULARY

sumimasen	I'm sorry
mō ichi-do onegaishimasu	one more time, please
mō ichi-do	one more time
mō	more
ichi-do	one time

Active Communication

1. Ask the people around you what their phone numbers are and make a list.

2. If you're in Japan, ask an employee of a restaurant or store what the establishment's phone number is.

SHOPPING

Japan is a shopper's paradise. From large and lavish department stores to small, hole-in-the-wall establishments in shopping arcades, the country abounds with shops. For the most part, price labels are attached to goods, although sometimes when the prices are not given or are written in *kanji* it is necessary to ask how much an item costs. Salesclerks are generally polite and helpful; upon entering a store or restaurant, a customer will almost always be greeted. The greeting is *irasshaimase*!

UNIT 2 GRAMMAR

Pronouns and Noun Modifiers

kore/sore/are wa noun desu

> *ex.* **Kore wa hon desu.** "This is a book."

■ Kore/Sore/Are

Whereas English has only "this" and "that," Japanese has three separate demonstrative pronouns: **kore**, **sore**, and **are**. **Kore** (see ① below) indicates something near the speaker, **sore** (see ② below) something near the listener, and **are** (see ③ below) something not near either person.

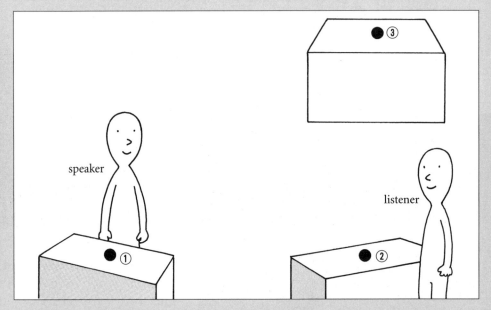

kono/sono/ano noun 1 wa noun 2 desu

> *ex.* **Kono hon wa watashi no desu.** "This book is mine."

■ Kono/Sono/Ano

Kono, **sono**, and **ano** have similar meanings to **kore**, **sore**, and **are**, but they modify nouns.

TARGET DIALOGUE

Mr. Smith goes to the department store, but it isn't open yet.

スミス：すみません、いま　なんじですか。

おんなの　ひと：９じ５０ぷんです。

スミス：デパートは　なんじからですか。

おんなの　ひと：１０じからです。

スミス：なんじまでですか。

おんなの　ひと：ごご　８じまでです。

スミス：ありがとうございます。

おんなの　ひと：どういたしまして。

■ デパートは　１０じから　８じまでです。

Sumisu: Sumimasen, ima nan-ji desu ka.
onna no hito: Ku-ji gojuppun desu.
Sumisu: Depāto wa nan-ji kara desu ka.
onna no hito: Jū-ji kara desu.
Sumisu: Nan-ji made desu ka.
onna no hito: Gogo hachi-ji made desu.
Sumisu: Arigatō gozaimasu.
onna no hito: Dō itashimashite.

■ **Depāto wa jū-ji kara hachi-ji made desu.**

Smith: Excuse me. What time is it?
woman: It's 9:50.
Smith: What time does the department store open?
woman: It opens at 10:00.
Smith: Until what time is it open?
woman: It's open till 8:00 p.m.
Smith: Thank you.
woman: You're welcome.

■ The department store is open from 10:00 to 8:00.

VOCABULARY

すみません	**sumimasen**	excuse me
いま	**ima**	now

なんじ	nan-ji	what time
〜じ	-ji	o'clock (counter)
おんなの　ひと	onna no hito	woman
おんな	onna	female, woman
ひと	hito	person
9じ	ku-ji	nine o'clock
50ぷん	gojuppun/gojippun	fifty minutes
50	gojū	fifty
〜ふん／ぷん	-fun/-pun	minute
から	kara	from (particle)
10じ	jū-ji	ten o'clock
まで	made	until (particle)
ごご	gogo	p.m., in the afternoon
8じ	hachi-ji	eight o'clock
どういたしまして	dō itashimashite	you're welcome; don't mention it

NOTES

1. (Depāto wa) jū-ji kara desu./(Depāto wa) gogo hachi-ji made desu.

When stating the hours that a business is open, use the "noun 1 **wa** noun 2 **desu**" pattern. However, if the topic of the sentence is clear from the context, it may be omitted, as it has been here. (See "Omission of the topic (noun 1)" in Unit 1 Grammar, p. 2.) The time the business opens is followed by **kara**, and the time that it closes is followed by **made**.

PRACTICE

WORD POWER

I. Services and activities:

1. **depāto**　　2. **sūpā**　　3. **resutoran**　　4. **yūbinkyoku**　　5. **ginkō**

VOCABULARY	**depāto**	department store	**ginkō**	bank
	sūpā	supermarket		
	resutoran	restaurant		
	yūbinkyoku	post office		

6. **shigoto**   7. **kaigi**   8. **hiru-yasumi**   9. **pātī**   10. **eiga**
(ē.)

II. Numbers:

10	**jū**	20	**nijū**	30	**sanjū**	100	**hyaku**
11	**jūichi**	21	**nijūichi**	40	**yonjū**		
12	**jūni**	22	**nijūni**	50	**gojū**		
13	**jūsan**	23	**nijūsan**	60	**rokujū**		
14	**jūyon/jūshi**	24	**nijūyon/nijūshi**	70	**nanajū**		
15	**jūgo**	25	**nijūgo**	80	**hachijū**		
16	**jūroku**	26	**nijūroku**	90	**kyūjū**		
17	**jūnana/ jūshichi**	27	**nijūnana/ nijūshichi**				
18	**jūhachi**	28	**nijūhachi**				
19	**jūku/jūkyū**	29	**nijūku/nijūkyū**				

III. Times:

1:00	**ichi-ji**	3:05	**san-ji go-fun**	3:10	**san-ji juppun**
2:00	**ni-ji**	3:15	**san-ji jūgo-fun**	3:20	**san-ji nijuppun**
3:00	**san-ji**	3:25	**san-ji nijūgo-fun**	3:30	**san-ji sanjuppun/san-ji han**
4:00	**yo-ji**	3:35	**san-ji sanjūgo-fun**	3:40	**san-ji yonjuppun**
5:00	**go-ji**	3:45	**san-ji yonjūgo-fun**	3:50	**san-ji gojuppun**
6:00	**roku-ji**	3:55	**san-ji gojūgo-fun**		
7:00	**shichi-ji**				
8:00	**hachi-ji**			4:00 a.m.	**gozen yo-ji**
9:00	**ku-ji**			9:00 p.m.	**gogo ku-ji**
10:00	**jū-ji**				
11:00	**jūichi-ji**				
12:00	**jūni-ji**				

NOTE: Hours and minutes are romanized here, but throughout the rest of the book they are spelled with numerals, e.g., **1-ji** for "1:00," **10-ji 20-pun** for "10:20," etc.

VOCABULARY			
shigoto	work, job	**pātī**	party
kaigi	meeting, conference	**eiga**	movie
hiru-yasumi	lunch break	**han**	half past (of time)
hiru	noon	**gozen**	a.m., in the morning
yasumi	break, rest		

KEY SENTENCES

1. **Ima 3-ji desu.**
2. **Shigoto wa 9-ji kara 5-ji made desu.**

1. It's 3:00.
2. Work is from 9:00 to 5:00.

EXERCISES

I. *State the time.* Practice telling the times indicated below.

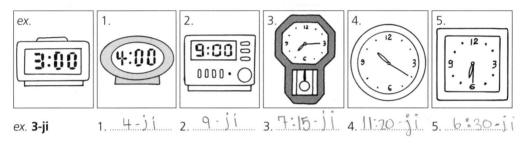

ex. **3-ji**   1. 4-ji   2. 9-ji   3. 7:15-ji   4. 11:20-ji   5. 6:30-ji

II. *Ask and give the time.* Make up dialogues following the pattern of the example. Substitute the underlined word with the times indicated in exercise I.

ex. **A: Ima nan-ji desu ka.**
     B: 3-ji desu.

1. A: Ima nan-ji desu ka
   B: 4-ji desu

2. A: Ima nan-ji desu ka
   B: 9 ji desu

3. A: Ima nan-ji desu ka
   B: 7:15-ji desu

4. A: Ima nan-ji desu ka
   B: 11:20-ji desu

5. A: Ima nan-ji desu ka
   B: 6:30-ji desu

III. Make up sentences following the patterns of the examples. Substitute the underlined word(s) with the alternatives given.

A. *State a department store's opening time.*

   ex. **Depāto wa 10-ji kara desu.**

   1. Depāto wa ku-ji kara desu   (9:00)

   2. Depāto wa jūichi-ji kara desu   (11:00)

B. *State what time work will finish.*

   ex. **Shigoto wa 5-ji made desu.**

   1. Shigoto wa shichi-ji made desu   (7:00)

   2. shingoto wa roku-ji han desu   (6:30)

C. *State what work hours are, from what time until what time.*

   ex. **Shigoto wa 9-ji kara 5-ji made desu.**

   1. shigoto wa ku-ji han kara roku-ji made desu   (9:30, 6:00)

   2. Shigoto wa jū-ji kara shichi-ji made desu   (10:00, 7:00)

IV. Make up dialogues following the patterns of the examples. Substitute the underlined words with the alternatives given.

A. *Ask and answer what time a business will open.*

   ex. **A: Ginkō wa nan-ji kara desu ka.**
       B: 9-ji kara desu.

   1. A: Sūpā wa nan-ji kara desu ka   (sūpā)
      B: Jūichi-ji kara desu   (11:00)

   2. A: Yūbinkyoku wa nan-ji kara desu ka   (yūbinkyoku)
      B: ku-ji kara desu   (9:00)

B. *Ask and answer what time something will end or close.*

   ex. **A: Pātī wa nan-ji made desu ka.**
       B: Gogo 9-ji made desu.

   1. A: Resutoran wa nan-ji made desu ka   (resutoran)
      B: Gogo jūichi-ji han made desu   (gogo 11:30)

   2. A: Kaigi wa nan-ji made desu ka   (kaigi)
      B: Jū-ji han made desu   (10:30)

C. *Ask and answer what an event's hours are.*

> ex. **A: Kaigi wa nan-ji kara nan-ji made desu ka.**
> **B: 1-ji kara 3-ji made desu.**

1. A: Hiru-yasumi wa nan-ji kara nan-ji made desu ka (hiru-yasumi)

   B: Jūni-ji han kara ichi-ji han made desu (12:30, 1:30)

2. A: Eiga wa nan-ji kara nan-ji made desu ka (eiga)

   B: Yo-ji jūgo fun kara roku-ji han made desu (4:15, 6:30)

V. *Find out when a service will begin or when a facility will open.* Make up dialogues following the pattern of the example. Substitute the underlined words with the alternatives given.

> ex. Mr. Smith is at a resort hotel. He asks the front desk when meals are served and when the hotel's facilities open.
>
> **Sumisu: Sumimasen. Asa-gohan wa nan-ji kara desu ka.**
> **furonto: 7-ji kara desu.**
> **Sumisu: Dōmo arigatō.**

1. Sumisu: Sumimasen. Ban-gohan wa nan-ji kara desu ka (ban-gohan)

   furonto: roku-ji kara desu (6:00)

   Sumisu: Dōmo arigatō.

2. Sumisu: Sumimasen. Pūru wa nan-ji kara desu ka (pūru)

   furonto: Gozen hachi-ji kara desu (8:00 a.m.)

   Sumisu: Dōmo arigatō.

3. Sumisu: Sumimasen. Jimu wa nan-ji kara desu ka (jimu)

   furonto: Gozen ku-ji kara desu (9:00 a.m.)

   Sumisu: Dōmo arigatō.

VI. Listen to the CD and fill in the blank based on the information you hear.

   Jimu wa 7:30 kara desu.

SHORT DIALOGUE

TRACK 12

Ms. Sasaki wants to call the London branch of her company.

Sasaki: **Nakamura-san, ima nan-ji desu ka.**
Nakamura: **4-ji han desu.**
Sasaki: **Rondon wa ima nan-ji desu ka.**
Nakamura: **Gozen 8-ji han desu.**
Sasaki: **Sō desu ka. Dōmo arigatō.**

Sasaki: Ms. Nakamura, what time is it?
Nakamura: It's 4:30.
Sasaki: What time is it in London?
Nakamura: It's 8:30 in the morning.
Sasaki: Is that so? Thank you very much.

VOCABULARY

sō desu ka   I see

NOTES

1. Sō desu ka.

This expression, meaning "I see" or "is that so?" is used as a comment on what someone else has said. It is spoken with falling intonation.

Active Communication

1. Ask someone for the time.

2. If you're in Japan, try asking for the business hours of a restaurant or other facilities you are interested in.

TARGET DIALOGUE

TRACK 13

Mr. Smith is shopping in a department store.

みせの　ひと：いらっしゃいませ。

スミス：(pointing) それを　みせてください。

みせの　ひと：はい、どうぞ。

スミス：ありがとう。これは　いくらですか。

みせの　ひと：3,000 えんです。

スミス：(pointing) それは　いくらですか。

みせの　ひと：これも　3,000 えんです。

スミス：じゃ、それを　ください。

みせの　ひと：はい、ありがとうございます。

mise no hito: Irasshaimase.
Sumisu: (*pointing*) **Sore o misete kudasai.**
mise no hito: Hai, dōzo.
Sumisu: Arigatō. Kore wa ikura desu ka.
mise no hito: Sanzen-en desu.
Sumisu: (*pointing*) **Sore wa ikura desu ka.**
mise no hito: Kore mo sanzen-en desu.
Sumisu: Ja, sore o kudasai.
mise no hito: Hai, arigatō gozaimasu.

salesperson: May I help you?
    Smith: Please show me that one.
salesperson: Yes, here it is.
    Smith: Thank you. How much is this?
salesperson: It's 3,000 yen.
    Smith: How much is that one?
salesperson: This is also 3,000 yen.
    Smith: I'll take that one, then.
salesperson: All right. Thank you.

VOCABULARY

みせ	**mise**	shop, store, restaurant
いらっしゃいませ	**irasshaimase**	may I help you?, welcome
それ	**sore**	that one
みせてください	**misete kudasai**	please show me
いくら	**ikura**	how much

3,000えん	sanzen-en	3,000 yen
～えん	-en	yen
も	mo	also, too, either (particle)
じゃ	ja	well then
ください	kudasai	please give me

NOTES

1. Sore o misete kudasai.

When you want to take a closer look at an item in a store, use "(something) **o misete kudasai**" ("please show me . . .").

2. Sanzen-en

The system of counting large numbers is different in Japanese and English. The chart below shows how to count from a thousand to a trillion.

1,000	**sen**
10,000	**ichi-man**
100,000	**jū-man**
1,000,000	**hyaku-man**
10,000,000	**sen-man**
100,000,000	**ichi-oku**
1,000,000,000	**jū-oku**
10,000,000,000	**hyaku-oku**
100,000,000,000	**sen-oku**
1,000,000,000,000	**it-chō**

chō oku man
2,222,222,222,222
nichō nisen nihyaku nijūni-oku nisen nihyaku nijūni-man nisen nihyaku nijūni

Decimals. (The word for "decimal point" is **ten**.)

0	**rei**
0.7	**rei ten nana**
0.29	**rei ten ni kyū**
0.538	**rei ten go san hachi**

Fractions. (**Bun** means "part.")

1/2	**ni-bun no ichi**		2/3	**san-bun no ni**
1/4	**yon-bun no ichi**			

3. Kore mo sanzen-en desu.

The particle **mo** means "too," "also," "either," etc. It is used in both affirmative and negative sentences.

> *ex.* **Sore wa sanzen-en desu. Kore mo sanzen-en desu.**
> "That one is 3,000 yen. This one is 3,000 yen, too."
> **Kore wa watashi no kasa dewa arimasen. Sore mo watashi no dewa arimasen.**
> "This is not my umbrella. That's not mine either."

4. Ja, kore o kudasai.

Ja and **dewa** correspond to "well" or "well then," interjections that express conclusion or resignation. **Kore o kudasai** means "I'll take this one" and is the phrase to use when you have decided what you want to buy.

PRACTICE

WORD POWER

TRACK 14

I. Electronic appliances:

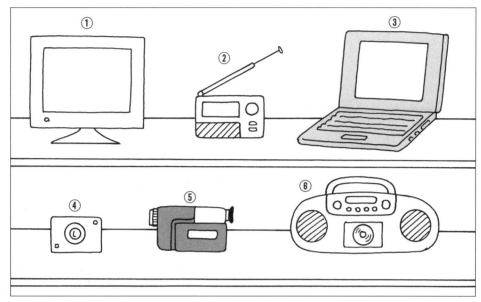

1. **terebi**   2. **rajio**   3. **pasokon**   4. **dejikame**   5. **bideo-kamera**   6. **CD-purēyā**

II. Numbers:

100	**hyaku**	1,000	**sen**	10,000	**ichiman**
200	**nihyaku**	2,000	**nisen**	20,000	**niman**
300	**sambyaku**	3,000	**sanzen**	30,000	**samman**
400	**yonhyaku**	4,000	**yonsen**	40,000	**yomman**
500	**gohyaku**	5,000	**gosen**	50,000	**goman**
600	**roppyaku**	6,000	**rokusen**	60,000	**rokuman**
700	**nanahyaku**	7,000	**nanasen**	70,000	**nanaman**
800	**happyaku**	8,000	**hassen**	80,000	**hachiman**
900	**kyūhyaku**	9,000	**kyūsen**	90,000	**kyūman**

Intermediate numbers are made by combining the numbers composing them.
   ex. 135 **hyaku-sanjū-go**   1,829 **sen-happyaku-nijūkyū**

NOTE: Large numbers are spelled out here, in romanized Japanese, but throughout the rest of the book, numerals are used to write them, e.g., **3,000-en** for "3,000 yen."

VOCABULARY			
terebi	television	**bideo-kamera**	video camera
rajio	radio	**bideo**	video
pasokon	(personal) computer	**kamera**	camera
dejikame	digital camera	**CD-purēyā**	CD player
		CD (=shīdī)	CD

III. Japanese currency:

1. **1-en**   2. **5-en**   3. **10-en**   4. **50-en**   5. **100-en**   6. **500-en**

7. **1,000-en**

8. **2,000-en**

9. **5,000-en**

10. **10,000-en**

KEY SENTENCES

> 1. **Sore wa terebi desu.**
> 2. **Are wa pasokon desu.**
> 3. **Kore wa 3,000-en desu. Are mo 3,000-en desu.**
>
> 1. That is a television set.
> 2. That over there is a personal computer.
> 3. This is 3,000 yen. That, too, is 3,000 yen.

VOCABULARY   **are**   that one over there

EXERCISES

 I. *State an item's price.* Look at the illustrations and state the price of each item.

ex. **gojū-en**
1. hachijū
2. hyaku

3. hyaku.nijū
4. sambyaku
5. happyakuroku jū

6. sen-nihyaku
7. sanzen-en
8. yonsen-happyaku

9. ichiman-nanasen
10. samman-kyūsen

 II. *Ask and give an item's price.* Make up dialogues following the pattern of the example and based on the information in the illustrations.

ex. **A: Kore wa ikura desu ka.**
    B: 500-en desu.

1. A: kore wa ikura desu ka
   B: roppyaku -en desu
2. A: kore wa ikura desu ka
   B: sambyaku -en desu
3. A: kore wa ikura desu ka
   B: nanahyaku-goju-en desu

III. *Identify objects in different locations.* Look at the illustration and make up sentences like the examples. Substitute the underlined words with the alternatives given.

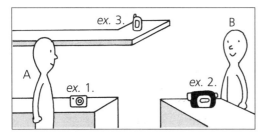
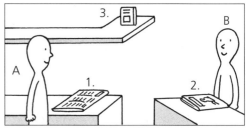

ex. 1. **A: Kore wa dejikame desu.**
ex. 2. **A: Sore wa bideo-kamera desu.**
ex. 3. **A: Are wa keitai desu.**

1. A: kore wa shimbun desu (shimbun)
2. A: sore wa zasshi desu (zasshi)
3. A: Are wa hon desu (hon)

IV. *Ask and give an item's price.* Use the information in the illustrations to make appropriate questions for each of the answers given.

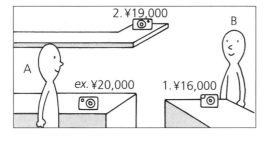
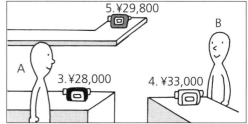

ex. **A: Kore wa ikura desu ka.**
    B: 20,000-en desu.

1. A: Sore wa ikura desu ka
   B: 16,000-en desu.

VOCABULARY **zasshi** magazine

33

2. A: Are wa ikura desu ka

B: 19,000-en desu.

3. A: Kore wa ikura desu ka

B: 28,000-en desu.

4. A: Sore wa ikura desu ka

B: 33,000-en desu.

5. A: Are wa ikura desu ka

B: 29,800-en desu.

V. *State that two things cost the same or are the same thing.* Make up sentences following the pattern of the example. Substitute the underlined words with the alternatives given.

ex. **Kore wa 800-en desu. Sore mo 800-en desu.**

1. Kore wa sen-gohyaku-en desu sore mo sen-gohyaku-en desu. (1,500-en)

2. Kore wa tokei desu. Sore mo tokei desu (tokei)

3. Kore wa sumisu-san no hon desu. Sore (Sumisu-san no hon)
mo sumisusan no hon desu.

VI. *Ask the price of more than one item.* Make up dialogues following the pattern of the example. Substitute the underlined words with the alternatives given.

ex. **Sumisu: Kore wa ikura desu ka.**
mise no hito: 8,000-en desu.
Sumisu: Are mo 8,000-en desu ka.
mise no hito: Iie, 8,000-en dewa arimasen.
**   7,500-en desu.**

1. Sumisu: Kore wa ikura desu ka

   mise no hito: nanasen-en desu (7,000-en)

   Sumisu: Are mo nanasen-en desu ka (7,000-en)

   mise no hito: Hai, so desu (7,000-en)

2. Sumisu: Kore wa ikura desu ka

   mise no hito: kyūsen-en desu (9,000-en)

   Sumisu: Are mo kyūsen-en desu ka (9,000-en)

   mise no hito: Hai, sō desu (9,000-en)

3. Sumisu Kore wa ikura desu ka

   mise no hito: Rokusen-gohyaku-en desu (6,500-en)

   Sumisu: Are mo rokusen-gohyaku-en desu ka (6,500-en)

   mise no hito: Hai, sō desu (6,500-en)

VII. ***Confirm what an item is.*** Make up dialogues following the pattern of the example. Substitute the underlined words with the alternatives given.

ex. Mr. Smith comes to a store.

Sumisu: Are wa <u>DVD</u> desu ka.
mise no hito: Iie, <u>CD</u> desu.
Sumisu: Sore wa <u>DVD</u> desu ka.
mise no hito: Hai, <u>DVD</u> desu.

1. Sumisu: Are wa shāpupenshiru desu ka (shāpupenshiru)

   mise no hito: Iie, bōrupen desu (bōrupen)

   Sumisu: Sore wa shāpupenshiru desu ka (shāpupenshiru)

   mise no hito: Hai, shāpupenshiru desu. (shāpupenshiru)

2. Sumisu: Are wa Furansu-go no jisho desu ka (Furansu-go no jisho)

   mise no hito: Iie, Eigo no jisho desu (Eigo no jisho)

   Sumisu: Sore wa Furansu-go no jisho desu ka (Furansu-go no jisho)

   mise no hito: Hai, Furansu-go no jisho desu (Furansu-go no jisho)

VIII. ***Buy something at a store.*** Make up dialogues following the pattern of the example. Substitute the underlined words with the alternatives given.

ex. **Sumisu:** Sumimasen. Are wa <u>bideo-kamera</u> desu ka.
mise no hito: Iie, <u>dejikame</u> desu.
Sumisu: Sore wa <u>bideo-kamera</u> desu ka.
mise no hito: Hai, sō desu.
Sumisu: Ikura desu ka.
mise no hito: <u>50,000-en</u> desu.
Sumisu: Ja, sore o kudasai.

1. Sumisu: Sumimasen. Are wa CD-purēyā desu ka (CD-purēyā)

   mise no hito: Iie, rajio desu (rajio)

   Sumisu: Sore wa CD-purēyā desu ka (CD-purēyā)

   mise no hito: Hai, sō desu

   Sumisu: Ikura desu ka

   mise no hito: ichiman-gosen-en desu (15,000-en)

   Sumisu: Ja, sore o kudasai

VOCABULARY	**DVD (=dībuidī)**	DVD	**Furansu-go**	French (language)
	shāpupenshiru	mechanical pencil	**Furansu**	France
	bōrupen	ballpoint pen	**-go**	language
			jisho	dictionary
			Eigo	English (language)

2. Sumisu: *Sumimasen. Are wa terebi desu ka* (terebi)

mise no hito: *Iie, pasokon desu* (pasokon)

Sumisu: *Sore wa terebi desu ka* (terebi)

mise no hito: *Hai, sō desu*

Sumisu: *Ikura desu ka*

mise no hito: *Jū-man-hachiman-en desu* (180,000-en)

Sumisu: *Ja sore o kudasai*

IX. Listen to the CD and fill in the blank based on the information you hear.

Bideo-kamera wa .... -en desu.

SHORT DIALOGUE

Mr. Smith is at a store, shopping.

Sumisu: **Kore o kudasai.**
mise no hito: **4,300-en desu.**
Sumisu: **Kādo demo ii desu ka.**
mise no hito: **Hai, kekkō desu.**

Smith: I'll take this.
salesperson: It's 4,300 yen.
Smith: Is it all right to use a credit card?
salesperson: Yes, it's fine.

VOCABULARY

kādo	(credit) card
demo ii desu ka	is . . . all right?
hai, kekkō desu	yes, it's fine

NOTES

1. Kādo demo ii desu ka.

The phrase **demo ii desu ka** is used to ask if something is permissible. It means "is . . . all right?"

Active Communication

If you're in Japan, try asking the prices of items at vendors where prices are not listed or are written in *kanji*.

SHOPPING, PART II

TARGET DIALOGUE

TRACK 17

Mr. Smith buys a T-shirt.

スミス：すみません。あの　Ｔシャツは　いくらですか。

みせの　ひと：どれですか。

スミス：あの　あおい　Ｔシャツです。

みせの　ひと：あれは　1,500 えんです。

スミス：その　あかい　Ｔシャツは　いくらですか。

みせの　ひと：1,000 えんです。

スミス：じゃ、それを　2まい　ください。

■ あかい　Ｔシャツは　1,000 えんです。

Sumisu: Sumimasen. Ano T-shatsu wa ikura desu ka.
mise no hito: **Dore desu ka.**
Sumisu: Ano aoi T-shatsu desu.
mise no hito: **Are wa 1,500-en desu.**
Sumisu: Sono akai T-shatsu wa ikura desu ka.
mise no hito: **1,000-en desu.**
Sumisu: Ja, sore o 2-mai kudasai.

■ **Akai T-shatsu wa 1,000-en desu.**

Smith: Excuse me. How much is that T-shirt over there?
salesperson: Which one?
Smith: That blue T-shirt.
salesperson: That's 1,500 yen.
Smith: How much is that red T-shirt?
salesperson: It's 1,000 yen.
Smith: Well then, give me two of those.

■ The red T-shirt is 1,000 yen.

VOCABULARY

あの	**ano**	that over there (used before a noun)
Ｔシャツ	**T-shatsu**	T-shirt
どれ	**dore**	which one
あおい	**aoi**	blue
その	**sono**	that (used before a noun)

あかい	**akai**	red
2まい	**2-mai**	two (shirts or other flat objects)
～まい	**-mai**	(counter for flat objects)

NOTES

1. Sore o 2-mai kudasai.

-Mai is a unit for counting thin, flat objects like shirts and pieces of paper. Japanese has two numerical systems: the **hitotsu, futatsu, mittsu** system and the abstract **ichi, ni, san** system. Counting things can be done in two ways: (1) using the **hitotsu, futatsu, mittsu** system independently (see Word Power II, p. 39), or (2) using the **ichi, ni, san** system combined with a counter such as **-mai** or **-hon** (**-bon, -pon**), the latter for long, slender objects like pencils and bottles.

ex. **Ringo o futatsu kudasai.** "Please give me two apples."

The **hitotsu, futatsu, mittsu** system, however, only goes as far as **tō** (10), after which the **ichi, ni, san** system is used: **jūichi, jūni, jūsan**, etc.

Note the word order here: thing + **o** + number (or number and counter) + **kudasai**.

PRACTICE

WORD POWER

I. Items for sale:

red   blue   black

1. **hagaki**	4. **akai**	7. **bīru**	10. **chiisai**
2. **kitte**	5. **aoi**	8. **ringo**	
3. **T-shatsu**	6. **kuroi**	9. **ōkii**	

VOCABULARY

hagaki	postcard	**aoi**	blue	**ōkii**	large, big
kitte	stamp	**kuroi**	black	**chiisai**	small, little
T-shatsu	T-shirt	**bīru**	beer		
akai	red	**ringo**	apple		

II. Numbers and counters:

	📄 👕 etc.	🍶 ☂ etc.	🍎 🍔 etc.
1	ichi-mai	ippon	hitotsu
2	ni-mai	ni-hon	futatsu
3	san-mai	sam-bon	mittsu
4	yon-mai	yon-hon	yottsu
5	go-mai	go-hon	itsutsu
6	roku-mai	roppon	muttsu
7	nana-mai	nana-hon	nanatsu
8	hachi-mai	happon	yattsu
9	kyū-mai	kyū-hon	kokonotsu
10	jū-mai	juppon	tō
11	jūichi-mai	jūippon	jūichi
12	jūni-mai	jūni-hon	jūni

ikutsu

KEY SENTENCES

1. **Kono T-shatsu wa 2,000-en desu.**
2. **Ano chiisai kamera wa 5,000-en desu.**
3. **Kore wa Suisu no tokei desu.**
4. **Sono ringo o futatsu kudasai.**

1. This T-shirt is 2,000 yen.
2. That little camera over there is 5,000 yen.
3. This is a Swiss watch.
4. Give me two of those apples.

VOCABULARY	**kono**	this (used before a noun)
	Suisu	Switzerland

EXERCISES

 I. ***Single out a specific item and state its price.*** Look at the illustration and state how much the umbrellas cost, following the pattern of the example.

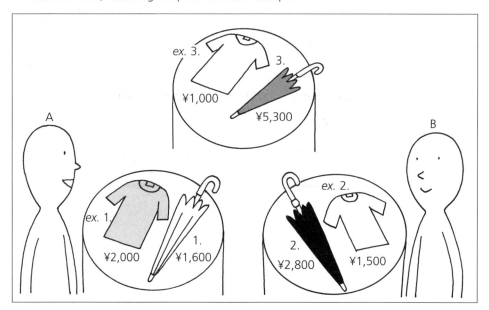

ex. 1. **A: Kono T-shatsu wa 2,000-en desu.**
ex. 2. **A: Sono T-shatsu wa 1,500-en desu.**
ex. 3. **A: Ano T-shatsu wa 1,000-en desu.**

1. A: sono T-shatsu wa nisen-en desu
2. A: kono T-shatsu wa sen-gohyaku-en desu
3. A: Ano T-shatsu wa _____

 II. ***Ask and give a specific item's price.*** Make up dialogues following the pattern of the example and based on the information in the illustration.

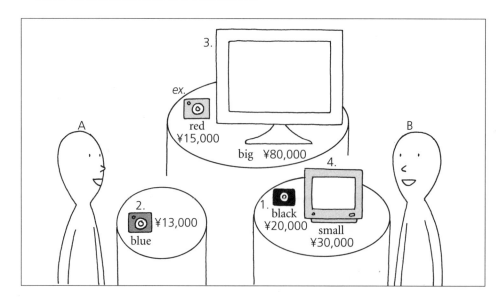

ex. **A: Ano akai kamera wa ikura desu ka.**
B: 15,000-en desu.

1. A: kono aoi kamera wa ikura desu ka

   B: ichiman-sanzen-en desu

2. A: Ano ōkii terebi wa ikura desu ka

   B: hachiman-en desu

3. A: sore kuroi kamera wa ikura desu ka

   B: niman-en desu

4. A: sore chiisai terebi wa ikura desu ka

   B: samman-en desu

III. Make up dialogues following the patterns of the examples. Substitute the underlined parts with the alternatives given.

A. *Ask and answer whether an item is from a given country.*

ex. **A: Kore wa Suisu no tokei desu ka.**
B: Iie, Suisu no dewa arimasen. Furansu no desu.

1. A: Kore wa Igirisu no kuruma desu ka (Igirisu no kuruma)

   B: Iie, Igirisu no. Itaria no desu (Igirisu no, Itaria no)

2. A: Kore wa Nihon no kamera desu ka (Nihon no kamera)

   B: Iie, Nihon no. Doitsu no desu (Nihon no, Doitsu no)

B. *Ask and answer what an item's country of origin is.*

ex. **A: Kore wa doko no pasokon desu ka.**
B: Kankoku no desu.

1. A: Kore wa doko no dejikame desu ka (dejikame)

   B: Nihon no desu (Nihon no)

2. A: Kore wa doko no bīru desu ka (bīru)

   B: Doitsu no desu. (Doitsu no)

VOCABULARY		
kuruma	car	
Itaria	Italy	
doko	where, which place	
Kankoku	South Korea	

IV. *Ask an item's price and whether it is a product of Japan.* Make up dialogues following the pattern of the example. Substitute the underlined parts with the alternatives given.

ex. Mr. Smith has gone to a store to shop.

Sumisu: <u>Ano kamera</u> wa ikura desu ka.
mise no hito: <u>20,000-en</u> desu.
Sumisu: <u>Are</u> wa Nihon no <u>kamera</u> desu ka.
mise no hito: Hai, Nihon no desu.

1. Sumisu: _Sono tokei wa ikura desu ka_ (sono tokei)

   mise no hito: _ichiman-gosen -en desu_ (15,000-en)

   Sumisu: _Sore wa nihon no tokei desu ka_ (sore, tokei)

   mise no hito: _Hai, Nihon no desu._

2. Sumisu: _kono terebi wa ikura desu ka_ (kono terebi)

   mise no hito: _yomman-sanzen -en desu_ (43,000-en)

   Sumisu: _Kore wa nihon no terebi desu ka_ (kore, terebi)

   mise no hito: _Hai, nihon no desu_

3. Sumisu: _kono kuruma ikura desu ka_ (kono kuruma)

   mise no hito: _hyakuman-gohyaku -en desu_ (1,500,000-en)

   Sumisu: _Kore wa nihon no kuruma desu ka_ (kore, kuruma)

   mise no hito: _Hai. Nihon no desu_

V. *Ask for more than one of an item at a store.* Make up sentences following the pattern of the example and based on the information in the illustration.

| VOCABULARY | **mikan** | tangerine |
| | **kiro** | kilogram |

42

ex. **Sumisu: Sono** <u>ringo</u> **o** <u>futatsu</u> **kudasai.**

1. Sumisu: sono chiisai ringo o mittsu kudasai

2. Sumisu: sono biru o ni-hon kudasai

3. Sumisu: sono t-shatsu o ni-mai kudasai

4. Sumisu: sono mikan o mittsu kudasai

VI. *Talk about an item's price and country of origin.* Make up dialogues following the pattern of the example. Substitute the underlined words with the words in parentheses.

ex. **Sumisu:** **Sumimasen. Sono** <u>wain</u> **wa ikura desu ka.**
mise no hito: 1,200-en desu.
Sumisu: **Sore wa doko no** <u>wain</u> **desu ka.**
mise no hito: Furansu no desu.
Sumisu: **Ja, sore o** <u>2-hon</u> **kudasai.**

1. Sumisu: sumimasen. sono kōhi-kappu wa ikura desu ka (kōhī-kappu)

   mise no hito: Gohyaku-en desu

   Sumisu: sore wa kōhi-kappu doko no desu ka (kōhī-kappu)

   mise no hito: itaria no desu (Itaria)

   Sumisu: Ja, sore o muttsu kudasai (muttsu)

2. Sumisu: sumimasen. kono taoru wa ikura desu ka (taoru)

   mise no hito: sen-roppyaku-en desu

   Sumisu: kore wa doko no taoru desu ka (taoru)

   mise no hito: igirisu no desu (Igirisu)

   Sumisu: Ja, kore o yon-mai kudasai (4-mai)

VII. Listen to the CD and choose the correct answers based on the information you hear.

TRACK 19

1. Where is the beer from?

   a) Nihon   b) Amerika   c) Doitsu

2. How much does the beer cost?

   a) 300-en   b) 200-en   c) 100-en

SHORT DIALOGUE

TRACK 20

At a confectionary:

mise no hito: Irasshaimase.
Chan: Shūkurīmu o mittsu kudasai.
mise no hito: Hai. 630-en desu.

salesperson: May I help you?
Chan: I'd like three cream puffs, please.
salesperson: All right. That will be 630 yen.

VOCABULARY

shūkurīmu   cream puff

Active Communication

1. Ask your classmates or colleagues where an item they own is from (i.e., what its country of origin is).

2. If you're in Japan, go shopping and buy more than one of an item. Be sure to use the pattern "number of items + **kudasai**."

Quiz 1 (Units 1–2)

I Fill in the blank(s) in each sentence with the appropriate particle. Where a particle is not needed, write in an *X*.

1. Kochira (_wa_) Sasaki-san desu.

2. Sumisu-san wa ABC Fūzu (_no_) bengoshi desu.

3. Buraun-san wa enjinia desu (_ka_), bengoshi desu (_ka_).
   Enjinia desu.

4. Kore wa watashi (_no_) hon dewa arimasen.
   Suzuki-san (_no_) desu.

5. Kaigi wa 9-ji (_kara_) 11-ji (_made_) desu.

6. Sore (_wa_) ikura desu ka.
   3,000-en desu.
   Are (_wa_) 3,000-en desu ka.
   Iie, 3,000-en dewa arimasen. 3,800-en desu.

7. Sono bīru (_X_) 5-hon (_O_) kudasai.

8. Sore wa doko (_X_) kamera desu ka.
   Doitsu (_no_) desu.

II Complete each sentence by filling in the blank(s) with the appropriate word.

1. Hofuman-san wa (_Doistu-jin_) desu ka.
   Hai, Doitsu-jin desu.

2. Sore wa (_nan_) desu ka.
   Tokei desu.

3. Kore wa (_Takahashi-san_) no kasa desu ka.
   Iie, Takahashi-san no dewa arimasen.
   (_Kasa_) no desu ka.
   Sumisu-san no desu.

4. Sumisu-san no uchi no denwa-bangō wa (_nan-ban_) desu ka.
   03-3459-9660 desu.

5. Hiru-yasumi wa (_nanji_) kara (_nanji_) made desu ka.
   12-ji kara 1-ji made desu.

6. Sono akai T-shatsu wa (_ikura_) desu ka.
   2,300-en desu.

7. Ano pasokon wa (_doko_) no desu ka.
   Nihon no desu.

UNIT
3

GETTING AROUND

Japan boasts one of the most convenient transportation systems in the
world. All major cities from Fukuoka
in southern Japan to Tokyo in the
east and Hachinohe in the north are
connected by bullet train. Other train
systems connect towns and outlying
suburbs of cities. In large metropoli-
tan areas such as Tokyo, Nagoya,
and Osaka, there are also extensive
subway systems. To an astounding
degree of accuracy, these modes of
transportation depart and arrive as
scheduled.

UNIT 3 GRAMMAR

Motion Verbs

> noun **wa** place **ni ikimasu**

ex. **Gurei-san wa ashita Kyōto ni ikimasu.** "Mr. Grey will go to Kyoto tomorrow."

■ Verbs

Japanese sentences end with a verb (or some other element followed by **desu**, which behaves like a verb). The endings of verbs show the tense and whether the verb is affirmative or negative.
Tenses of Japanese verbs can be divided roughly into two categories:
1. The present form. The present, or **-masu** form—so called because verbs in this tense end in **-masu**—encompasses both the simple present (used for expressing habitual action) and future tenses.

ex. **Gurei-san wa mainichi kaisha ni ikimasu.**
"Mr. Grey goes to the office (*lit.*, 'company') every day."
(Watashi wa) ashita kaerimasu. "(I) return/am returning/will return tomorrow."

2. The past form. The past, or **-mashita** form, on the other hand, includes not only the simple past tense but also the present perfect.

ex. **(Watashi wa) senshū Kyōto ni ikimashita.** "Last week (I) went to Kyoto."
Gurei-san wa mō uchi ni kaerimashita. "Mr. Grey has already gone home."

The chart below summarizes the tenses of Japanese verbs and shows the endings—affirmative and negative—that correspond to each.

PRESENT FORM		PAST FORM	
aff.	*neg.*	*aff.*	*neg.*
-masu	**-masen**	**-mashita**	**-masendeshita**

■ The particle **ni**

The role of the preposition "to" in English is played by the particle **ni** in Japanese. **Ni** is placed after a noun that denotes a place. It indicates the direction of movement with verbs such as **ikimasu** ("go"), **kimasu** ("come"), and **kaerimasu** ("return").

ex. **Tōkyō ni ikimasu.** "I am going to Tokyo." (*lit.*, "'Tokyo-ward' I am going.")
In this pattern, the particle **e** can also be used in place of **ni.**

> noun **wa** place **ni ikimasu ka**
> **Hai,** (noun **wa** place **ni**) **ikimasu**
> **Iie,** (noun **wa** place **ni**) **ikimasen**

ex. **Gurei-san wa ashita Kyōto ni ikimasu ka.** "Mr. Grey, will you go to Kyoto tomorrow?"
Hai, ikimasu. "Yes, (I) will go."
Iie, ikimasen. "No, (I) will not go."

■ Questions that contain verbs

To ask a question like "will you go?" that contains a verb, simply add **ka** to the verb. Answers to such questions can be brief, as in the examples above.

CONFIRMING SCHEDULES

 TARGET DIALOGUE

Mr. Smith phones Mr. Takahashi of Nozomi Department Store to confirm the time of Friday's meeting.

スミス：もしもし、ＡＢＣの　スミスです。

たかはし：たかはしです。おはようございます。

スミス：あした　そちらに　いきます。かいぎは　３じからですね。

たかはし：はい、３じからです。ひとりで　きますか。

スミス：いいえ、かいしゃの　ひとと　いきます。

たかはし：そうですか。では、あした。

スミス：しつれいします。

■スミスさんは　あした　かいしゃの　ひとと　のぞみデパートに　いきます。

    Sumisu: Moshimoshi, ABC no Sumisu desu.
Takahashi: Takahashi desu. Ohayō gozaimasu.
    Sumisu: Ashita sochira ni ikimasu. Kaigi wa 3-ji kara desu ne.
Takahashi: Hai, 3-ji kara desu. Hitori de kimasu ka.
    Sumisu: Iie, kaisha no hito to ikimasu.
Takahashi: Sō desu ka. Dewa, ashita.
    Sumisu: Shitsureishimasu.

■ **Sumisu-san wa ashita kaisha no hito to Nozomi Depāto ni ikimasu.**

    Smith: Hello, this is Smith from ABC.
Takahashi: This is Takahashi. Good morning.
    Smith: I'll go to your company (*lit.*, "there") tomorrow. The meeting is from 3:00, right?
Takahashi: Yes, it starts at 3:00. Are you coming alone?
    Smith: No, I'll go with someone from the company.
Takahashi: Is that so? Well then, till tomorrow . . .
    Smith: Good-bye.

■ Mr. Smith is going to Nozomi Department Store with a colleague tomorrow.

VOCABULARY

もしもし	**moshimoshi**	hello (on the telephone)
おはようございます	**ohayō gozaimasu**	good morning
あした	**ashita**	tomorrow
そちら	**sochira**	there (where your listener is)

に	ni	to (particle; see Unit 3 Grammar, p. 48)
いきます	ikimasu	go
ね	ne	right?; isn't it? (particle; see Notes 3 below)
ひとりで	hitori de	alone (*lit.*, "by one person")
きます	kimasu	come
と	to	with, together with (particle)
では	dewa	well then, in any case (formal way of saying **ja**)
しつれいします	shitsureishimasu	good-bye (*lit.*, "I'm going to be rude.")

NOTES

1. Moshimoshi

This is the conventional beginning of a telephone conversation and may be repeated during the call to confirm whether the other party is still on the line.

2. Ashita sochira ni ikimasu.

Relative time expressions like **ashita** "tomorrow," **raishū** ("next week"), **kongetsu** ("this month"), and **kyonen** ("last year") generally do not take particles.

3. Kaigi wa 3-ji kara desu ne.

The particle **ne** comes at the end of a sentence or phrase and, like "isn't it?" in English, seeks confirmation and agreement from the other person. It is spoken with rising intonation.

4. Hitori de kimasu ka.
Iie, kaisha no hito to ikimasu.

The phrase **kaiasha no hito to ikimasu** means "I'll go with someone from the company." The Japanese verbs **ikimasu** and **kimasu** are always used from the point of view of the speaker. **Ikimasu** expresses the idea of moving from where the speaker is now to some other place. **Kimasu**, on the other hand, expresses the idea of moving toward the place where the speaker is now. Therefore, unlike in English, a speaker talking about going to the place where the listener is located, as in the above exchange, uses **ikimasu** rather than **kimasu**.

The particle **to** ("with") in **kaisha no hito to ikimasu** is used to indicate accompaniment.

5. Shitsureishimasu.

This expression is used as a form of "good-bye" when hanging up the phone or leaving a house or room. It is also used when entering a house or room, passing in front of someone, leaving in the middle of a gathering, and so on to mean "excuse me."

PRACTICE

WORD POWER

I. Destinations:

| 1. **kūkō** | 2. **eki** | 3. **shisha** | 4. **kōen** | 5. **tomodachi no uchi** |

II. Verbs:

| 1. **ikimasu** | 2. **kimasu** | 3. **kaerimasu** |

III. Time expressions:

	LAST	THIS	NEXT
day	**kinō**	**kyō**	**ashita**
week	**senshū**	**konshū**	**raishū**
month	**sengetsu**	**kongetsu**	**raigetsu**
year	**kyonen**	**kotoshi**	**rainen**

KEY SENTENCES

1. Sumisu-san wa ashita ginkō ni ikimasu.
2. Sumisu-san wa senshū Honkon ni ikimashita.
3. Chan-san wa kinō tomodachi to resutoran ni ikimashita.
4. Chan-san wa kyonen Nihon ni kimashita.
5. Sumisu-san wa rainen Amerika ni kaerimasu.

1. Mr. Smith is going to the bank tomorrow.
2. Mr. Smith went to Hong Kong last week.
3. Ms. Chan went to a restaurant with a friend yesterday.
4. Ms. Chan came to Japan last year.
5. Mr. Smith will return to the United States next year.

EXERCISES

I. *Practice conjugating verbs.* Repeat the verbs below and memorize their forms—present and past, affirmative and negative.

	PRESENT FORM		PAST FORM	
	aff.	*neg.*	*aff.*	*neg.*
go	ikimasu	ikimasen	ikimashita	ikimasendeshita
come	kimasu	kimasen	kimashita	kimasendeshita
return, go home	kaerimasu	kaerimasen	kaerimashita	kaerimasendeshita

II. Make up sentences following the patterns of the examples. Substitute the underlined words with the alternatives given.

A. *State where someone will go.*

ex. **Sumisu-san wa <u>ginkō</u> ni ikimasu.**

1. Sumisu-san wa kūkō ni ikimasu. _____ (kūkō)
2. Sumisu-san wa Tōkyō Eki ni ikimasu _____ (Tōkyō Eki)
3. Sumisu-san wa Ōsaka-shisha ni ikimasu _____ (Ōsaka-shisha)
4. Sumisu-san wa Ginza no depāto ni ikimasu _____ (Ginza no depāto)

B. *State when someone will go to Kyoto.*

ex. **Sumisu-san wa <u>ashita</u> Kyōto ni ikimasu.**

1. Sumisu-san wa raishu Kyōto ni ikimasu _____ (raishū)
2. Sumisu-san wa raigetsu Kyōto ni ikimasu _____ (raigetsu)
3. Sumisu-san wa asette Kyōto ni ikimasu _____ (asatte)

VOCABULARY			
Honkon	Hong Kong	**Ginza**	Ginza (famous shopping district in Tokyo)
Tōkyō Eki	Tokyo Station	**Kyōto**	Kyoto
Ōsaka-shisha	Osaka (branch) office	**asatte**	the day after tomorrow
Ōsaka	Osaka		

C. *State when someone went to Hong Kong.*

　　ex. **Sumisu-san wa** <u>**kinō**</u> **Honkon ni ikimashita.**

　　1. Sumisu-san wa senshū Honkon ni ikimashita (senshū)

　　2. Sumisu-san wa sengatsu Honkon ni ikimashita (sengetsu)

　　3. Sumisu-san wa kyonen Honkon ni ikimashita (kyonen)

III. Make up dialogues following the patterns of the examples. Substitute the underlined words with the alternatives given.

A. *Ask and answer whether someone will go to a particular place.*

　　ex. **A: Sumisu-san wa ashita** <u>**Kyōto**</u> **ni ikimasu ka.**
　　　　B: Hai, ikimasu.

　　1. A: Sumisu-san wa ashita yūbinkyoku ni ikimasu ka (yūbinkyoku)

　　　 B: Hai, ikimasu

　　2. A: Sumisu-san wa ashita Ginza no depāto ni ikimasu ka (Ginza no depāto)

　　　 B: Hai, ikimasu.

B. *Ask and answer whether someone will go to a particular place.*

　　ex. **A: Sumisu-san wa ashita** <u>**ginkō**</u> **ni ikimasu ka.**
　　　　B: Iie, ikimasen.

　　1. A: Sumisu-san wa ashita Ōsaka-shisha ni ikimasu ka (Ōsaka-shisha)

　　　 B: Iie, ikimasen

　　2. A: Sumisu-san wa ashita kūkō ni ikimasu ka (kūkō)

　　　 B: Iie, ikimasen

C. *Ask and answer whether someone went to a particular place.*

　　ex. **A: Sumisu-san wa kinō** <u>**Honkon**</u> **ni ikimashita ka.**
　　　　B: Hai, ikimashita.

　　1. A: Sumisu-san wa kinō kōen ni ikimashita ka (kōen)

　　　 B: Hai, ikimashita

　　2. A: Sumisu-san wa kinō tomodachi no uchi ni ikimashita ka (tomodachi no uchi)

　　　 B: Hai, ikimashita.

D. *Ask and answer whether someone went to a particular place.*

    ex. **A: Sumisu-san wa kinō** <u>taishikan</u> **ni ikimashita ka.**
    B: Iie, ikimasendeshita.

    1. A: Sumisu-san wa kinō Nozomi Depāto ni ikimashita ka (Nozomi Depāto)

        B: Iie, ikimasendeshita

    2. A: Sumisu-san wa kinō Ginkō ni ikimashita ka (ginkō)

        B: Iie, ikimasendeshita

IV. Make up dialogues following the patterns of the examples. Substitute the underlined words with the alternatives given.

A. *Ask and answer where someone will go.*

    ex. **A: Sumisu-san wa ashita doko ni ikimasu ka.**
    B: <u>Nozomi Depāto</u> **ni ikimasu.**

    1. A: Sumisu-san wa ashita doko ni ikimasu ka

        B: Kyōto ni ikimasu (Kyōto)

    2. A: Sumisu-san wa ashita doko ni ikimasu ka

        B: Tomodachi no uchi ni ikimasu (tomodachi no uchi)

B. *Ask and answer when someone will go to a particular place.*

    ex. **A: Katō-san wa itsu Ōsaka-shisha ni ikimasu ka.**
    B: <u>Raishū</u> **ikimasu.**

    1. A: Katō-san wa itsu Ōsaka-shisha ni ikimasu ka

        B: ashita ikimasu (ashita)

    2. A: Katō-san wa itsu Ōsaka-shisha ni ikimasu ka

        B: raigetsu ikimasu (raigetsu)

V. *State whom someone will go somewhere with.* Make up sentences following the pattern of the example. Substitute the underlined word with the alternatives given.

    ex. **Chan-san wa** <u>tomodachi</u> **to resutoran ni ikimasu.**

    1. Chan-san wa Nakamura-san to resutoran ni ikimasu (Nakamura-san)

    2. Chan-san wa Suzuki-san to resutoran ni ikimasu (Suzuki-san)

    3. Chan-san wa Sumisu-san to resutoran ni ikimasu (Sumisu-san)

VOCABULARY   **itsu**   when

VI. *Ask and answer whom someone will go somewhere with.* Make up dialogues following the pattern of the example. Substitute the underlined word with the alternatives given.

ex. **A: Sumisu-san wa ashita dare to Nozomi Depāto ni ikimasu ka.**
    B: <u>Katō-san</u> to ikimasu.

1. A: Sumisu-san wa ashita dare to Nozomi Depato ni ikimasu ka

   B: chan-san to ikimasu _____ (Chan-san)

2. A: sumisu-san wa ashita dare to Nozomi Depāto ni ikimasu ka

   B: sasaki-san to ikimasu _____ (Sasaki-san)

VII. Make up sentences following the patterns of the examples. Substitute the underlined words with the alternatives given.

A. *State who came to Japan.*

ex. **<u>Sumisu-san</u> wa kyonen Nihon ni kimashita.**

1. chan-san wa kyonen Nihon ni Kimashita _____ (Chan-san)

2. Gurin-san wa kyonen Nihon ni Kimashita _____ (Gurīn-san)

B. *State who will return to America.*

ex. **<u>Sumisu-san</u> wa rainen Amerika ni kaerimasu.**

1. Gurin-san wa rainen Amerika ni kaerimasu (Gurīn-san)

2. Sumisu-san no tomodachi wa rainen Amerika ni kaerimasu (Sumisu-san no tomodachi)

VIII. **State when, where, and with whom someone will travel.** Make up sentences following the pattern of the example and based on the information in the illustration.

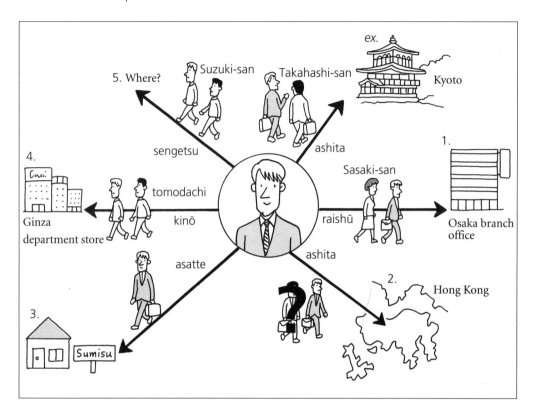

ex. **Sumisu-san wa ashita Takahashi-san to Kyōto ni ikimasu.**

1. Sumisu-san wa raishu Sasaki-san to Ōsaka shisha ni ikimasu
2. Sumisu-san wa ashita donata to Honkon ni ikimasu ka
3. Sumisu-san wa asatte hitori de uchi ni kaerimasu
4. Sumisu-san wa kino tomodachi to Ginza Depāto ni ikimashita
5. Sumisu-san wa sengetsu Suzuki-san to doko ni ikimashita ka

| VOCABULARY | **Yokohama-shisha** | Yokohama (branch) office |
| | **Yokohama** | Yokohama (port city southwest of Tokyo) |

56

IX. *Talk about a plan.* Make up dialogues following the pattern of the example. Substitute the underlined words with the words in parentheses.

ex. Mr. Smith is talking on the phone with a person from the Yokohama branch office.

Yokohama-shisha no hito: Sumisu-san wa itsu Yokohama-shisha ni kimasu ka.
Sumisu: **<u>Ashita</u> ikimasu.**
Yokohama-shisha no hito: Dare to kimasu ka.
Sumisu: **<u>Chan-san</u> to ikimasu.**
Yokohama-shisha no hito: Sō desu ka.

1. Yokohama-shisha no hito: Sumisu-san wa itsu Yokohama-shisha ni kimasu ka

    Sumisu: Raishū ikimasu (raishū)

    Yokohama-shisha no hito: Dare to kimasu ka

    Sumisu: Katō-san (Katō-san)

    Yokohama-shisha no hito: Sō desu ka

2. Yokohama-shisha no hito: Sumisu-san wa itsu Yokohama-shisha ni kimasu

    Sumisu: asatte ikimasu (asatte)

    Yokohama-shisha no hito: Dare to kimasu ka

    Sumisu: sasaki-san (Sasaki-san)

    Yokohama-shisha no hito: Sō desu ka

X. Listen to the CD and fill in the blanks based on the information you hear.

Sumisu-san wa asatte .... to .... ni ikimasu.

SHORT DIALOGUES

I. Ms. Chan sees Mr. Suzuki in front of ABC Foods carrying a large piece of luggage.

Chan: A, Suzuki-san, shutchō desu ka.
Suzuki: Ee, Ōsaka-shisha ni ikimasu. Asatte Tōkyō ni kaerimasu.
Chan: Sō desu ka. Itterasshai.

Chan: Oh, Mr. Suzuki, are you going on a business trip?
Suzuki: Yes, I'm going to the Osaka branch office. I'll come back to Tokyo the day after tomorrow.
Chan: Really? Have a good trip.

VOCABULARY

a	oh (interjection used to get someone's attention)
shutchō	business trip
itterasshai	good-bye, have a nice trip

II. At a bus stop, Mr. Smith asks the driver a question before boarding.

Sumisu:	**Sumimasen. Kono basu wa Shibuya ni ikimasu ka.**
basu no untenshu:	**Iie, ikimasen.**
Sumisu:	**Dono basu ga ikimasu ka.**
basu no untenshu:	**88-ban no basu ga ikimasu.**
Sumisu:	**Arigatō gozaimasu.**

Smith:	Excuse me. Does this bus go to Shibuya?
bus driver:	No, it doesn't.
Smith:	Which bus goes there?
bus driver:	The number 88 bus goes there.
Smith:	Thank you.

VOCABULARY

basu	bus
Shibuya	Shibuya (district in Tokyo)
untenshu	driver
dono	which (used before a noun)
ga	(particle that marks the subject of a sentence; see Note 2 below)
-ban	number . . . (counter; used as a suffix after a number)

NOTES

1. **Dono basu**
   Dore is used alone to mean "which," but if "which" is to be followed by a noun, then **dono** is used.
   ex. **dore**, "which one"
      dono basu, "which bus"

2. **Dono basu ga ikimasu ka.**
   88-ban no basu ga ikimasu.
   The particle **ga** is used instead of the topic marker **wa** after interrogatives like **dore** and **dono**. In the case of **dono**, it follows the noun: **dono basu ga**. Ga is repeated in replies to questions of the **dore ga** or **dono . . . ga** pattern, as in the exchange here.

Active Communication

Ask someone where they are going tomorrow, next week, next month, and so on.

VISITING ANOTHER COMPANY

TARGET DIALOGUE

Mr. Smith goes to Nozomi Department Store on business with Ms. Chan on Friday.

たかはし：スミスさん、チャンさん、どうぞ　おはいりください。

スミス：しつれいします。

チャン：しつれいします。

たかはし：どうぞ　こちらへ。

スミス、チャン：ありがとうございます。

たかはし：くるまで　きましたか。

スミス：いいえ、ちかてつで　きました。

■スミスさんは　きんようびに　チャンさんと　ちかてつで　のぞみ　デパートに　いきました。

      Takahashi: Sumisu-san, Chan-san, dōzo ohairikudasai.
         Sumisu: Shitsureishimasu.
          Chan: Shitsureishimasu.
      Takahashi: Dōzo kochira e.
    Sumisu, Chan: Arigatō gozaimasu.
      Takahashi: Kuruma de kimashita ka.
         Sumisu: Iie, chikatetsu de kimashita.

■ **Sumisu-san wa kin-yōbi ni Chan-san to chikatetsu de Nozomi Depāto ni ikimashita.**

    Takahashi: Mr. Smith, Ms. Chan, please come in.
        Smith: Excuse me.
         Chan: Excuse me.
    Takahashi: Come right this way.
  Smith, Chan: Thank you.
    Takahashi: Did you come by car?
        Smith: No, we came by subway.

■ On Friday, Mr. Smith went with Ms. Chan to Nozomi Department Store by subway.

VOCABULARY

おはいりください	**ohairikudasai**	please come in
どうぞ　こちらへ	**dōzo kochira e**	come right this way
で	**de**	by means of (particle indicating means)
ちかてつ	**chikatetsu**	subway
きんようび	**kin-yōbi**	Friday
に	**ni**	at, on, in (particle indicating time; see Note 2 below)

NOTES

1. Kuruma de kimashita ka.

The function of the particle **de** ("by means of"), which follows nouns, is to express means of conveyance.

ex. **basu de**, "by bus"

takushī de, "by taxi"

But to say "by foot," use **aruite**, e.g., **aruite kimashita**, "(I) walked here."

To ask the means by which someone will go somewhere, use **nan de**:

ex. **Nan de ikimasu ka.** "How will you go?"

Basu de ikimasu. "I'll go by bus."

2. Kin-yōbi ni . . . ikimashita.

Unlike relative time expressions (see Note 2, p. 50), specific time expressions take the particle **ni**.

ex. **5-ji ni**, "at 5:00"

do-yōbi ni, "on Saturday"

12-nichi ni, "on the twelfth"

2006-nen ni, "in 2006"

PRACTICE

WORD POWER

I. Dates:

YEARS		
1998-nen	**sen kyūhyaku kyūjūhachi-nen**	the year 1998
2006-nen	**nisen roku-nen**	the year 2006

DAYS OF THE WEEK	
nichi-yōbi	Sunday
getsu-yōbi	Monday
ka-yōbi	Tuesday
sui-yōbi	Wednesday
moku-yōbi	Thursday
kin-yōbi	Friday
do-yōbi	Saturday

VOCABULARY   **-nen**   year (counter)

               -yōbi   day (of the week)

MONTHS	
ichi-gatsu	January
ni-gatsu	February
san-gatsu	March
shi-gatsu	April
go-gatsu	May
roku-gatsu	June
shichi-gatsu	July
hachi-gatsu	August
ku-gatsu	September
jū-gatsu	October
jūichi-gatsu	November
jūni-gatsu	December

DAYS OF THE MONTH			
tsuitachi	1st	**jūshichi-nichi**	17th
futsuka	2nd	**jūhachi-nichi**	18th
mikka	3rd	**jūku-nichi**	19th
yokka	4th	**hatsuka**	20th
itsuka	5th	**nijūichi-nichi**	21st
muika	6th	**nijūni-nichi**	22nd
nanoka	7th	**nijūsan-nichi**	23rd
yōka	8th	**nijūyokka**	24th
kokonoka	9th	**nijūgo-nichi**	25th
tōka	10th	**nijūroku-nichi**	26th
jūichi-nichi	11th	**nijūshichi-nichi**	27th
jūni-nichi	12th	**nijūhachi-nichi**	28th
jūsan-nichi	13th	**nijūku-nichi**	29th
jūyokka	14th	**sanjū-nichi**	30th
jūgo-nichi	15th	**sanjūichi-nichi**	31st
jūroku-nichi	16th		

NOTE: Months and dates are romanized here, but elsewhere in the book numerals are used to write them, e.g., **1-gatsu** for "January," **11-nichi** for "the eleventh," etc.

II. Means of transportation:

1. **densha** 2. **chikatetsu** 3. **kuruma** 4. **takushī** 5. **shinkansen** 6. **hikōki**

KEY SENTENCES

1. **Kaigi wa sui-yōbi desu.**
2. **Buraun-san wa 3-gatsu 26-nichi ni Igirisu kara Nihon ni kimashita.**
3. **Jonson-san wa raishū no kin-yōbi ni Nihon ni kimasu.**
4. **Sumisu-san wa shinkansen de Ōsaka ni ikimasu.**

1. The meeting is Wednesday.
2. Ms. Brown came to Japan from the United Kingdom on March 26.
3. Mr. Johnson will come to Japan next Friday.
4. Mr. Smith is going to Osaka on the Shinkansen.

VOCABULARY		
-gatsu	month	
-nichi	day (of the month) (counter)	
densha	train	
chikatetsu	subway	
kuruma	car	

takushī	taxi
shinkansen	the Shinkansen (Japan's bullet train)
hikōki	airplane
kara	from (particle indicating origin or point of departure)
Jonson	Johnson (surname)

EXERCISES

I. *State when a meeting will be held.* Make up sentences following the pattern of the example. Substitute the underlined word with the alternatives given.

ex. **Kaigi wa sui-yōbi desu.**

1. kaigi wa getsu-yōbi desu .... (getsu-yōbi)

2. Kaigi wa shi-gatsu hatsuka desu .... (4-gatsu hatsuka)

II. Make up dialogues following the patterns of the examples. Substitute the underlined parts with the alternatives given.

A. *Ask and answer when a festival will be held.*

ex. **A: O-matsuri wa nan-gatsu desu ka.**
    B: 9-gatsu desu.

1. A: O-matsuri wa nan-nichi desu ka ..... (nan-nichi)

   B: Jūshichi-nichi desu .... (17-nichi)

2. A: o-matsuri wa nan-yōbi desu ka (nan-yōbi)

   B: ka-yōbi desu .... (ka-yōbi)

B. *Ask and answer when an event will take place.*

ex. **A: Tanjōbi wa itsu desu ka.**
    B: 8-gatsu 19-nichi desu.

1. A: kaigi wa itsu desu ka .... (kaigi)

   B: shichi-gatsu tsuitachi .... (7-gatsu tsuitachi)

2. A: Pātī wa itsu desu ka .... (pātī)

   B: raishū no do-yōbi desu (raishū no do-yōbi)

C. *Ask and answer when an event will take place, from when and until when.*

ex. **A: Natsu-yasumi wa itsu kara itsu made desu ka.**
    B: 8-gatsu mikka kara 28-nichi made desu.

1. A: Shutchō wa itsu kare itsu made desu ka (shutchō)

   B: getsu-yōbi kara moku-yōbi made desu (getsu-yōbi, moku-yōbi)

2. A: RYOKŌ wa itsu kara itsu made desu ka (ryokō)

   B: shi-gatsu nijūku nichi kara
      go-gatsu itsuka made desu (4-gatsu 29-nichi, 5-gatsu itsuka)

III. *State when someone came to a place.* Make up sentences following the pattern of the example. Substitute the underlined word with the alternatives given.

ex. **Buraun-san wa 4-gatsu ni Igirisu kara kimashita.**

1. Buraun-san wa jūni-gatsu ni Igirisu kara kimashita (11-gatsu)

2. Buraun-san wa san-gatsu nijū roku nichi ni Igirisu kara kimashita (3-gatsu 26-nichi)

3. Buraun-san wa nisen yon-nen ni Igirisu (2004-nen)

IV. *Ask and answer when someone will come to Japan.* Make up dialogues following the pattern of the example. Substitute the underlined word with the alternatives given.

ex. **A: Jonson-san wa itsu Nihon ni kimasu ka.**
B: Sui-yōbi ni kimasu.

1. A: Jonson-san wa itsu Nihon ni kimasu ka

   B: Nichi-yōbi ni kimasu (nichi-yōbi)

2. A: Jonson-san wa itsu Nihon ni kimasu ka

   B: raishū no kin-yōbi ni kimasu (raishū no kin-yōbi)

V. *State how someone got home.* Make up sentences following the pattern of the example. Substitute the underlined part with the alternatives given.

ex. **Sumisu-san wa chikatetsu de uchi ni kaerimashita.**

1. Sumisu-san wa takushi de uchi ni kaerimashita (takushi de)

2. Sumisu-san wa densha de uchi ni kaerimashita (densha de)

3. Sumisu-san wa aruite uchi ni kaerimashita (aruite)

VI. *Ask and answer how someone will get to Osaka.* Make up dialogues following the pattern of the example. Substitute the underlined word with the words in parentheses.

ex. **A: Sumisu-san wa nan de Ōsaka ni ikimasu ka.**
B: Kuruma de ikimasu.

1. A: Sumisu-san wa nan de Osaka ni ikimasu ka

   B: shinkansen de ikimasu (shinkansen)

2. A: Sumisu-san wa nan de Osaka ni ikimasu ka

   B: hikōki de ikimasu (hikōki)

| VOCABULARY | aruite | by foot, by walking |
| | nan de | by what means |

VII. ***State when and how someone will reach his destination.*** Look at the illustration and make up
sentences following the pattern of the example.

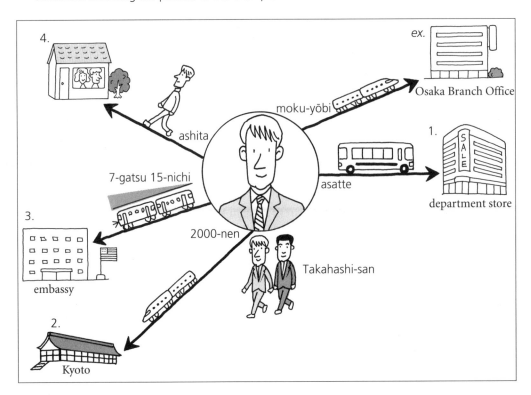

ex. **Sumisu-san wa moku-yōbi ni shinkansen de Ōsaka-shisha ni ikimasu.**

1. sumisu-san wa asatte basu de Depāto ni ikimasu

2. sumisu-san wa nisen-nen ni shinkansen de kyoto ni ikimasushita
   Takahashi-san to

3. sumisu-san wa shichigatsu jūgo-nichi ni chikatetsu de taishikan ni ikimasu

4. sumisu-san wa ashita aruite tomodachi no uchi ni ikimasu

VIII. *Describe a schedule.* Look at the page from Mr. Smith's weekly planner and make up sentences following the pattern of the example and based on the information provided.

ex.	Mon.	12:00	Go to Tokyo Hotel (by taxi, with Mr. Suzuki)
	Tue.		
1.	Wed.		Go to Osaka branch office (by airplane, alone)
	Thu.		
2.	Fri.	12:00	Go to the restaurant (with my secretary)
		4:00	Go to Yokohama branch office (with Ms. Sasaki)
		6:00	Go to the American Embassy
	Sat.		
3.	Sun.	9:00 a.m.	Go to the park (with friends)
		7:00 p.m.	Go to a friend's house (with Mr. Suzuki)

ex. **Sumisu-san wa getsu-yōbi no 12-ji ni Suzuki-san to takushī de Tōkyō Hoteru ni iki-masu.**

1. Sui-yōbi ni hikōki de Ōsaka-shisha ni ikimasu
   <small>hitori</small>

2. Kin-yōbi no jūni-ji ni nishe to resutoran ni ikimasu sorekara
   yo-ji ni Suzuki-san to Yokohama-shisha ni ikimasu sorekara
   roku-ji ni Amerika taishikan ni ikimasu

3. Do-yōbi no ku-ji ni tomodachi to kōen ni ikimasu
   <small>gozen</small>
   sorekara gogo shichi-ji ni suzuki-san to tomodachi no uchi ni ikimasu.

IX. *Talk about a plan.* Make up dialogues following the pattern of the example. Substitute the underlined words with the words in parentheses.

ex. **Ōsaka-shisha no hito: Raishū no getsu-yōbi ni sochira ni ikimasu.**
Sumisu: **Nan-ji ni kimasu ka.**
Ōsaka-shisha no hito: **10-ji ni ikimasu.**
Sumisu: **Nan de kimasu ka.**
Ōsaka-shisha no hito: **Shinkansen de ikimasu.**
Sumisu: **Sō desu ka.**

1. Ōsaka-shisha no hito: Raishū no getsu-yōbi ni sochira ni ikimasu

   Sumisu: Nan-ji ni kimasu ka

   Ōsaka-shisha no hito: ku-ji ni ikimasu (9-ji)

   Sumisu: Nan de kimasu ka

   Ōsaka-shisha no hito: Hikōki de ikimasu (hikōki)

   Sumisu: Sō desu ka

VOCABULARY   **Tōkyō Hoteru**   Tokyo Hotel (fictitious hotel name)
hoteru   hotel

2. Ōsaka-shisha no hito: <u>Raishū no getsu-yōbi ni sochira ni ikimasu</u>

   Sumisu: <u>Nan-ji ni kimasu ka</u>

   Ōsaka-shisha no hito: <u>Jūichi-ji ni ikimasu</u> (11-ji)

   Sumisu: <u>Nan de kimasu ka</u>

   Ōsaka-shisha no hito: <u>shinkansen de ikimasu</u> (shinkansen)

   Sumisu: <u>sō desu ka</u>

TRACK 27

X. Listen to the CD and choose the correct answers to the questions asked.

1. a) getsu-yōbi   b) moku-yōbi   c) sui-yōbi

2. a) 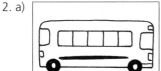   b) 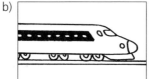   c)

SHORT DIALOGUE

TRACK 28

A conversation while drinking tea at Nozomi Department Store:

Takahashi: Chan-san wa itsu Nihon ni kimashita ka.
Chan: Kyonen no 10-gatsu ni Honkon kara kimashita.
Takahashi: Sō desu ka. Natsu-yasumi ni Honkon ni kaerimasu ka.
Chan: Iie, kaerimasen. Tomodachi to Okinawa ni ikimasu.

Takahashi: Ms. Chan, when did you come to Japan?
Chan: I came in October of last year, from Hong Kong.
Takahashi: Really? Will you go back to Hong Kong for summer vacation?
Chan: No, I won't. I'm going to Okinawa with a friend.

VOCABULARY

Okinawa   Okinawa (islands on the southwestern tip of Japan)

Active Communication

1. Ask people when their birthdays are.

2. Ask people when their summer vaca-
   tions are.

A WEEKEND EXCURSION

In the vicinity of Tokyo lie a number of places to visit for pleasure. From the historical sites of Nikko in the north to the gorgeous lakes surrounding Mt. Fuji in the southwest, these locations are only about two hours away from the city. Other popular places include Kamakura, a historical town that dates back to the twelfth century; Okutama, a region abound with rivers, gorges, and mountains; and Hakone, an attractive place to enjoy *onsen*. *Onsen* are Japanese spas, and to visit one is a small luxury that the Japanese enjoy tremendously.

UNIT ■
4 GRAMMAR

Existence of People and Things

| place **ni** noun **ga arimasu/imasu** |

> *ex.* **1-kai ni resutoran ga arimasu.** "There is a restaurant on the first floor."
> **Uketsuke ni onna no hito ga imasu.** "There is a woman at the reception desk."

■ The verbs **arimasu** and **imasu**

Both verbs express "being." **Arimasu** is used for inanimate things (books, buildings, trees), and **imasu** for animate things (people, animals, insects).

■ The particle **ni**

Existence in or at a place is indicated by the particle **ni**.

■ The subject marker **ga**

When a subject is introduced for the first time, or when the speaker believes the information to be new to the listener, the subject marker **ga** is used after the noun. **Ga** should be used, for instance, when stating that someone or something unknown to your listener is in or at a particular place.

| noun **wa** place **ni arimasu/imasu** |

> *ex.* **Resutoran wa 1-kai ni arimasu.** "The restaurant is on the first floor."

■ Ga → wa

To state that a thing or person exists in a particular location, use **ga arimasu/imasu**, as in **1-kai ni resutoran ga arimasu**. But if you want to comment about that thing or person—even to say where it or he/she exists—use **wa** instead of **ga**, as in **Resutoran wa 1-kai ni arimasu**, where "the restaurant" is the topic of the sentence. Note the difference in translation: "There is a restaurant on the first floor" for the first sentence, versus "The restaurant is on the first floor" for the second.

TARGET DIALOGUE

Mr. Kato and Ms. Chan are talking about Nikko.

かとう：どようびに　かぞくと　にっこうに　いきます。

チャン：そうですか。にっこうに　なにが　ありますか。

かとう：おおきい　おてらや　じんじゃが　あります。おんせんも
　　　　あります。

チャン：おんせんって　なんですか。

かとう：(*shows her a pamphlet and points*) これです。にほんの　スパですよ。

チャン：いいですね。

■ かとうさんは　どようびに　かぞくと　にっこうに　いきます。
　にっこうに　おおきい　おてらや　じんじゃが　あります。

> **Katō:** Do-yōbi ni kazoku to Nikkō ni ikimasu.
> **Chan:** Sō desu ka. Nikkō ni nani ga arimasu ka.
> **Katō:** Ōkii o-tera ya jinja ga arimasu. Onsen mo arimasu.
> **Chan:** Onsen tte nan desu ka.
> **Katō:** (*shows her a pamphlet and points*) **Kore desu. Nihon no supa desu yo.**
> **Chan:** Ii desu ne.

The Toshogu Shrine (Nikko)

■ **Katō-san wa do-yōbi ni kazoku to Nikkō ni ikimasu.
Nikkō ni ōkii o-tera ya jinja ga arimasu.**

> Kato: On Saturday I'm going to Nikko with my family.
> Chan: Really? What is there in Nikko?
> Kato: There are large temples and shrines. There are also *onsen*.
> Chan: What are *onsen*?
> Kato: These. Japanese spas.
> Chan: That's nice.

■ Mr. Kato will go to Nikko with his family on Saturday. There are
large temples and shrines (and other such things) in Nikko.

Nikko

VOCABULARY

かぞく	**kazoku**	family
にっこう	**Nikkō**	Nikko (scenic area north of Tokyo)
なに	**nani**	what
あります	**arimasu**	be, exist
おてら	**o-tera**	Buddhist temple

や	ya	and, and so on (particle; see Note 1 below)
じんじゃ	jinja	Shinto shrine
おんせん	onsen	hot spring (resort)
～って なんですか	-tte nan desu ka	what is a/an . . . ?
スパ	supa	spa
よ	yo	(particle; see Note 2 below)
いいですね	ii desu ne	that's nice

NOTES

1. **(Nikkō ni) o-tera ya jinja ga arimasu.**

   The particle **ya** is used for "and" when listing two or more things or people and implying the existence of others. Another particle, **to**, also means "and," but it does not imply the existence of other people or things.

   > *ex.* **1-kai ni ginkō to kombini ga arimasu.**

   > "There is a bank and a convenience store on the first floor (and nothing else)."

   Note that unlike "and" in English, both **ya** and **to** are used only to connect nouns. They cannot be used to connect verbs or clauses.

2. **Nihon no supa desu yo.**

   The particle **yo** is added to the end of a sentence to call attention to information the speaker thinks the other person does not know.

PRACTICE

WORD POWER

I. Parts of a building:

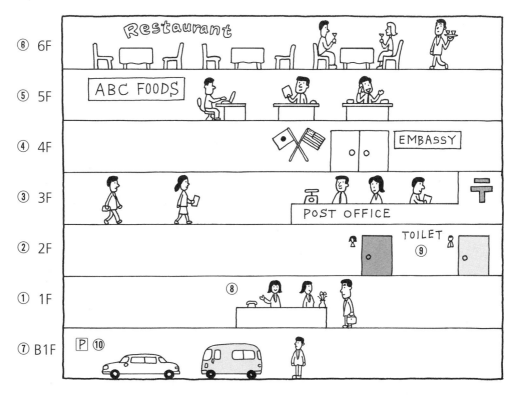

1. **ikkai**	4. **yon-kai**	7. **chika ikkai**	10. **chūshajō**
2. **ni-kai**	5. **go-kai**	8. **uketsuke**	
3. **san-gai**	6. **rokkai**	9. **o-tearai**	

NOTE: Floors are romanized here, but elsewhere in the book they are spelled with numerals, e. g., **1-kai** for "first floor," **3-gai** for "third floor," etc.

II. Things in a hotel room:

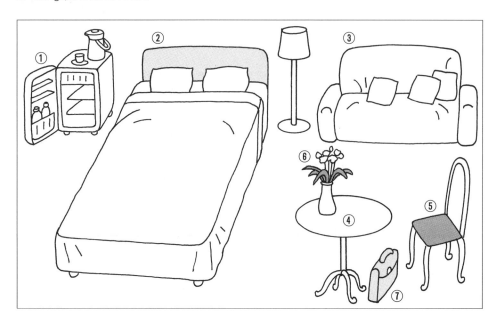

1. **reizōko**   2. **beddo**   3. **sofā**   4. **tēburu**   5. **isu**   6. **hana**   7. **kaban**

III. Positions:

1. **ue**

2. **shita**

3. **mae**

4. **ushiro**

5. **naka**

6. **tonari**

7. **chikaku**

VOCABULARY						
reizōko	refrigerator	**hana**	flower	**ushiro**	back, behind
beddo	bed	**kaban**	briefcase, tote bag	**naka**	inside, middle
sofā	sofa	**ue**	top, above	**tonari**	next to
tēburu	table	**shita**	bottom, below, under	**chikaku**	vicinity, nearby
isu	chair	**mae**	front, before		

KEY SENTENCES

1. 1-kai ni ginkō ga arimasu.
2. Uketsuke ni onna no hito ga imasu.
3. Tēburu no ue ni shimbun to hana ga arimasu.
4. Kaban no naka ni kagi ya hon ga arimasu.
5. Tēburu no ue ni nani mo arimasen.
6. 2-kai ni dare mo imasen.

1. There is a bank on the first floor.
2. There is a woman at the reception desk.
3. There is a newspaper and some flowers on the table.
4. Inside the briefcase there are keys and books and so on.
5. There is nothing on the table.
6. There is no one on the second floor.

EXERCISES

I. *Practice conjugating verbs.* Repeat the verbs below and memorize their forms—present and past, affirmative and negative.

	PRESENT FORM		PAST FORM	
	aff.	*neg.*	*aff.*	*neg.*
be	arimasu	arimasen	arimashita	arimasendeshita
be	imasu	imasen	imashita	imasendeshita

II. Make up sentences following the patterns of the examples. Substitute the underlined words with the words in the parentheses.

A. *State what is in or at a particular place.*

ex. **Nikkō ni <u>o-tera</u> ga arimasu.**

1. Nikkō ni jinja ga arimasu. (jinja)
2. Nikkō ni mizummi ga arimasu (mizuumi)

B. *State who is at a particular place.*

ex. **Uketsuke ni <u>onna no hito</u> ga imasu.**

1. Uketsuke ni otoko no hito ga imasu (otoko no hito)
2. Uketsuke ni Tanaka-san ga imasu (Takahashi-san)

VOCABULARY				
imasu	be, exist (only of animate objects)	**mizuumi**	lake
to	and (particle; see Note 1, p. 70)	**otoko no hito**	man
nani mo . . . -masen	nothing	**otoko**	male, man
dare mo . . . -masen	no one		

III. Make up dialogues following the patterns of the examples. Substitute the underlined words with the words in parentheses.

A. *Ask and answer what is at a particular place.*

ex. **A: 1-kai ni nani ga arimasu ka.**
B: Ginkō ga arimasu.

1. A: Ni-kai ni nani ga arimasu ka _____ (2-kai)

   B: yūbinkyoku _____ (yūbinkyoku)

2. A: san-kai ni nani ga arimasu ka (3-gai)

   B: taishikan _____ (taishikan)

B. *Ask and answer who is at a particular place.*

ex. **A: Uketsuke ni dare ga imasu ka.**
B: Takahashi-san ga imasu.

1. A: Chūshajō ni dare ga imasu ka _____ (chūshajō)

   B: Otoko no hito ga imasu _____ (otoko no hito)

2. A: 3-gai ni dare ga imasu ka _____ (3-gai)

   B: Sumisu-san ga imasu _____ (Sumisu-san)

IV. *State where a thing is located.* Make up sentences following the pattern of the example. Substitute the underlined part with the alternatives given.

ex. **Tēburu no ue ni saifu ga arimasu.**

1. Kaban no naka ni saifu ga arimasu (kaban no naka)
2. shimbun no shita ni saifu ga arimasu (shimbun no shita)

V. Make up dialogues following the patterns of the examples. Substitute the underlined part(s) with the alternatives given.

A. *Ask and answer what is inside another thing.*

ex. **A: Kaban no naka ni nani ga arimasu ka.**
B: Pen ga arimasu.

1. A: Kaban no naka ni nani ga arimasu ka

   B: kagi ga arimasu _____ (kagi)

2. A: kaban no naka ni nani ga arimasu ka

   B: keitai ga arimasu _____ (keitai)

VOCABULARY	**pen**	pen
	saifu	wallet

3. A: kanban no naka ni nani ga arimasu ka

   B: saifu ga arimasu. _____ (saifu)

4. A: kanban no naka ni nani ga arimasu ka

   B: Nihon-go no hon ga arimasu (Nihon-go no hon)

B. *Ask and answer what is on, in, or nearby another thing.*

  ex. **A: <u>Tēburu no ue</u> ni nani ga arimasu ka.**
      B: <u>Shimbun to hana</u> ga arimasu.

1. A: sofā no ue ni nani ga arimasu ka (sofā no ue)

   B: hon to sētā ga arimasu. _____ (hon to sētā)

2. A: reizōko no naka ni nani ga arimasu ka (reizōko no naka)

   B: mizu ya bīru ga arimasu _____ (mizu ya bīru)

3. A: beddo no chikaku ni nani ga arimasu ka (beddo no chikaku)

   B: denwa ga arimasu _____ (denwa)

C. *Ask and answer what is in or on another thing.*

  ex. **A: <u>Hikidashi no naka</u> ni nani ga arimasu ka.**
      B: Nani mo arimasen.

1. A: isu no ue ni nani ga arimasu ka (isu no ue)

   B: nani mo arimasen _____

2. A: poketto no naka ni nani ga arimasu ka (poketto no naka)

   B: nani mo arimasen _____

D. *Ask and answer who is at a particular place.*

  ex. **A: <u>2-kai</u> ni dare ga imasu ka.**
      B: Dare mo imasen.

1. A: 5-kai ni dare ga imasu ka (5-kai)

   B: dare mo imasen

2. A: uketsuke ni dare ga imasu ka (uketsuke)

   B: dare mo arimasen.

VOCABULARY	**Nihon-go**	Japanese (language)	**hikidashi**	drawer
	sētā	sweater	**poketto**	pocket
	mizu	(cold) water		

location no

VI. *State or ask where someone or something is located.* Make up sentences following the pattern of the example and based on the information in the illustrations.

ex. **2-kai ni ginkō ga arimasu.**

1. 3-gai ni resutoran ga arimasu
2. 1-kai ni tanaka-san ga imasu
3. 4-kai ni nani-ga arimasu ka? chika ikkai
4. ~ ni dare ga imasu ka.
5. Isu no ue ni kaban ga arimasu
6. Tēburu no ue ni hana to hon ga arimasu
7. Beddo no tonari ni tanaka-san ga imasu.
8. Reizōko no naka ni nani ga arimasu

VII. *Talk about a tourist destination.* Make up dialogues following the pattern of the example. Substitute the underlined parts with the alternatives given.

ex. **Katō:** Nichi-yōbi ni kuruma de **Hakone** ni ikimasu.
Sumisu: Sō desu ka. **Hakone** ni nani ga arimasu ka.
Katō: **Mizuumi ya onsen** ga arimasu.
Sumisu: Ii desu ne.

1. Katō: Nichi-yōbi ni kuruma de kamakura ni ikimasu (Kamakura)

   Sumisu: Sō desu ka. kamakura ni nani ga arimasu ka (Kamakura)

   Katō: Jinja ya o-tera ga arimasu. (jinja ya o-tera)

   Sumisu: Ii desu ne.

VOCABULARY

Hakone   Hakone (national park southwest of Tokyo)

Kamakura   Kamakura (historic town southwest of Tokyo)

Odaiba   Odaiba (new town with a shopping center, built on reclaimed land in Tokyo Bay)

2. Katō: Nichi-yōbi ni kuruma de Odaiba ni ikimasu (Odaiba)

Sumisu: Sō desu ka. Odaiba ni nani ga arimasu ka (Odaiba)

Katō: mizuumi ya onsen ga arimasu (hoteru ya onsen)

Sumisu: Iie desu ne

VIII. Listen to the CD and fill in the blanks based on the information you hear.

1. 1-kai ni .... ga arimasu.

2. 2-kai ni .... ga arimasu.

3. 3-gai ni .... ga arimasu.

SHORT READING

Mr. Kato stays at a famous inn in Nikko.

Ryokan no chikaku ni ōkii mizuumi ya taki ga arimasu.
Ryokan no tonari ni soba-ya ga arimasu. Ryokan no mae ni chiisai kōen ga arimasu.

Near the inn are things like a large lake and waterfalls. Next to the inn is a buckwheat noodle shop. In front of the inn is a small park.

VOCABULARY

ryokan	traditional Japanese inn
taki	waterfall
soba-ya	buckwheat noodle shop
-ya	shop (suffix)

Active Communication

Using the vocabulary you have learned so far, ask someone what is in his or her hometown or nearby his or her house.

LOOKING FOR A PARKING LOT

🔊 TARGET DIALOGUE

TRACK 32

Mr. Kato has come to Nikko. He asks a salesperson at a store where to find a parking lot.

かとう：すみません。この　ちかくに　ちゅうしゃじょうが

　　　　ありますか。

みせの　ひと：ええ、ありますよ。

かとう：どこですか。

みせの　ひと：あそこに　コンビニが　ありますね。

　　　　ちゅうしゃじょうは　あの　コンビニの　となりです。

かとう：どうも　ありがとう。

■ ちゅうしゃじょうは　コンビニの　となりに　あります。

　　　　Katō: Sumimasen. Kono chikaku ni chūshajō ga arimasu ka.
mise no hito: **Ee, arimasu yo.**
　　　　Katō: Doko desu ka.
mise no hito: **Asoko ni kombini ga arimasu ne. Chūshajō wa ano kombini no tonari desu.**
　　　　Katō: Dōmo arigatō.

■ **Chūshajō wa kombini no tonari ni arimasu.**

　　　Kato: Excuse me. Is there a parking lot in the vicinity?
salesperson: Yes, there is.
　　　Kato: Where is it?
salesperson: There's a convenience store over there, right? The parking lot is next to the convenience store.
　　　Kato: Thank you.

■ The parking lot is next to the convenience store.

only for location

koko here　*soko (where the listener)*

VOCABULARY

| あそこ | asoko | over there |
| コンビニ | kombini | convenience store |

NOTES

1. Chūshajō wa kombini no tonari desu.

When the verb is understood, **desu** sometimes takes its place at the end of the sentence.

ex. **Terebi wa doko ni arimasu ka.** "Where is the TV set?"
Tēburu no ue desu (instead of **Tēburu no ue ni arimasu**). "It's on the table."

If it is uncertain whether there is a TV set, **desu** cannot be substituted, and **arimasu** must be repeated to make the meaning clear.

ex. **Tēburu no ue ni terebi ga arimasu ka.** "Is there a TV set on the table?"
Hai, arimasu./Hai, terebi ga arimasu. "Yes, there is./Yes, there is a TV set."

PRACTICE

WORD POWER

I. Things near a train station:

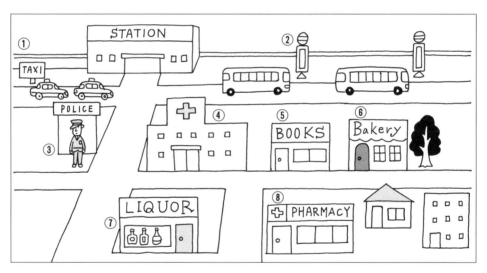

1. **takushī-noriba**	3. **kōban**	5. **hon-ya**	7. **saka-ya**
2. **basu-noriba**	4. **byōin**	6. **pan-ya**	8. **kusuri-ya**

VOCABULARY

takushī-noriba	taxi stand	**hon-ya**	bookstore	**kusuri-ya**	drugstore
basu-noriba	bus terminal	**pan-ya**	bakery	**kusuri**	medicine
kōban	police box	**pan**	bread		
byōin	hospital, clinic	**saka-ya**	liquor store		

II. Office supplies:

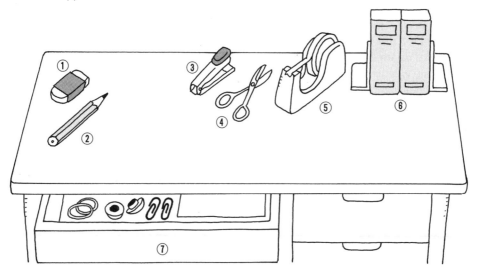

1. **keshigomu**
2. **empitsu**
3. **hotchikisu**
4. **hasami**
5. **sero-tēpu**
6. **fairu**
7. **hikidashi**

III. Numbers of people:

	hitori
	futari
	san-nin
	yo-nin
	go-nin
?	**nan-nin**

NOTE: Other than **hitori** and **futari**, numbers of people from now on will be expressed with numerals: **3-nin**, **4-nin**, etc.

VOCABULARY					
keshigomu	eraser	**sero-tēpu**	Scotch tape	**san-nin**	three people
empitsu	pencil	**fairu**	file	**-nin**	person (counter)
hotchikisu	stapler	**hitori**	one person	**nan-nin**	how many people
hasami	scissors	**futari**	two people		

80

KEY SENTENCES

1. **Tēburu no ue ni bīru ga 2-hon arimasu.**
2. **Kombini no mae ni otoko no hito ga futari imasu.**
3. **Takushī-noriba wa eki no chikaku ni arimasu.**
4. **Yūbinkyoku wa ano biru no naka desu.**

1. There are two bottles of beer on the table.
2. There are two men in front of the convenience store.
3. The taxi stand is in the vicinity of the station.
4. The post office is inside that building over there.

EXERCISES

 I. Make up sentences following the patterns of the examples. Substitute the underlined words with the words in parentheses.

A. *State how many of a certain object are in a drawer.*

ex. **Hikidashi no naka ni <u>pen</u> ga <u>5-hon</u> arimasu.**

1. Hikidashi no naka ni meishi ga 3-mai arimasu (meishi, 3-mai).
2. Hikidashi no naka ni keshigomu ga futatsu arimasu (keshigomu, futatsu)
3. Hikidashi no naka ni fairu ga takusan arimasu (fairu, takusan)

B. *State how many people are in front of a building.*

ex. **Kombini no mae ni <u>otoko no hito</u> ga <u>futari</u> imasu.**

1. Kombini no mae ni onna no hito ga 3-nin imasu. (onna no hito, 3-nin)
2. Kombini no mae ni otoko no ko ga hitori imasu (otoko no ko, hitori)
3. Kombini no mae ni onna no ko ga takusan imasu (onna no ko, takusan)

 II. Make up dialogues following the patterns of the examples. Substitute the underlined words with the words in parentheses.

A. *Ask and answer how many of a certain object are on a table.*

ex. **A: Tēburu no ue ni <u>ringo</u> ga <u>ikutsu</u> arimasu ka.**
    B: <u>Mittsu</u> arimasu.

1. A: Tēburu no ue ni kitte ga nan-mai arimasu ka (kitte, nan-mai)
   B: go mai arimasu (5-mai)
2. A: Tēburu no ue ni bīru ga nan bon arimasu ka (bīru, nan-bon)
   B: nihon arimasu (2-hon)

VOCABULARY			
takusan	a lot, many, much	**ikutsu**	how many (small objects)
otoko no ko	boy	**nan-mai**	how many (flat objects)
ko	child	**nan-bon**	how many (long, thin objects)
onna no ko	girl		

81

3. A: Tēburu no ue ni kōhī-kappu ga ikutsu *arimasu ka* (kōhī-kappu, ikutsu)

   B: Yottsu arimasu .... (yottsu)

B. *Ask and answer how many people are in front of a building.*

   ex. **A: Ginkō no mae ni otoko no hito ga nan-nin imasu ka.**
   B: Hitori imasu.

   1. A: Ginkō no mae ni onna no hito ga nan-*nin imasu ka* (onna no hito)

      B: Yo-nin imasu .... (4-nin)

   2. A: Ginkō no mae ni otoko no ko ga nan-*nin imasu ka* (otoko no ko)

      B: Futari imasu .... (futari)

   3. A: Ginkō no mae ni gakusei ga nan-nin *imasu ka* (gakusei)

      B: Takusan imasu .... (takusan)

III. *Indicate where a facility or store is located.* Make up sentences following the pattern of the example and based on the information in the illustrations.

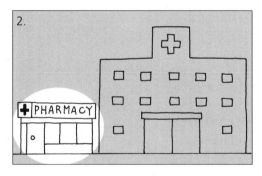

   ex. **Chūshajō wa kombini no tonari ni arimasu.**

   1. Takūshī-noriba wa eki no mae ni *arimasu* (takushī-noriba, eki no mae)

   2. Kusuri-ya wa byōin no tonari ni *arimasu* (kusuri-ya, byōin no tonari)

   3. Kōban wa asoko ni arimasu .... (kōban, asoko)

IV. Make up dialogues following the patterns of the examples. Substitute the underlined parts with the alternatives given.

A. *Ask and answer where something is.*

ex. **A: Chūshajō** wa doko ni arimasu ka.
    B: Kombini no tonari ni arimasu.

1. A: Takushī-noriba wa doko ni arimasu ka (takushī-noriba)
   B: eki no mae ni arimasu (eki no mae)

2. A: Hon-ya wa doko ni arimasu ka (hon-ya)
   B: depāto no tonari ni arimasu (depāto no tonari)

3. A: kyō no shimbun wa doko ni arimasu ka (kyō no shimbun)
   B: koko ni arimasu (koko)

4. A: Kuruma no kagi wa doko ni arimasu ka (kuruma no kagi)
   B: kaban no naka ni arimasu (kaban no naka)

B. *Ask and answer where someone is.*

ex. **A: Sumisu-san** wa doko ni imasu ka.
    B: 2-kai ni imasu.

1. A: Takahashi san wa doko ni imasu ka (Takahashi-san)
   B: niwa ni imasu (niwa)

2. A: Gurīn-san wa doko ni imasu ka (Gurīn-san)
   B: 3-gai ni imasu (3-gai)

3. A: Sasaki-san wa doko ni imasu ka (Sasaki-san)
   B: kaigishitsu ni imasu ka (kaigishitsu)

C. *Ask and answer where something or someone is.*

ex. **A: Kōban** wa doko desu ka.
    B: Eki no mae desu.

1. A: O-tearai wa doko desu ka (o-tearai)
   B: asoko desu (asoko)

2. A: hasami wa doko desu ka (hasami)
   B: tēburu no ue desu (tēburu no ue)

VOCABULARY	koko	here
	niwa	garden
	kaigishitsu	conference room

3. A: <u>Bīru wa doko desu ka</u> (bīru)

   B: <u>reizōko no naka desu</u> (reizōko no naka)

4. A: <u>Sumisu-san wa doko desu ka</u> (Sumisu-san)

   B: <u>2 kai desu</u> (2-kai)

V. ***Ask where a facility or store at an airport is located.*** Make up sentences following the pattern of the example and based on the information in the illustration.

ex. **Chan: <u>Chekkuin-kauntā wa doko ni arimasu ka.</u>**

1. Chan: <u>takushī-noriba wa doko ni arimasu ka</u>

2. Chan: <u>Ginkō wa doko ni arimasu ka</u>

3. Chan: <u>kāto wa doko ni arimasu ka</u>

4. Chan: <u>kusuri-ya wa doko ni arimasu ka</u>

5. Chan: <u>Toshokan wa doko ni arimasu ka</u>

6. Chan: <u>O-tearai wa doko ni arimasu ka</u>

VOCABULARY	**kāto**	cart (for luggage)
	chekkuin-kauntā	check-in counter

VI. *Talk about where a facility is located.* Make up dialogues following the pattern of the example. Substitute the underlined parts with the alternatives given.

ex. **otoko no hito: Sumimasen. Kono chikaku ni <u>takushī-noriba</u> ga arimasu ka.**
Chan: Ee, arimasu yo.
otoko no hito: Doko desu ka.
Chan: <u>Takushī-noriba</u> wa <u>eki no mae</u> desu.
otoko no hito: Dōmo arigatō gozaimasu.

1. otoko no hito: .... (basutei)

   Chan: ....

   otoko no hito: ....

   Chan: .... (kombini no mae)

   otoko no hito: ....

2. otoko no hito: .... (yūbinkyoku)

   Chan: ....

   otoko no hito: ....

   Chan: .... (ano biru no naka)

   otoko no hito: ....

3. otoko no hito: .... (chikatetsu no iriguchi)

   Chan: ....

   otoko no hito: ....

   Chan: .... (asoko)

   otoko no hito: ....

VII. Listen to the CD and fill in the blank based on the information you hear.

TRACK
34

    Chūshajō wa .... desu.

VOCABULARY	**basutei**	bus stop
	iriguchi	entrance

SHORT DIALOGUES

TRACK 35

I. Mr. Kato is looking for today's newspaper.

Katō: **Kyō no shimbun wa doko ni arimasu ka.**
Chan: **Koko ni arimasu. Hai, dōzo.**

Kato: Where is today's paper?
Chan: It's here. Here you go.

II. Mr. Kato calls Mr. Suzuki on his cell phone while Mr. Suzuki is out on a sales visit.

Katō: **Suzuki-san, ima doko desu ka.**
Suzuki: **Ima Nozomi Depāto ni imasu.**
Katō: **Nan-ji goro kaisha ni kaerimasu ka.**
Suzuki: **3-ji ni kaerimasu.**

Kato: Mr. Suzuki, where are you now?
Suzuki: I'm at Nozomi Department Store.
Kato: About what time are you coming back to the office?
Suzuki: I'll be back at 3:00.

VOCABULARY

nan-ji goro   about/approximately what time

goro   about (used of time; see Note 1 below)

NOTES

1. Nan-ji goro . . .

The suffix **goro** is used to indicate an approximate point in time. Unlike "about" in English, however, it cannot be used to express an approximate period.

Active Communication

If you're in Japan, go out on the street and ask people if there is a station, department store, post office, etc. in the vicinity.

DINING OUT

Japanese cuisine is not just sushi and tempura; in fact, most Japanese people only have these dishes occasionally. There are many different kinds of foods in Japan and, consequently, many specialty restaurants. The inexpensive restaurants typically showcase their dishes—sometimes the real thing, but more often than not plastic replicas—in their front windows. Among the most expensive establishments are sushi bars and tempura restaurants. Ginza, an upscale shopping district in Tokyo that features in this unit, is famous for its restaurants and bars.

5 GRAMMAR

Verbs That Take a Grammatical Object

| person **wa** noun **o** verb |

    ex. **Gurei-san wa eiga o mimasu.** "Mr. Grey will see a movie."

■ The particle **o**

Placed after a noun, **o** indicates that the noun is the object of the sentence. **O** is used with verbs like **mimasu** ("see"), **yomimasu** ("read"), **nomimasu** ("drink"), **kaimasu** ("buy"), and a host of others.

| person 1 **wa** person 2 **ni** verb |

    ex. **Gurei-san wa Yoshida-san ni aimasu.** "Mr. Grey will meet Mr. Yoshida."

■ The particle **ni**

The particle **ni** can also serve as an object marker, as in the example here, where Mr. Yoshida is the object of the verb **aimasu** ("meet"). Essentially, **ni** indicates the person or thing an action is directed at.

| person 1 **wa** person 2/place **ni** noun **o** verb |

    ex. **Gurei-san wa Yoshida-san ni tegami o kakimashita.**
    "Mr. Grey wrote a letter to Mr. Yoshida."
    Gurei-san wa taishikan ni tegami o kakimashita.
    "Mr. Grey wrote a letter to the embassy."

■ The particle **ni**

With verbs like **tegami o kakimasu** ("write a letter"), **nimotsu o okurimasu** ("send luggage"), and **denwa o shimasu** ("telephone"), **ni** indicates the receiver of the action. In English, the receiver corresponds to the indirect object.

MAKING PLANS FOR THE WEEKEND

 TARGET DIALOGUE

Ms. Sasaki and Mr. Smith are talking about their plans for the weekend.

スミス：しゅうまつに　なにを　しますか。

ささき：どようびに　ともだちと　かぶきを　みます。

スミス：そうですか。

ささき：スミスさんは？

スミス：にちようびに　ぎんざで　すずきさんと　てんぷらを
　　　　たべます。

ささき：いいですね。

■ ささきさんは　どようびに　ともだちと　かぶきを　みます。
　スミスさんは　にちようびに　ぎんざで　すずきさんと　てんぷらを
　たべます。

Sumisu: Shūmatsu ni nani o shimasu ka.
 Sasaki: Do-yōbi ni tomodachi to Kabuki o mimasu.
Sumisu: Sō desu ka.
 Sasaki: Sumisu-san wa?
Sumisu: Nichi-yōbi ni Ginza de Suzuki-san to tempura o tabemasu.
 Sasaki: Ii desu ne.

■ **Sasaki-san wa do-yōbi ni tomodachi to Kabuki o mimasu.**
 Sumisu-san wa nichi-yōbi ni Ginza de Suzuki-san to tempura o tabemasu.

 Smith: What are you going to do during the weekend?
 Sasaki: I'm going to see Kabuki with a friend on Saturday.
 Smith: Oh, really.
 Sasaki: What about you?
 Smith: I'm going to eat tempura in Ginza with Mr. Suzuki on Sunday.
 Sasaki: Sounds good.

■ Ms. Sasaki is going to see Kabuki with a friend on Saturday. Mr. Smith is going to eat tempura
 in Ginza with Mr. Suzuki on Sunday.

VOCABULARY

しゅうまつ	**shūmatsu**	weekend
します	**shimasu**	do
かぶき	**Kabuki**	Kabuki (a traditional form of theater)
みます	**mimasu**	see

で	de	(particle indicating the location where an action takes place)
てんぷら	tempura	tempura (deep-fried seafood/vegetables)
たべます	tabemasu	eat

NOTES

1. Ginza de Suzuki-san to tempura o tabemasu.
Nouns and place names concerned with actions such as where things are bought, seen, eaten, sold and so on take the particle **de**.

PRACTICE

WORD POWER

I. Food:

1. **asa-gohan**	4. **kōhī**	7. **sake**	10. **jūsu**
2. **hiru-gohan**	5. **kōcha**	8. **sūpu**	11. **sandoitchi**
3. **ban-gohan**	6. **o-cha**	9. **miruku**	12. **sarada**

VOCABULARY	**asa-gohan**	breakfast	**kōcha**	tea	**miruku**	milk
	hiru-gohan	lunch	**o-cha**	green tea	**jūsu**	juice
	ban-gohan	dinner	**sake**	sake (Japanese rice wine)	**sandoitchi**	sandwich
90	**kōhī**	coffee	**sūpu**	soup	**sarada**	salad

II. Verbs:

1. **tabemasu**   2. **nomimasu**   3. **kaimasu**   4. **yomimasu**   5. **kikimasu**

6. **mimasu**   7. **tenisu o shimasu**   8. **benkyō o shimasu**   9. **kaimono o shimasu**   10. **shigoto o shimasu**

NOTE: For more on the "noun **o shimasu**" verb type, see p. 246

III. Time expressions:

	DAY	MORNING	EVENING	WEEK
every	**mainichi**	**maiasa**	**maiban**	**maishū**

KEY SENTENCES

1. **Sumisu-san wa ashita eiga o mimasu.**
2. **Sumisu-san wa mainichi jogingu o shimasu.**
3. **Sumisu-san wa kinō resutoran de ban-gohan o tabemashita.**

1. Mr. Smith is going to see a movie tomorrow.
2. Mr. Smith jogs every day.
3. Mr. Smith ate dinner at a restaurant yesterday.

VOCABULARY

tabemasu	eat	mimasu	see	mainichi	every day
nomimasu	drink	tenisu o shimasu	play tennis	maiasa	every morning
kaimasu	buy	benkyō o shimasu	study	maiban	every evening
yomimasu	read	kaimono o shimasu	shop	maishū	every week
kikimasu	listen (to)	shigoto o shimasu	work	jogingu o shimasu	jog

EXERCISES

 I. **Practice conjugating verbs.** Repeat the verbs below and memorize their forms—present and past, affirmative and negative.

	PRESENT FORM		PAST FORM	
	aff.	*neg.*	*aff.*	*neg.*
eat	**tabemasu**	**tabemasen**	**tabemashita**	**tabemasendeshita**
drink	**nomimasu**	**nomimasen**	**nomimashita**	**nomimasendeshita**
buy	**kaimasu**	**kaimasen**	**kaimashita**	**kaimasendeshita**
read	**yomimasu**	**yomimasen**	**yomimashita**	**yomimasendeshita**
listen (to)	**kikimasu**	**kikimasen**	**kikimashita**	**kikimasendeshita**
see	**mimasu**	**mimasen**	**mimashita**	**mimasendeshita**
do	**shimasu**	**shimasen**	**shimashita**	**shimasendeshita**

 II. Make up sentences following the patterns of the examples. Substitute the underlined words with the words in parentheses.

A. *State what someone will see.*

   ex. **Suzuki-san wa <u>terebi</u> o mimasu.**

   1. .... (eiga)

   2. .... (Kabuki)

B. *State what someone will listen to.*

   ex. **Suzuki-san wa <u>ongaku</u> o kikimasu.**

   1. .... (CD)

   2. .... (rajio)

III. Make up sentences or dialogues following the patterns of the examples and based on the information in the illustrations.

ex.  1.  2.  coffee 3.  80 4.

A. *State what someone will do.*

ex. **Sumisu-san wa sutēki o tabemasu.**

1. ....

2. ....

3. ....

4. ....

B. *Ask and answer what someone will do.*

ex. **A: Sumisu-san wa nani o tabemasu ka.**
B: Sutēki o tabemasu.

1. A: ....

   B: ....

2. A: ....

   B: ....

3. A: ....

   B: ....

4. A: ....

   B: ....

IV. Make up sentences following the patterns of the examples. Substitute the underlined words with the alternatives given.

A. *State where someone will drink beer.*

ex. **Suzuki-san wa <u>uchi</u> de bīru o nomimasu.**

1. .... (resutoran)

2. .... (hoteru no bā)

| VOCABULARY | sutēki | steak |
| | bā | bar |

93

B. *State where someone will buy a magazine.*

   ex. **Suzuki-san wa** <u>hon-ya</u> **de zasshi o kaimasu.**

   1. .... (kombini)

   2. .... (kūkō)

V. Make up sentences following the patterns of the examples and based on the information in the illustrations.

A. *State where someone will do something.*

   ex. **Sumisu-san wa resutoran de ban-gohan o tabemasu.**

   1. ....

   2. ....

   3. ....

   4. ....

B. *Ask and answer where someone will do something.*

   ex. **A: Sumisu-san wa doko de ban-gohan o tabemasu ka.**
   B: Resutoran de tabemasu.

   1. A: ....

      B: ....

   2. A: ....

      B: ....

   3. A: ....

      B: ....

   4. A: ....

      B: ....

VOCABULARY		
toshokan	library	
supōtsu-kurabu	gym, fitness/sports club	
supōtsu	sport(s)	
kurabu	club	

VI. *State what someone does regularly.* Make up sentences following the pattern of the example and based on the information in the illustrations.

ex. every day — inu

1. every morning — yasai-jūsu

2. every evening — okusan / jog

3. every week — supōtsu kurabu

ex. **Katō-san wa mainichi inu to sampo o shimasu.**

1. ....

2. ....

3. ....

VII. *Talk about the events of a weekend.* Make up dialogues following the pattern of the example. Substitute the underlined words with the alternatives given.

ex. **Katō:** **Shūmatsu ni nani o shimashita ka.**
Sumisu: **Tomodachi to gorufu o shimashita.**
Katō: **Doko de shimashita ka.**
Sumisu: **Hakone de shimashita.**
Katō: **Sō desu ka.**

1. Katō: ....

   Sumisu: .... (Gurīn-san, tenisu)

   Katō: ....

   Sumisu: .... (hoteru no tenisu-kōto)

   Katō: ....

2. Katō: ....

   Sumisu: .... (Suzuki-san, kaimono)

   Katō: ....

   Sumisu: .... (Ginza no depāto)

   Katō: ....

VOCABULARY			
inu	dog	**sampo o shimasu**	go for a walk
yasai-jūsu	vegetable juice	**gorufu o shimasu**	play golf
yasai	vegetable	**tenisu-kōto**	tennis court
okusan	(another person's) wife		

VIII. Listen to the CD and fill in the blanks based on the information you hear.

1. Chan-san wa Kamakura de .... o mimashita.

2. Chan-san wa .... hiru-gohan o tabemashita.

SHORT DIALOGUE

Mr. Suzuki phones the tempura specialty restaurant Tenmasa to make a reservation.

mise no hito:	**Temmasa de gozaimasu.**
Suzuki:	**Yoyaku o onegaishimasu.**
mise no hito:	**Hai, arigatō gozaimasu.**
Suzuki:	**Nichi-yōbi no 7-ji ni onegaishimasu. Futari desu.**
mise no hito:	**Hai, wakarimashita. Dewa, o-namae to o-denwa-bangō o onegai-shimasu.**

restaurant employee:	This is Tenmasa.
Suzuki:	I'd like to make a reservation.
restaurant employee:	All right. Thank you.
Suzuki:	Sunday at seven o'clock, please, for two people.
restaurant employee:	Yes. Well, then, please give me your name and telephone number.

VOCABULARY

Temmasa de gozaimasu	this is Tenmasa (speaking on the phone)
Temmasa	Tenmasa (fictitious restaurant name)
de gozaimasu	(humble form of **desu**)
yoyaku	reservation
wakarimashita	understood; I see; I understand
wakarimasu	understand
o-namae	(another person's) name (polite word for **namae**)

NOTES

1. Yoyaku o onegaishimasu.
This is the phrase to use when you want to make a reservation. **Onegaishimasu** can be used to order food or drink, too.
    ex. **Kōhī o onegaishimasu.** "I'll have (a cup of) coffee, please."

Active Communication

1. Talk to someone about your plans for the weekend.

2. Tell someone about what you did the previous weekend.

LESSON 11 — AT A TEMPURA RESTAURANT

 TARGET DIALOGUE

Mr. Smith and Mr. Suzuki have arrived at a tempura restaurant in Ginza.

みせの　ひと：いらっしゃいませ。

　　すずき：すずきです。

みせの　ひと：すずきさまですね。どうぞ　こちらへ。

　　スミス：(*a few moments later, at the table*) いい　みせですね。

　　　　　　すずきさんは　よく　この　みせに　きますか。

　　すずき：ええ、ときどき　きます。おいしいですから。

　　スミス：(*fifteen minutes later, after their dishes have arrived*) すずきさん、

　　　　　　この　さかなは　なんですか。

　　すずき：キスです。

　　スミス：おいしいですね。

■ スミスさんは　すずきさんと　ぎんざの　てんぷらやに　いきました。
　スミスさんは　すずきさんに　さかなの　なまえを　ききました。

mise no hito: Irasshaimase.
　　Suzuki: Suzuki desu.
mise no hito: Suzuki-sama desu ne. Dōzo kochira e.
　　Sumisu: (*a few moments later, at the table*) Ii mise desu ne. Suzuki-san wa
　　　　yoku kono mise ni kimasu ka.
　　Suzuki: Ee, tokidoki kimasu. Oishii desu kara.
　　Sumisu: (*fifteen minutes later, after their dishes have arrived*) Suzuki-san, kono
　　　　sakana wa nan desu ka.
　　Suzuki: Kisu desu.
　　Sumisu: Oishii desu ne.

■ **Sumisu-san wa Suzuki-san to Ginza no tempura-ya ni ikimashita. Sumisu-san wa Suzuki-san ni sakana no namae o kikimashita.**

restaurant employee: Welcome.
　　Suzuki: I'm Suzuki.
restaurant employee: Oh, Mr. Suzuki. Right this way, please.
　　Smith: This is a nice restaurant, isn't it? Do you come to this restaurant often, Mr.
　　　　Suzuki?
　　Suzuki: Yes, I come sometimes. Because (this restaurant's tempura) is so delicious.
　　Smith: Mr. Suzuki, what's this fish?

Suzuki: It's whiting.
Smith: It's delicious, isn't it?

■ Mr. Smith went to a tempura restaurant in Ginza with Mr. Suzuki. Mr. Smith asked Mr. Suzuki the name of the fish.

VOCABULARY

すずきさま	Suzuki-sama	Mr. Suzuki
～さま	-sama	Mr., Ms., Mrs., Miss (more polite than **-san**)
よく	yoku	often (see Appendix I, p. 248)
ときどき	tokidoki	sometimes (see Appendix I, p. 248)
おいしいです	oishii desu	be delicious, be tasty
から	kara	because (particle)
さかな	sakana	fish
キス	kisu	whiting (kind of fish) (NOTE: Names of fish, fruits, vegetables, etc. are sometimes written in *katakana*.)
てんぷらや	tempura-ya	tempura restaurant
ききます	kikimasu	ask

NOTES

1. (Kono mise no tempura wa) oishii desu kara.
Kara follows a sentence or clause that explains the reason for something. Here, the topic phrase **kono mise no tempura wa** is being omitted. (For more on **kara**, see Note 3, p.142.)

PRACTICE

WORD POWER

I. Verbs:

1. **denwa o shimasu**   2. **kakimasu**   3. **okurimasu**   4. **aimasu**

VOCABULARY

denwa o shimasu	telephone
kakimasu	write
okurimasu	send
aimasu	meet

II. Family:

1. **Takahashi-san no otōsan**
2. **Takahashi-san no okāsan**
3. **Takahashi-san no okusan**
4. **chichi**
5. **haha**
6. **tsuma/kanai**
7. **Sasaki-san no go-shujin**
8. **otto/shujin**

KEY SENTENCES

> 1. **Sumisu-san wa tomodachi ni denwa o shimasu.**
> 2. **Sumisu-san wa ashita Takahashi-san ni aimasu.**
> 3. **Chan-san wa yoku okāsan ni tegami o kakimasu.**
> 4. **Chan-san wa amari terebi o mimasen.**
>
> 1. Mr. Smith is going to phone a friend.
> 2. Mr. Smith is going to see Mr. Takahashi tomorrow.
> 3. Ms. Chan often writes letters to her mother.
> 4. Ms. Chan doesn't watch television very much.

VOCABULARY	**otōsan**	(another person's) father	**haha**	(my) mother	**otto/shujin**	(my) husband
	okāsan	(another person's) mother	**tsuma/kanai**	(my) wife	**tegami**	letter
	okusan	(another person's) wife	**go-shujin**	(another person's) husband	**amari . . . -masen**	not much (see Appendix I, p. 248)
	chichi	(my) father	**go-**	(honorific prefix)		

EXERCISES

I. *Practice conjugating verbs.* Repeat the verbs below and memorize their forms—present and past, affirmative and negative.

	PRESENT FORM		PAST FORM	
	aff.	*neg.*	*aff.*	*neg.*
telephone	denwa o shimasu	denwa o shimasen	denwa o shimashita	denwa o shimasendeshita
write	kakimasu	kakimasen	kakimashita	kakimasendeshita
send	okurimasu	okurimasen	okurimashita	okurimasendeshita
meet	aimasu	aimasen	aimashita	aimasendeshita

II. Make up sentences following the patterns of the examples. Substitute the underlined words with the words in parentheses.

A. *State whom someone will write to.*

ex. **Sumisu-san wa tomodachi ni tegami o kakimasu.**

1. Sumisu-san wa otōsan ni tegami o kakimasu (otōsan)
2. Sumisu-san wa Takahashi-san ni tegami o kakimasu (Takahashi-san)
3. Sumisu-san wa taishikan ni tegami o kakimasu (taishikan)

B. *State whom someone will telephone.*

ex. **Sumisu-san wa resutoran ni denwa o shimasu.**

1. Sumisu-san wa okāsan ni denwa o shimasu (okāsan)
2. Sumisu-san wa kaisha no hito ni denwa o shimasu (kaisha no hito)
3. Sumisu-san wa Nozomi Depāto ni denwa o shimasu (Nozomi Depāto)

III. Make up sentences or dialogues following the patterns of the examples and based on the information in the illustration.

1.

2.

3.
mēru

ex. 1. Takahashi-san

1) tomodachi

2) Nozomi Depāto no shachō

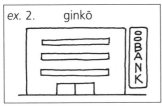

ex. 2. ginkō

3) Ginza no hoteru

4) Nihon-go no gakkō

A. *State who will write to, call, or e-mail whom.*

ex. 1. **Sumisu-san wa Takahashi-san ni tegami o kakimasu.**

ex. 2. **Sumisu-san wa ginkō ni tegami o kakimasu.**

1. 1) Sumisu-san wa Ginza no hoteru ni tegami o kakimasu.

2) Sumisu-san wa tomodachi ni tegami o kakimasu

3) Sumisu-san wa Nihon-go no gakkō ni tegami o kakimasu

4) Sumisu-san wa Nozomi Depāto no sachō ni tegami o kakimasu

2. 1) Sumisu-san wa tomodachi ni denwa o shimasu

2) Sumisu-san wa Ginza no hoteru ni denwa o shimasu

3) Sumisu-san wa Nihongo no gakkō ni denwa o shimasu

4) Sumisu-san wa Nozomi Depāto no shachō ni denwa o shimasu

3. 1) Sumisu-san wa tomodachi ni mēru o okurimasu

2) Sumisu-san wa Nozomi Depāto no shachō ni mēru o okurimasu

3) Sumisu-san wa Ginza no hoteru ni mēru o okurimasu

4) Sumisu-san wa Nihon-go gakkō ni mēru o okurimasu

VOCABULARY	gakkō	school
	shachō	president (of a company)
	mēru	e-mail

B. *Ask and answer who will write to, call, or e-mail whom.*

    ex. 1. **A: Sumisu-san wa dare ni tegami o kakimasu ka.**
          B: Takahashi-san ni kakimasu.
    ex. 2. **A: Sumisu-san wa doko ni tegami o kakimasu ka.**
          B: Ginkō ni kakimasu.

1. 1) A: Sumisu-san wa dare ni denwa o shimasu ka
     B: Tomodachi ni denwa o shimasu

   2) A: Sumisu-san wa doko ni denwa o shimasu ka
     B: Ginza no hoteru ni denwa o shimasu

   3) A: Sumisu-san wa dare ni denwa o shimasu ka
     B: Nozomi depāto no shachō ni denwa o shimasu

   4) A: Sumisu-san wa doko ni denwa o shimasu ka
     B: Nihon-go gakkō ni denwa o shimasu

2. 1) A: Sumisu-san wa dare ni tegami o kakimasu
     B: tomodachi ni tegami o kakimasu

   2) A: ....
     B: ....

   3) A: ....
     B: ....

   4) A: ....
     B: ....

3. 1) A: ....
     B: ....

   2) A: ....
     B: ....

   3) A: ....
     B: ....

   4) A: ....
     B: ....

IV. *Describe a schedule.* Make up sentences following the pattern of the example and based on the information in the planner.

ex.	Mon.	4:00	Tōkyō Eki	Suzuki-san
1.	Tue.	10:00	Nozomi Depāto	Takahashi-san
2.	Wed.	7:00	Resutoran Rōma	Sasaki-san no go-shujin
3.	Thu.	11:00	Sapporo-shisha	shisha no hito
4.	Fri.	6:30	hoteru no robī	Nakamura-san

ex. **Sumisu-san wa getsu-yōbi no 4-ji ni Tōkyō Eki de Suzuki-san ni aimasu.**

1. sumisu-san wa ka-yōbi no jū-ji Nozomi Depāto de sumisu-san wa   Takahashi-san ni aimasu

2. sumisu-san   suiyobi no shichiji restoran Roma de sasaki-san no goshuji ni arimasu

3. wa muku-yōbi no jūnichi-ji ni sapporo - shisha de shisha no hito ni aimasu

4.

V. *Give a qualified answer in response to a question.* Answer the questions below using the words in parentheses and the appropriate verb.

ex. **A: Sumisu-san wa yoku bīru o nomimasu ka.**
   B: Hai, yoku nomimasu.

1. A: Takahashi-san wa yoku sushi o tabemasu ka.

   B: Hai, tokidoki nomimasu _____ (hai, tokidoki)

2. A: Suzuki-san wa yoku tomodachi ni denwa o shimasu ka.

   B: Iie, anari shimasen _____ (iie, amari . . . -masen)

3. A: Chan-san wa yoku eiga o mimasu ka.

   B: Iie, zenzen mimasen _____ (iie, zenzen . . . -masen)

VI. *Give a reason for an answer.* Answer the questions below using the example as a guide. Substitute the underlined word with the words in parentheses.

ex. **A: Sumisu-san wa yoku tenisu o shimasu ka.**
   B: Hai. Uchi no chikaku ni <u>tenisu-kōto</u> ga arimasu kara.

1. A: Sasaki-san wa yoku sampo o shimasu ka.

   B: Hai. Uchi no chikaku ni kōen ga arimasu kara (kōen)

2. A: Chan-san wa yoku sushi o tabemasu ka.

   B: Hai. Uchi no chikaku ni sushi- ya ga arimasu kara (sushi-ya)

VOCABULARY				
Resutoran Rōma	Restaurant Roma (fictitious restaurant name)	**sushi**	sushi
Rōma	Rome		
Sapporo-shisha	Sapporo (branch) office	**zenzen . . . -masen**	not at all (see Appendix I, p. 248.)
Sapporo	Sapporo (city on the island of Hokkaido)		
robī	lobby	**sushi-ya**	sushi restaurant

VII. *Order at a restaurant.* Make up dialogues following the pattern of the example and based on the information in the illustration.

ex. **Sumisu: Bīru o 2-hon onegaishimasu.**
mise no hito: Hai.

1. Sumisu: <u>wain o ippon onegaishimasu</u>

    mise no hito: <u>Hai</u>

2. Sumisu: <u>sarada o futatsu onegaishimasu</u>

    mise no hito: <u>Hai</u>

3. Sumisu: <u>aisu-kurīmu o yottsu onegaishimasu</u>

    mise no hito: <u>Hai</u>

VOCABULARY   **aisu-kurimu**   ice cream

VIII. **Talk about a weekend plan.** Make up dialogues following the pattern of the example. Substitute the underlined parts with the alternatives given.

ex. Suzuki: **Kondo no shūmatsu ni nani o shimasu ka.**
Chan: <u>**Shibuya Toshokan**</u> **ni ikimasu.**
Suzuki: **Chan-san wa yoku** <u>**Shibuya Toshokan**</u> **ni ikimasu ka.**
Chan: **Ee,** <u>**Eigo no bideo**</u> **ga takusan arimasu kara.**

1. Suzuki: ....

    Chan: .... (ABC Supōtsu-kurabu)

    Suzuki: .... (ABC Supōtsu-kurabu)

    Chan: .... (mashīn)

2. Suzuki: ....

    Chan: .... (Resutoran Doragon)

    Suzuki: .... (Resutoran Doragon)

    Chan: .... (kuni no ryōri)

 IX. Listen to the CD and fill in the blank based on the information you hear.

TRACK 42

Chan-san wa yoku okāsan ni .... masu.

SHORT DIALOGUES

 I. Mr. Green comes to the restaurant Tenmasa with his wife.

TRACK 43

Gurin:	**Sumimasen. Matsu-kōsu o futatsu onegaishimasu.**
mise no hito:	**Hai. O-nomimono wa?**
Gurin:	**Nama-bīru o futatsu onegaishimasu.**
mise no hito:	**Hai.**

Green:	Excuse me, two "pine" meals please.
restaurant employee:	All right. What about a beverage?
Green:	Two draft beers, please.
restaurant employee:	All right.

VOCABULARY

matsu-kōsu	"pine" meal (the most expensive set meal at a traditional restaurant)
o-nomimono	beverage
nama-bīru	draft beer

VOCABULARY	**kondo**	this coming	**kuni**	(my) country
	mashin	machine	**ryōri**	cooking, cuisine
	Resutoran Doragon	Restaurant Dragon (fictitious restaurant name)		

105

II. Mr. Green pays for his meal at Tenmasa. He needs a receipt.

Gurīn: **Sumimasen. O-kanjō o onegaishimasu.**
mise no hito: Hai.
Gurīn: **Sumimasen. Ryōshūsho o onegaishimasu.**
mise no hito: Hai. O-namae wa?

Green: Excuse me, I'd like the check, please.
restaurant employee: All right.
Green: Excuse me. I'd like a receipt.
restaurant employee: All right. What is your name?

VOCABULARY

o-kanjō   bill, check

ryōshūsho   receipt (requiring signature from the restaurant or
                     store where the purchase was made and usually
                     necessary when applying for reimbursement of
                     expenses incurred)

Active Communication

Go to a restaurant and try ordering food
and a beverage in Japanese.

Quiz 2 (Units 3–5)

I Fill in the blank(s) in each sentence with the appropriate particle. Where a particle is not needed, write in an *X*.

1. Tēburu no ue ni hana (   ) shimbun ga arimasu. (Hint: There are other things in addition to these two.)

2. Yūbinkyoku no mae (   ) onna no hito (   ) otoko no ko ga imasu. (Hint: No one else is there.)

3. 1-kai ni dare (   ) imasu ka.
    Sumisu-san (   ) imasu.

4. Basu-noriba (   ) doko (   ) arimasu ka.
    Depāto (   ) mae desu.

5. Takahashi-san wa ashita kaisha no hito (   ) Ōsaka (   ) ikimasu.

6. Sumisu-san wa Sasaki-san (   ) denwa o shimashita.

7. Takahashi-san wa kaisha no chikaku no resutoran (   ) hiru-gohan (   ) tabe-mashita.

8. Watashi wa basu (   ) uchi (   ) kaerimasu.

9. Watashi wa maiasa (   ) uchi (   ) shimbun (   ) yomimasu.

10. Sumisu-san wa itsu (   ) Nihon ni kimashita ka.
    5-gatsu 18-nichi (   ) kimashita.

11. Yoku tenisu o shimasu ka.
    Ee, uchi no chikaku ni tenisu-kōto ga arimasu (   ). (Hint: This sentence is giving the reason.)

II Complete each question by filling in the blank(s) with the appropriate word.

1. Hon-ya no mae ni (   ) ga imasu ka.
    Takahashi-san no okusan ga imasu.

2. Takushī-noriba wa (   ) desu ka.
    Asoko desu.

3. Eki no chikaku ni (   ) ga arimasu ka.
    Basu-noriba ya yūbinkyoku ya depāto ga arimasu.

4. Tēburu no ue ni ringo ga (   ) arimasu ka.
    Mittsu arimasu.

5. Eki no mae ni otoko no hito ga (   ) imasu ka.
    Futari imasu.

6. Chan-san no tanjōbi wa (   ) desu ka.
    1-gatsu 29-nichi desu.

7. (   ) ga Kyōto-shisha ni denwa o shimashita ka.
    Sumisu-san ga shimashita.

8. Takahashi-san wa kinō (   ) ni ikimashita ka.
    Kūkō ni ikimashita.

9. (   ) ni Buraun-san ni aimashita ka.
    3-ji ni aimashita.

10. Buraun-san wa (   ) Amerika ni kaerimashita ka.
    Senshū no do-yōbi ni kaerimashita.

11. Kinō (　　　　) o shimashita ka.
    Tegami o kakimashita.
    (　　　　) ni kakimashita ka.
    Haha ni kakimashita.

III Choose one of the two words in parentheses to complete the sentence in a way that makes sense in the context.

1. Tēburu no ue ni shashin ya hon ga (arimasu, imasu).

2. Isu no ue ni nani mo (arimasu, arimasen).

3. Yoku Resutoran Sakura ni ikimasu ka.
   Iie, amari (ikimasu, ikimasen).

4. Tokidoki terebi o (mimasu, mimasen) ka.
   Iie, zenzen (mimasu, mimasen).

5. Chan-san wa (yoku, amari) tomodachi ni denwa o shimasu.

VISITING A JAPANESE HOME

In Japan, it is usual to offer guests green tea and Japanese sweets, or *wagashi*. *Wagashi* convey a sense of the seasons. The soft, moist sweets given in spring, for example, are modeled on cherry blossom flowers, while summer *wagashi* take the form of refreshing jellies made from adzuki beans and agar. *Wagashi* are perfect for both entertaining guests and appreciating the seasons. They also make nice gifts. Throughout Japan there are confectionaries that specialize in these unique treats. Some of the oldest and most successful ones have been in business for centuries.

6 GRAMMAR

Adjectives

adjective + noun

 ex. **Sakura wa kireina hana desu.** "Cherry blossoms are pretty flowers."

noun **wa** adjective **desu**

 ex. **Gurei-san no uchi wa ōkii desu.** "Mr. Grey's house is big."

Japanese adjectives can either modify nouns by directly preceding them, or act as predicates. In this they resemble English adjectives. There are two kinds of adjectives: **-i** adjectives and **-na** adjectives.

MODIFYING NOUN: ADJECTIVE + NOUN		
-I ADJ.	**ōkii kōen**	big park
-NA ADJ.	**kireina hana**	pretty flower

Unlike English adjectives, Japanese adjectives are inflected for tense and mood as shown below.

AS PREDICATE: ADJECTIVE + **DESU**				
	PRESENT FORM		PAST FORM	
	aff.	*neg.*	*aff.*	*neg.*
-I ADJ.	**ōkii desu**	**ōkikunai desu**	**ōkikatta desu**	**ōkikunakatta desu**
-NA ADJ.	**kirei desu**	**kirei dewa arimasen**	**kirei deshita**	**kirei dewa arimasen-deshita**

Giving and Receiving

person 1 **wa** person 2 **ni** noun **o agemasu**

 ex. **Okada-san wa Gurei-san ni tokei o agemashita.** "Ms. Okada gave Mr. Grey a watch."

person 1 **wa** person 2 **ni** noun **o moraimasu**

 ex. **Gurei-san wa Okada-san ni tokei o moraimashita.**
 "Mr. Grey received a watch from Ms. Okada."

The sentence pattern used with the verbs **agemasu** ("give") and **moraimasu** ("receive") is the same as the one introduced in Unit 5: "person 1 **wa** person 2 **ni** noun **o** verb." With **agemasu**, the person who is given something is marked by the particle **ni**, and the thing he or she is given is marked by **o**. But with **moraimasu**, **ni** indicates the giver rather than the receiver. Here **ni** corresponds to "from." **NOTE: Agemasu** cannot be used in the sense of "someone gives something to me (the speaker)." For this meaning, the verb **kuremasu** is used.

TARGET DIALOGUE

Mr. Smith has been invited to the home of his client Mr. Takahashi for the first time.

たかはし：おちゃを　どうぞ。

　スミス：ありがとうございます。

たかはし：おかしは　いかがですか。

　スミス：はい、　いただきます。　きれいな　おかしですね。

　　　　　　にほんの　おかしですか。

たかはし：ええ、そうです。

　スミス：とても　おいしいです。

たかはし：おちゃを　もう　1ぱい　いかがですか。

　スミス：いいえ、もう　けっこうです。

■スミスさんは　たかはしさんの　うちで　きれいな　にほんの　おかしを
　たべました。おちゃを　1ぱい　のみました。

Takahashi: O-cha o dōzo.
　Sumisu: Arigatō gozaimasu.
Takahashi: O-kashi wa ikaga desu ka.
　Sumisu: Hai, itadakimasu. Kireina o-kashi desu ne. Nihon no o-kashi desu ka.
Takahashi: Ee, sō desu.
　Sumisu: Totemo oishii desu.
Takahashi: O-cha o mō 1-pai ikaga desu ka.
　Sumisu: Iie, mō kekkō desu.

■ **Sumisu-san wa Takahashi-san no uchi de kireina Nihon no o-kashi o tabemashita.**
　O-cha o 1-pai nomimashita.

Takahashi: Have some tea.
　Smith: Thank you.
Takahashi: How about some sweets?
　Smith: Yes, I'll have some. These are pretty sweets. Are they Japanese sweets?
Takahashi: Yes, they are.
　Smith: They're very tasty.
Takahashi: How about another cup of tea?
　Smith: No thanks, I'm fine.

■ Mr. Smith ate some pretty Japanese sweets at Mr. Takahashi's home. He drank one cup of tea.

どうぞ	**dōzo**	please (see Note 1 below)
おかし	**o-kashi**	sweets
いかがですか	**ikaga desu ka**	how about . . . ? (see Note 2 below)
いただきます	**itadakimasu**	(said before eating; see Note 3 below)
きれい（な）	**kireina**	pretty
とても	**totemo**	very
1ぱい	**1-pai (=ippai)**	one cup
〜はい／ばい／ぱい	**-hai/-bai/-pai**	cupful, glassful (counter)
いいえ、もう　けっこうです	**iie, mō kekkō desu**	no thank you, I'm fine (see Note 4 below)
けっこうです	**kekkō desu**	no thank you

NOTES

1. O-cha o dōzo.

"(Thing) **o dōzo**" ("please help yourself to . . .") is used to offer something to someone.

2. O-kashi wa ikaga desu ka.

Ikaga desu ka is often used when politely offering things like food or drink. It means "would you like one?" or "how about some?"

3. Hai, itadakimasu.

This phrase is spoken when taking something that is offered. It implies both acceptance and gratitude.

4. Iie, mō kekkō desu.

This is a polite way of refusing a second helping of food or drink. If you want to refuse the first time you are offered something, say **iie, kekkō desu**.

PRACTICE

WORD POWER

I. **-i** adjectives:

1. **ōkii desu**

2. **chiisai desu**

3. **takai desu**

4. **yasui desu**

5. **atarashii desu**

6. **furui desu**

7. **chikai desu**

8. **tōi desu**

9. **muzukashii desu**

10. **yasashii desu**

11. **amai desu**

12. **karai desu**

13. **atsui desu**

14. **samui desu**

15. **ii desu**

16. **omoshiroi desu**

17. **isogashii desu**

18. **oishii desu**

VOCABULARY

ōkii desu	big	**furui desu**	old (not used of people)	**muzukashii desu**	difficult
chiisai desu	small			**yasashii desu**	easy
takai desu	expensive	**chikai desu**	near	**amai desu**	sweet
yasui desu	inexpensive	**tōi desu**	far	**karai desu**	hot, spicy
atarashii desu	new, fresh			**atsui desu**	hot

samui desu	cold
ii desu	good, nice
omoshiroi desu	interesting
isogashii desu	busy
oishii desu	delicious

113

II. **-na** adjectives:

1. **nigiyaka desu**

2. **shizuka desu**

3. **benri desu**

4. **yūmei desu**

5. **kirei desu**

6. **shinsetsu desu**

7. **hima desu**

KEY SENTENCES

1. **Takahashi-san no uchi wa atarashii desu.**
2. **Kore wa omoshiroi hon desu.**
3. **Tōkyō no chikatetsu wa benri desu.**
4. **Sumisu-san wa senshū yūmeina resutoran de shokuji o shimashita.**

1. Mr. Takahashi's house is new.
2. This is an interesting book.
3. The Tokyo subway is convenient.
4. Mr. Smith had a meal at a famous restaurant last week.

EXERCISES

I. *Practice conjugating -i adjectives.* Repeat the adjectives below and memorize their forms.

| | AS PREDICATE: PRESENT FORM | | MODIFYING NOUN |
	aff.	neg.	
big	**ōkii desu**	**ōkikunai desu**	**ōkii**
small	**chiisai desu**	**chiisakunai desu**	**chiisai**
expensive	**takai desu**	**takakunai desu**	**takai**
inexpensive	**yasui desu**	**yasukunai desu**	**yasui**

okikuarimasen

VOCABULARY

nigiyaka desu	lively	**yūmei desu**	famous	**hima desu**	free, not busy
shizuka desu	quiet	**kirei desu**	pretty, clean	**shokuji o shimasu**	have a meal
benri desu	convenient	**shinsetsu desu**	kind, helpful		

	AS PREDICATE: PRESENT FORM		MODIFYING NOUN
	aff.	*neg.*	
new, fresh	atarashii desu	atarashikunai desu	atarashii
old	furui desu	furukunai desu	furui
near	chikai desu	chikakunai desu	chikai
far	tōi desu	tōkunai desu	tōi
difficult	muzukashii desu	muzukashikunai desu	muzukashii
easy	yasashii desu	yasashikunai desu	yasashii
sweet	amai desu	amakunai desu	amai
hot, spicy	karai desu	karakunai desu	karai
hot	atsui desu	atsukunai desu	atsui
cold	samui desu	samukunai desu	samui
good, nice	ii desu	yokunai desu	ii
interesting	omoshiroi desu	omoshirokunai desu	omoshiroi
busy	isogashii desu	isogashikunai desu	isogashii
delicious	oishii desu	oishikunai desu	oishii

II. *State a thing's characteristic.* Make up sentences following the pattern of the example. Substitute the underlined parts with the alternatives given.

> ex. **Kono kuruma wa ōkii desu.**

1. Kono kamura wa yasui desu .... (kono kamera, yasui desu)
2. Takahashi-san no uchi wa atarashi desu .... (Takahashi-san no uchi, atarashii desu)

III. Make up dialogues following the patterns of the examples. Substitute the underlined parts with the alternatives given. Be sure to use the same grammatical forms as in the examples.

A. *Ask and answer how something tastes.*

> ex. **A: Sukiyaki wa oishii desu ka.**
> **B: Hai, oishii desu.**

1. A: kono kēki wa amai desu .... (kono kēki, amai desu)
   B: Hai, amai desu .... (amai desu)

2. A: kono karē wa karai desu .... (kono karē, karai desu)
   B: Hai karai desu .... (karai desu)

VOCABULARY

sukiyaki	sukiyaki
kēki	cake
karē	curry

B. *Ask and give one's opinion about something.*

> *ex.* **A: Nihon-go wa muzukashii desu ka.**
> **B: Iie, muzukashikunai desu.**

1. A: Kono gēmu wa omoshiroi desu. _____ (kono gēmu, omoshiroi desu)

   B: Iie, omoshirokunai desu. _____ (omoshiroi desu)

2. A: Ano jisho wa ii desu _____ (ano jisho, ii desu)

   B: Ii desu _____ (ii desu)

IV. *Describe something.* Make up sentences following the pattern of the example and based on the information in the illustrations.

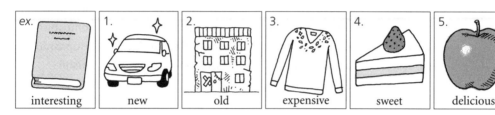

ex.	1.	2.	3.	4.	5.
interesting	new	old	expensive	sweet	delicious

> *ex.* **Kore wa omoshiroi hon desu.**

1. Kore wa atarashii kuruma desu
2. Kore wa furui gakko desu
3. Kore wa takai sēto desu
4. Kore wa amai cake desu
5. Kore wa oiishi ringo desu

V. *Practice conjugating -na adjectives.* Repeat the adjectives below and memorize their forms.

	AS PREDICATE: PRESENT FORM		MODIFYING NOUN
	aff.	*neg.*	
lively	**nigiyaka desu**	**nigiyaka dewa arimasen**	**nigiyakana**
quiet	**shizuka desu**	**shizuka dewa arimasen**	**shizukana**
convenient	**benri desu**	**benri dewa arimasen**	**benrina**
famous	**yūmei desu**	**yūmei dewa arimasen**	**yūmeina**
pretty, clean	**kirei desu**	**kirei dewa arimasen**	**kireina**
kind, helpful	**shinsetsu desu**	**shinsetsu dewa arimasen**	**shinsetsuna**
free, not busy	**hima desu**	**hima dewa arimasen**	**himana**

VOCABULARY   **gēmu**   game

VI. **Describe someone or something.** Make up sentences following the pattern of the example. Substitute the underlined parts with the alternatives given.

ex. **Howaito-san wa shinsetsu desu.**

1. _Gurin-san no okusan wa kirei desu_ (Gurīn-san no okusan, kirei desu)

2. _Tōkyō no chikatetsu wa benri desu_ (Tōkyō no chikatetsu, benri desu)

VII. Make up dialogues following the patterns of the examples. Substitute the underlined part(s) with the alternatives given.

A. **Ask and give one's opinion about a place.**

ex. **A: Ano resutoran wa shizuka desu ka.**
    B: Hai, shizuka desu.

1. A: _Roppongi wa nigiyaka desu ka_ (Roppongi, nigiyaka desu)

   B: _Hai, nigiyaka desu._ (nigiyaka desu)

2. A: _Ano kōen wa kieri desu ka_ (ano kōen, kirei desu)

   B: _hai, kirei desu._ (kirei desu)

B. **Ask and answer whether one is free.**

ex. **A: Ashita hima desu ka.**
    B: Iie, hima dewa arimasen. Isogashii desu.

1. A: _Ashita no gogo hima desu ka_ (ashita no gogo)

   B: _Iie, hima dewa arimasen. Isogashii desu_

2. A: _Asatte no ban hima desu ka_ (asatte no ban)

   B: _Iie, hima dewa arimasen. Isogashii desu_

VIII. **Describe a restaurant where someone had a meal.** Make up sentences following the pattern of the example and based on the information in the illustrations.

famous

quiet

pretty

ex. **Sumisu-san wa senshū yūmeina resutoran de shokuji o shimashita.**

1. _Sumisu-san wa senshū shizuka resutoran de shokuji o shimashita_

2. _Sumisu-san wa senshū kireina resutoran de shokuji o shimashita_

VOCABULARY

Howaito — White (surname)

Roppongi — Roppongi (district in Tokyo)

117

IX. Make up dialogues following the patterns of the examples. Substitute the underlined words with the words in parentheses.

A. *Ask and give one's opinion about a hotel.*

ex. **A: Tōkyō Hoteru wa kireina hoteru desu ka.**
B: Hai, kireina hoteru desu.

1. A: Tōkyō Hoteru wa atarashii hoteru desu ka (atarashii)

   B: Hai, atarashii hoteru desu (atarashii)

2. A: .... (ōkii)

   B: .... (ōkii)

B. *Ask and give one's opinion about a restaurant.*

ex. **A: Resutoran Ginza wa yūmeina resutoran desu ka.**
B: Iie, yūmeina resutoran dewa arimasen.

1. A: .... (shizukana)

   B: .... (shizukana)

2. A: .... (ii)

   B: .... (ii)

C. *Ask and give one's opinion about a place.*

ex. **A: Shūmatsu ni Nikkō ni ikimasu.**
B: Nikkō wa donna tokoro desu ka.
A: Kireina tokoro desu yo.

1. A: .... (Asakusa)

   B: .... (Asakusa)

   A: .... (nigiyakana)

2. A: .... (Odaiba)

   B: .... (Odaiba)

   A: .... (omoshiroi)

VOCABULARY

donna	what kind of
tokoro	place
Asakusa	Asakusa (district in Tokyo)

118

X. *Compliment someone's possessions.* Mr. Smith is visiting Mr. Takahashi's house. Compliment Mr. Takahashi's house and the things (numbered in the picture) he owns, assuming the role of Mr. Smith. Make up sentences following the pattern of the example.

ex. big

1. (a) close to the station
   (b) convenient

e

2. interesting   3. very old   4. pretty

ex. **Sumisu: <u>Ōkii uchi</u> desu ne.**

1. Sumisu: (a) chikaii eki desu ne

   (b) benri desu ne

2. Sumisu: omoshiroi e desu ne

3. Sumisu: totemo furui desu ne

4. Sumisu: kire hana kabin desu ne

XI. Make up dialogues following the patterns of the examples. Substitute the underlined parts with the alternatives given.

A. *Talk about the weather.*

ex. **Sumisu:** **Kyō wa ii tenki desu ne.**
Takahashi: Ee, hontō ni ii tenki desu ne.

1. Sumisu: .... (atsui)

   Takahashi: .... (atsui)

2. Sumisu: .... (samui)

   Takahashi: .... (samui)

B. *Ask and answer whether a facility is far from where one is.*

ex. **Chan:** **Sumimasen. Chikatetsu no eki wa koko kara tōi desu ka.**
otoko no hito: Iie, tōkunai desu. Aruite 5-fun gurai desu yo.
Chan: **Sō desu ka. Arigatō gozaimasu.**

1. Chan: .... (basutei)

   otoko no hito: ....

   Chan: ....

2. Chan: .... (kōen)

   otoko no hito: ....

   Chan: ....

XII. Listen to the CD and fill in the blank based on the information you hear.

TRACK
46

Hakone wa .... *donna* .... tokoro desu.

VOCABULARY	tenki	weather	5-fun gurai	about five minutes
	hontō ni	really	5-fun	for five minutes
			gurai	about, approximately (particle; used of a period, price, amount, etc., but not of a specific point in time)

SHORT DIALOGUES

TRACK
47

I. Mr. Smith visits Mr. Takahashi's home. He rings the security system intercom.

Takahashi: Hai.
Sumisu: Sumisu desu.
Takahashi: A, chotto matte kudasai. (*Takahashi goes to answer the door.*)
Takahashi: Yoku irasshaimashita.
Sumisu: Ojamashimasu.

Takahashi: Yes?
Mr. Smith: It's me, Smith.
Takahashi: Oh, please wait a minute. (*Takahashi goes to answer the door.*)
Takahashi: Welcome!
Mr. Smith: May I come in? (*lit.*, "I'm going to disturb you.")

VOCABULARY

chotto matte kudasai	please wait a minute
chotto	a little bit
yoku irasshaimashita	welcome
ojamashimasu	may I come in? (said when entering someone's home)

II. Mr. Smith is at an antique shop in Tokyo.

Sumisu: Kore wa ikura desu ka.
mise no hito: 8,000-en desu.
Sumisu: Chotto takai desu ne.
mise no hito: Kore wa 6,500-en desu.
Sumisu: Ja, sore o kudasai.

Smith: How much is this?
salesperson: It's 8,000 yen.
Smith: It's a little bit expensive, isn't it?
salesperson: This is 6,500 yen.
Smith: Well then, I'll have that one.

Active Communication

Start a conversation with someone by talking about the weather. Say whether it is a nice day, a cold day, or a hot day. Refer to Exercise XI-A as necessary.

GIVING COMPLIMENTS

TARGET DIALOGUE

Mr. Takahashi and Mr. Smith are talking about the flower vase that Mr. Takahashi received from Ms. Hoffman.

スミス：きれいな　かびんですね。

たかはし：ええ、たんじょうびに　ともだちの　ホフマンさんに

　　　　　　　もらいました。

スミス：いい　いろですね。

たかはし：ええ、わたしの　すきな　いろです。

■ たかはしさんは　たんじょうびに　ホフマンさんに　かびんを
　もらいました。

Sumisu: Kireina kabin desu ne.
Takahashi: Ee, tanjōbi ni tomodachi no Hofuman-san ni moraimashita.
Sumisu: Ii iro desu ne.
Takahashi: Ee, watashi no sukina iro desu.

■ **Takahashi-san wa tanjōbi ni Hofuman-san ni kabin o moraimashita.**

Smith: That's a pretty vase, isn't it?
Takahashi: Yes, I received it from my friend Ms. Hoffman for my birthday.
Smith: That's a nice color, isn't it?
Takahashi: Yes, it's my favorite color.

■ Mr. Takahashi received a vase for his birthday from Ms. Hoffman.

VOCABULARY

かびん	**kabin**	vase
もらいました	**moraimashita**	received
もらいます	**moraimasu**	receive
いろ	**iro**	color
すきな	**sukina**	favorite (**-na** adj.)

NOTES

1. Tomodachi no Hofuman-san
This **no** is not possessive but appositive: "my friend Ms. Hoffman."

PRACTICE

WORD POWER

I. Verbs:

1. **agemasu**   2. **moraimasu**

II. Flower vocabulary:

1. **bara**   2. **kānēshon**   3. **chūrippu**   4. **hanataba**

VOCABULARY				
	agemasu	give	chūrippu	tulip
	moraimasu	receive	hanataba	bouquet
	bara	rose		
	kānēshon	carnation		123

III. Gifts:

1. **iyaringu**
2. **nekkuresu**
3. **yubiwa**
4. **sukāfu**
5. **burausu**
6. **eiga no kippu**
7. **rekishi no hon**
8. **bōshi**
9. **nekutai**
10. **kōto**
11. **Kyōto no o-miyage**

KEY SENTENCES

1. **Sumisu-san wa Chan-san ni hana o agemashita.**
2. **Chan-san wa Sumisu-san ni hana o moraimashita.**

1. Mr. Smith gave Ms. Chan some flowers.
2. Ms. Chan received some flowers from Mr. Smith.

EXERCISES

I. *Practice conjugating verbs.* Repeat the verbs below and memorize their forms—present and past, affirmative and negative.

	PRESENT FORM		PAST FORM	
	aff.	*neg.*	*aff.*	*neg.*
give	**agemasu**	**agemasen**	**agemashita**	**agemasendeshita**
receive	**moraimasu**	**moraimasen**	**moraimashita**	**moraimasendeshita**

VOCABULARY

iyaringu	earring	**burausu**	blouse	**nekutai**	necktie
nekkuresu	necklace	**kippu**	ticket	**kōto**	coat
yubiwa	ring	**rekishi**	history	**o-miyage**	gift, souvenir
sukāfu	scarf	**bōshi**	hat, cap		

II. *State what someone will give to, or receive from, another.* Make up sentences following the pattern of the example. Substitute the underlined words with the alternatives given.

    ex. **Sumisu-san wa Chan-san ni <u>hana</u> o agemasu.**
        Chan-san wa Sumisu-san ni <u>hana</u> o moraimasu.

    1. .... (kireina hana)

    2. .... (eiga no kippu)

    3. .... (rekishi no hon)

III. Make up dialogues following the patterns of the examples and based on the information in the illustration.

A. *Ask and answer whom someone gave something to.*

    ex. **A: Sumisu-san wa dare ni <u>eiga no kippu</u> o agemashita ka.**
        B: <u>Chan-san</u> ni agemashita.

    1. A: ....

        B: ....

    2. A: ....

        B: ....

B. *Ask and answer whom someone received something from.*

    ex. **A: <u>Chan-san</u> wa dare ni <u>eiga no kippu</u> o moraimashita ka.**
        B: Sumisu-san ni moraimashita.

    1. A: ....

        B: ....

2. A: ....

   B: ....

C. *Ask and answer what someone gave to another.*

   ex. **A: Sumisu-san wa <u>Chan-san</u> ni nani o agemashita ka.**
   B: <u>Eiga no kippu</u> o agemashita.

   1. A: ....

      B: ....

   2. A: ....

      B: ....

IV. Make up sentences or dialogues following the patterns of the examples and based on the information in the illustration.

A. *State who gave what to whom, and who received what from whom, on a specific day.*

   ex. 1. **Suzuki-san wa Kurisumasu ni Chan-san ni denshi-jisho o agemashita.**
   Chan-san wa Kurisumasu ni Suzuki-san ni denshi-jisho o moraimashita.

   1. ....

   2. ....

B. *Ask and answer what someone gave to another on a specific day.*

    ex. 1. **A: Suzuki-san wa Kurisumasu ni Chan-san ni nani o agemashita ka.**
          B: Denshi-jisho o agemashita.

    1. A: ....

        B: ....

    2. A: ....

        B: ....

C. *Ask and answer whom someone gave something to on a specific day.*

    ex. 1. **A: Suzuki-san wa Kurisumasu ni dare ni denshi-jisho o agemashita ka.**
          B: Chan-san ni agemashita.

    1. A: ....

        B: ....

    2. A: ....

        B: ....

D. *Ask and answer when someone gave something to another.*

    ex. 1. **A: Suzuki-san wa itsu Chan-san ni denshi-jisho o agemashita ka.**
          B: Kurisumasu ni agemashita.

    1. A: ....

        B: ....

    2. A: ....

        B: ....

E. *Ask and answer what someone received on a specific day.*

    ex. 2. **A: Suzuki-san wa Barentaindē ni Chan-san ni nani o moraimashita ka.**
          B: Furansu no chokorēto o moraimashita.

    3. A: ....

        B: ....

    4. A: ....

        B: ....

F. *Ask and answer whom someone received something from on a specific day.*

    ex. 2. **A: Suzuki-san wa Barentaindē ni dare ni Furansu no chokorēto o moraimashita ka.**
          B: Chan-san ni moraimashita.

    3. A: ....

        B: ....

    4. A: ....

        B: ....

G. *Ask and answer when someone received something from another.*

> *ex. 2.* **A: Suzuki-san wa itsu Chan-san ni Furansu no chokorēto o moraimashita ka.**
> **B: Barentaindē ni moraimashita.**

3. A: ....

   B: ....

4. A: ....

   B: ....

V. Make up dialogues following the patterns of the examples. Substitute the underlined parts with the alternatives given.

A. *Ask someone whether he or she will give a birthday present to another.*

> *ex.* **Chan: Katō-san, ashita wa <u>Sumisu-san</u> no tanjōbi desu ne. <u>Sumisu-san</u> ni purezento o agemasu ka.**
> **Katō: Ee, <u>nekutai</u> o agemasu.**
> **Chan: Sō desu ka.**

1. Chan: .... (Gurīn-san)

   Katō: .... (rekishi no hon)

   Chan: ....

2. Chan: .... (okusan)

   Katō: .... (atarashii kaban)

   Chan: ....

B. *Talk about presents to be given on special occasions.*

> *ex.* **Sumisu: Katō-san, <u>Haha no hi</u> ni <u>okāsan</u> ni nani o agemasu ka.**
> **Katō: <u>Akai kānēshon</u> o agemasu.**
> **Sumisu: Sō desu ka.**

1. Sumisu: .... (Chichi no hi, otōsan)

   Katō: .... (dejikame)

   Sumisu: ....

2. Sumisu: .... (kekkon-kinembi, okusan)

   Katō: .... (bara no hanataba)

   Sumisu: ....

VOCABULARY			
purezento	present	**kekkon-kinembi**	wedding anniversary
Haha no hi	Mother's Day	**kekkon**	marriage
Chichi no hi	Father's Day	**kinembi**	anniversary

C. *Talk about an article someone is wearing.*

    ex. Ms. Chan has a new necklace.

       Suzuki: <u>Kireina nekkuresu</u> desu ne.
       Chan: Ee, <u>tanjōbi</u> ni tomodachi ni moraimashita.
       Suzuki: Yoku niaimasu ne.
       Chan: Arigatō gozaimasu.

  1. Suzuki: .... (ii tokei)

      Chan: .... (Kurisumasu)

      Suzuki: ....

      Chan: ....

  2. Suzuki: .... (kireina sukāfu)

      Chan: .... (tanjōbi)

      Suzuki: ....

      Chan: ....

VI. Listen to the CD and answer the question based on the information you hear.

....

SHORT DIALOGUES

I. Mr. Smith is visiting Mr. Takahashi's house today. He glances at his watch.

  Sumisu: Ja, sorosoro shitsureishimasu.
                Kyō wa dōmo arigatō gozaimashita.
  Takahashi: Dō itashimashite.

  Smith: Well, I'll have to be leaving soon.
             Thank you for (inviting me) today.
  Takahashi: You're welcome.

VOCABULARY

sorosoro shitsureishimasu	it's time to be going; I'd better get going
sorosoro	in just a short while
dōmo arigatō gozaimashita	thank you very much (used to thank someone who has done you a favor or shown you kindness)

| **VOCABULARY** | **yoku** | well |
| | **niaimasu** | suit, look good on |

II. Mrs. Matsui, who lives next door to the Greens, has received a bunch of peaches from a friend, so she brings some to Mrs. Green.

Matsui: Tomodachi ni momo o takusan moraimashita. Kore, dōzo.
Gurin: Dōmo arigatō gozaimasu.

Matsui: I received a lot of peaches from a friend. Please take some.
Green: Thank you very much.

VOCABULARY

momo   peach

Active Communication

Notice an item of clothing or an accessory that someone else is wearing and compliment him or her on it. Refer to Exercise V-C as necessary.

EXPRESSING GRATITUDE

TARGET DIALOGUE

Mr. Smith, who visited Mr. Takahashi's house yesterday, phones Mr. Takahashi. Before getting to the point of the call, Mr. Smith thanks Mr. Takahashi for his hospitality.

スミス：もしもし、たかはしさんの　おたくですか。

たかはし：はい、そうです。

スミス：スミスです。

たかはし：あ、スミスさん。

スミス：きのうは　どうも　ありがとうございました。とても

たのしかったです。

たかはし：いいえ、どういたしまして。わたしたちも　たのしかった

です。どうぞ　また　きてください。

スミス：どうも　ありがとうございます。

■スミスさんは　たかはしさんの　うちに　でんわを　しました。

Sumisu: Moshimoshi, Takahashi-san no o-taku desu ka.
Takahashi: Hai, sō desu.
Sumisu: Sumisu desu.
Takahashi: A, Sumisu-san.
Sumisu: Kinō wa dōmo arigatō gozaimashita. Totemo tanoshikatta desu.
Takahashi: Iie, dō itashimashite. Watashitachi mo tanoshikatta desu. Dōzo mata kite kudasai.
Sumisu: Dōmo arigatō gozaimasu.

■ Sumisu-san wa Takahashi-san no uchi ni denwa o shimashita.

Smith: Hello, is this the Takahashi residence?
Takahashi: Yes, it is.
Smith: This is Smith.
Takahashi: Oh, Mr. Smith.
Smith: Thank you very much for yesterday. It was a lot of fun.
Takahashi: Oh, you're welcome. We had a lot of fun, too. Please come again.
Smith: Thank you very much.

■ Mr. Smith phoned Mr. Takahashi's home.

VOCABULARY

おたく	o-taku	(another person's) house

たのしかったです	**tanoshikatta desu**	was fun
たのしいです	**tanoshii desu**	be fun
わたしたち	**watashitachi**	we
また	**mata**	again
きてください	**kite kudasai**	please come

NOTES

1. Takahashi-san no o-taku
When speaking politely about your listener's house, use **o-taku** instead of **uchi**.

PRACTICE

WORD POWER

I. **-i** adjectives:

1. **tanoshii desu**   2. **tsumaranai desu**   3. **warui desu**

II. Events:

1. **o-matsuri**   2. **konsāto**   3. **bāgen-sēru**   4. **shō**

VOCABULARY			
tanoshii desu	fun, enjoyable	**konsāto**	concert
tsumaranai desu	boring, tedious	**bāgen-sēru**	clearance sale
warui desu	bad	**shō**	show
o-matsuri	festival		

KEY SENTENCES

1. **Kinō wa samukatta desu.**
2. **Kinō no o-matsuri wa nigiyaka deshita.**

1. It was cold yesterday.
2. Yesterday's festival was lively.

EXERCISES

I. Repeat the adjectives below and memorize their forms—present and past, affirmative and negative.

A. *Practice conjugating -i adjectives.*

	PRESENT FORM		PAST FORM	
	aff.	*neg.*	*aff.*	*neg.*
cold	**samui desu**	**samukunai desu**	**samukatta desu**	**samukunakatta desu**
hot	**atsui desu**	**atsukunai desu**	**atsukatta desu**	**atsukunakatta desu**
fun	**tanoshii desu**	**tanoshikunai desu**	**tanoshikatta desu**	**tanoshikunakatta desu**
good	**ii desu**	**yokunai desu**	**yokatta desu**	**yokunakatta desu**
bad	**warui desu**	**warukunai desu**	**warukatta desu**	**warukunakatta desu**
interesting	**omoshiroi desu**	**omoshirokunai desu**	**omoshirokatta desu**	**omoshiroku-nakatta desu**
tasty	**oishii desu**	**oishikunai desu**	**oishikatta desu**	**oishikunakatta desu**
boring	**tsumaranai desu**	**tsumaranakunai desu**	**tsumaranakatta desu**	**tsumaranaku-nakatta desu**

B. *Practice conjugating -na adjectives.*

	PRESENT FORM		PAST FORM	
	aff.	*neg.*	*aff.*	*neg.*
pretty	**kirei desu**	**kirei dewa arimasen**	**kirei deshita**	**kirei dewa arimasendeshita**
quiet	**shizuka desu**	**shizuka dewa arimasen**	**shizuka deshita**	**shizuka dewa arimasendeshita**
lively	**nigiyaka desu**	**nigiyaka dewa arimasen**	**nigiyaka deshita**	**nigiyaka dewa arimasendeshita**

II. Make up sentences following the patterns of the examples. Substitute the underlined parts with the alternatives given, using the same grammatical forms as in the examples.

A. *Give one's opinion about a movie.*

　　ex. **Kinō no eiga wa omoshirokatta desu.**

　　1. Kinō no eiga wa ii desu .... (ii desu)

　　2. kinō no eiga wa tanoshii desu .... (tanoshii desu)

B. *Give one's opinion about a party.*

　　ex. **Kinō no pāti wa tanoshikunakatta desu.**

　　1. Kinō no pāti wa omoshiroi desu .... (omoshiroi desu)

　　2. Kinō no pāti wa ii desu .... (ii desu)

C. *Give one's opinion about a show.*

　　ex. **Kinō no shō wa kirei deshita.**

　　　　kinō no shō wa nigiyaka desu .... (nigiyaka desu)

D. *Give one's opinion about a festival.*

　　ex. **Kinō no o-matsuri wa nigiyaka dewa arimasendeshita.**

　　　　Kinō no o-matsuri wa kirei desu .... (kirei desu)

III. Make up sentences following the patterns of the examples and based on the information in the illustrations. Use the words in parentheses as a guide.

A. *Ask someone's opinion about an experience.*

　　ex. **Nakamura: Kinō no eiga wa omoshirokatta desu ka.**
　　　　Chan:　　Hai, omoshirokatta desu.
　　　　Sumisu:　Iie, omoshirokunakatta desu.

　　1. Nakamura: Kinō no pāti no ryōri wa oishii desu ka (pāti no ryōri, oishii desu)

　　　　Chan:　　Hai, oishii katta desu

　　　　Sumisu:　Iie, oishikunakatta desu

　　2. Nakamura: Kinō no omatsuri wa nigiyaka desu ka (o-matsuri, nigiyaka desu)

　　　　Chan:　　Hai, nigiyaka deshita

　　　　Sumisu:　Iie, nigiyaka dewa arimasendeshita

ex.	1.	2.
very	not very	very	not very	very	not very

B. *Ask and give one's opinion about an experience.*

ex. **Katō:** **Kinō no p͟atī wa dō deshita ka.**
Chan: **Totemo tanoshikatta desu.**
Sumisu: Amari tanoshikunakatta desu.

1. Katō: Kinō no konsāto wa dō deshita ka (konsāto)

   Chan: totemo ii desu (ii desu)

   Sumisu: amari yokunakatta desu (ii desu)

2. Katō: Kinō no bāgen-sēru wa do desu ka (bāgen-sēru)

   Chan: totemo yasui desu (yasui desu)

   Sumisu: amari yasukunakatta desu (yasui desu)

 IV. Make up dialogues following the patterns of the examples. Substitute the underlined parts with the alternatives given, using the same grammatical forms as in the examples.

A. *Use appropriate expressions when giving or receiving gifts.*

ex. **Chan:** **Sh͟umatsu ni K͟yōto ni ikimashita. Kore, K͟yōto no o-miyage desu. Dōzo.**
Suzuki: Arigatō gozaimasu. K͟yōto wa dō deshita ka.
Chan: **Totemo kirei deshita.**

1. Chan: Shūmatsu ni Sapporo ni ikimashita. Kore, Sapporo no omiyage desu. Dōzo. (Sapporo)

   Suzuki: Arigatō gozaimasu. Sapporo wa dō deshita ka (Sapporo)

   Chan: Totemo samui desu (samui desu)

2. Chan: Shūmatsu ni Hakone no onsen ni ikimashita. Kore, Hakone no onsen. dōzo (Hakone no onsen)

   Suzuki: Arigatō gozaimasu. Hakone no onsen dō deshita ka (onsen)

   Chan: tanoshii desu (tanoshii desu)

VOCABULARY	**dō deshita ka**	how was . . . ?
	dō	how

B. *Thank someone for a gift one received.*

ex. Ms. Chan received a box of chocolates from Ms. Nakamura on her birthday.

Chan: Nakamura-san, <u>chokorēto</u> o arigatō gozaimashita. Totemo <u>oishikatta desu</u>.
Nakamura: Sō desu ka. Yokatta desu.

1. Chan: Nakamura-san, konsāto no kippu o arigatō gozaimashita. Totemo tanoshii desu

(konsāto no kippu, tanoshii desu)

Nakamura: So desu ka. Yokatta desu

2. Chan: Nakamura-san, kabuki no hon o arigatō gozaimashita. totemo omoshiori desu.

(kabuki no hon, omoshiroi desu)

Nakamura: sō desu ka Yokatta desu.

C. *Make a telephone call.*

ex. **Suzuki:** Moshimoshi, <u>Nakamura-san</u> no o-taku desu ka.
Nakamura-san no kazoku: Hai, sō desu.
Suzuki: Suzuki desu. <u>Mayumi-san</u> wa irasshaimasu ka.
Nakamura-san no kazoku: Hai. Chotto o-machi kudasai.

1. Suzuki: Moshimoshi, sasaki-san no otaku desu ka

(Sasaki-san)

Sasaki-san no kazoku: Hai, so desu

Suzuki: suzuki desu. Okusan wa irasshaimasu ka

(okusan)

Sasaki-san no kazoku: Hai, Chotto omachi kudasai

2. Suzuki: Moshimoshi, Kāto-san no o-taku desu ka

(Katō-san)

Katō-san no kazoku: Hai, sō desu

Suzuki: suzuki desu. Go-shujin wa irasshaimasu ka

(go-shujin)

Katō-san no kazoku: Hai, Chotto o-machi kudasai

V. Listen to the CD and fill in the blanks based on the information you hear.

TRACK 54

Chan-san wa .... ni o-matsuri o mimashita. O-matsuri wa totemo ....

....

VOCABULARY

yokatta desu   that's good   **irasshaimasu**   be (honorific word for **imasu**)

Mayumi   Mayumi (female first name)   **chotto o-machi kudasai**   please wait a minute (politer way of saying **chotto matte kudasai**)

SHORT DIALOGUE

The morning after receiving some peaches from Mrs. Matsui, Mrs. Green happens to run into Mrs. Matsui. She thanks her for the peaches.

Gurīn: **Ohayō gozaimasu.**
Matsui: Ohayō gozaimasu.
Gurīn: **Kinō wa momo o arigatō gozaimashita. Totemo oishikatta desu.**
Matsui: Sō desu ka. Yokatta desu.

Green: Good morning.
Matsui: Good morning.
Green: Thank you for the peaches you gave us yesterday. They were very tasty.
Matsui: Were they? That's good.

Active Communication

Ask people for their impressions of places, movies, or other things or events. Refer to Exercise III.

GOING TO A FESTIVAL

The Japanese calendar is lined with seasonal festivals and events. Seasonal festivals such as cherry blossom viewing in spring and firework displays in the heat of summer are held to appreciate nature at its best. Festivals to celebrate a good harvest are held mainly in autumn, whereas those meant to invoke one are held in spring. At these fêtes, people carry around portable shrines, or *o-mikoshi*, and the men often wear *happi* coats designating neighborhood associations. Many festivals attract large crowds, and famous ones such as the Sapporo Snow Festival or the Gion Festival in Kyoto are always packed with people.

Inviting Someone to Do Something and Making Suggestions

| verb-**masen ka** |

| verb-**mashō** |

> *ex.* **Issho ni Asakusa ni ikimasen ka.**
> "Won't you go to Asakusa with (me)?/What do you say to going to Asakusa together?"
> **Ee/Hai, ikimashō.** "Yes, let's go."

The verb-**masen ka** pattern is used to invite someone to do something. Appropriate replies are as follows.

1. Acceptance:
   a. **Ee/Hai,** verb-**mashō.** "Yes, let's [verb]."
   b. **Ee/Hai, zehi.** "Yes, I'd love to."
2. Refusal: **Zannen desu ga, tsugō ga warui desu.**
   "I'm sorry, but it wouldn't be convenient (for me)."

The verb-**mashō** pattern is generally translatable as "let's."

| verb-**mashō ka** |

> *ex.* **Doko de aimashō ka.** "Where should we meet?"

The verb-**mashō ka** pattern is used to invite someone to decide a time, place, etc. for something.

Offering to Do Something

| verb-**mashō ka** |

> *ex.* **Nimotsu o mochimashō ka.** "Shall I carry your luggage?"

The verb-**mashō ka** pattern is also used when offering to do something for someone. Appropriate replies are as follows.
1. Acceptance: **Ee/Hai, onegaishimasu.** "Yes, please."
2. Refusal: **Iie, kekkō desu.** "No, thank you."

INVITATIONS

TARGET DIALOGUE

Mr. Kato invites Mr. Smith to a festival in Asakusa.

かとう：スミスさん、こんしゅうの　どようびに　あさくさで　おま
　　　　つりが　あります。いっしょに　いきませんか。

スミス：いいですね。いきましょう。なんで　いきましょうか。

かとう：ちかてつで　いきませんか。

スミス：そう　しましょう。どこで　あいましょうか。

かとう：あさくさえきの　かいさつぐちで　あいませんか。

スミス：はい。なんじに　あいましょうか。

かとう：10じは　どうですか。

スミス：10じですね。じゃ、どようびに。

■こんしゅうの　どようびに　あさくさで　おまつりが　あります
　から、スミスさんは　かとうさんと　あさくさに　いきます。

　　Katō: Sumisu-san, konshū no do-yōbi ni Asakusa de o-matsuri ga arimasu. Issho ni
　　　　ikimasen ka.
Sumisu: Ii desu ne. Ikimashō. Nan de ikimashō ka.
　　Katō: Chikatetsu de ikimasen ka.
Sumisu: Sō shimashō. Doko de aimashō ka.
　　Katō: Asakusa Eki no kaisatsuguchi de aimasen ka.
Sumisu: Hai. Nan-ji ni aimashō ka.
　　Katō: 10-ji wa dō desu ka.
Sumisu: 10-ji desu ne. Ja, do-yōbi ni.

■ **Konshū no do-yōbi ni Asakusa de o-matsuri ga arimasu kara, Sumisu-san wa Katō-
san to Asakusa ni ikimasu.**

　Kato: Mr. Smith, there is a festival in Asakusa this Saturday. Won't you go with me?
Smith: That would be nice. Let's go. How should we go?
　Kato: Would you like to go by subway?
Smith: Let's do that. Where should we meet?
　Kato: Would you like to meet at the ticket gate at Asakusa Station?
Smith: All right. What time should we meet?
　Kato: How about 10:00?
Smith: 10:00, then. Well, I'll see you on Saturday.

■ On Saturday there is a festival in Asakusa, so Mr. Smith is going to Asakusa with Mr. Kato.

VOCABULARY

あります	**arimasu**	there is/are going to be (see Note 1 below)
いっしょに	**issho ni**	together
いきませんか	**ikimasen ka**	won't you go (with me)?
いきましょう	**ikimashō**	let's go
いきましょうか	**ikimashō ka**	shall we go?
あさくさえき	**Asakusa Eki**	Asakusa Station
かいさつぐち	**kaisatsuguchi**	ticket gate
どうですか	**dō desu ka**	how is . . . ?
から	**kara**	because (particle; see Note 3 below)

NOTES

1. **Asakusa de o-matsuri ga arimasu.**
   Arimasu can also be used in the sense of "take place" or "happen." The place where the event happens is followed by the particle **de**.

2. **Ja, do-yōbi ni.**
   Do-yōbi ni is short for **do-yōbi ni aimashō**, "let's meet on Saturday." Japanese people often refer to the next meeting rather than saying good-bye.
   ex. **Ja, mata ashita.** "Well then, (see you) again tomorrow."

3. **Konshū no do-yōbi ni Asakusa de o-matsuri ga arimasu kara, Sumisu-san wa Katō-san to Asakusa ni ikimasu.**
   This complex sentence consists of two clauses. The first clause, ending with the particle **kara**, expresses a reason for what is stated in the second clause.

PRACTICE

WORD POWER

I. Events:

1. **hanabi-taikai**   2. **yuki-matsuri**   3. **sakkā no shiai**

VOCABULARY					
hanabi-taikai	fireworks display	**yuki-matsuri**	snow festival	**sakkā**	soccer
hanabi	fireworks	**yuki**	snow	**shiai**	game, match
taikai	large gathering				

II. Parts of a station:

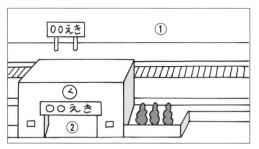

1. **hōmu**
2. **iriguchi**

3. **nishiguchi**
4. **higashiguchi**
5. **kitaguchi**
6. **minamiguchi**

III. Variations on the **-masu** form:

	go	see	do	meet
V-**masu**	ikimasu	mimasu	shimasu	aimasu
V-**mashō**	ikimashō	mimashō	shimashō	aimashō
V-**mashō ka**	ikimashō ka	mimashō ka	shimashō ka	aimashō ka
V-**masen ka**	ikimasen ka	mimasen ka	shimasen ka	aimasen ka

KEY SENTENCES

1. **Shūmatsu ni issho ni eiga o mimasen ka.**
2. **Eiga o mimashō.**
3. **Nani o tabemashō ka.**
4. **Do-yōbi ni Asakusa de o-matsuri ga arimasu.**
5. **2-kai ni resutoran ga arimasu kara, resutoran de shokuji o shimasen ka.**

1. Would you like to see a movie with me over the weekend?
2. Let's see a movie.
3. What should we eat?
4. There's a festival in Asakusa on Saturday.
5. There's a restaurant on the second floor, so won't you have a meal with me there?

VOCABULARY

hōmu	platform	**kitaguchi**	north exit
iriguchi	entrance	**minamiguchi**	south exit
nishiguchi	west exit		
higashiguchi	east exit		

EXERCISES

I. *Invite someone to do something.* Make up sentences as in the example.

> ex. **hiru-gohan o tabemasu** → **Hiru-gohan o tabemasen ka.**

1. kōhī o nomimasu → Kōhī o nomimasen ka

2. gorufu o shimasu → gorufu o shimasen ka

II. Make up dialogues following the patterns of the examples and based on the information in the illustrations.

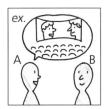  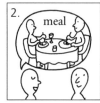  

A. *Invite someone to do something and accept one's invitation.*

> ex. **A: Shūmatsu ni issho ni eiga o mimasen ka.**
> **B: Ee, mimashō.**

1. A: shūmatsu ni issho ni Ginza o ikimasen ka
   B: Ee, ikimashō

2. A: shūmatsu ni issho ni
   B: Ee, tabemashō.

3. A: shūmatsu ni issho ni sumō o mimasen ka
   B: Hai, arigatō gozaimasu

4. A: shūmatsu ni issho ni hiru-gohan o tabemasen ka
   B: ee, tabemashō

B. *Invite someone to do something and refuse one's invitation.*

> ex. **A: Shūmatsu ni issho ni eiga o mimasen ka.**
> **B: Zannen desu ga, tsugō ga warui desu.**

1. A: shūmatsu ni issho ni hiru-gohan o tabemasen ka
   B: Zannen desu ga, tsugō ga warui desu.

2. A: Shūmatsu ni isshoni sumō o mimasen ka

B: zannen desu ga, tsugō ga warui desu

3. A: ....

B: ....

4. A: Shōmatsu ni issho ni Ginza o ikimasen ka

B: zannen desu ga. tsugō ga warui desu.

III. Make up dialogues following the patterns of the examples. Substitute the underlined parts with the alternatives given, using the same grammatical forms as in the examples.

A. *Decide what to do.*

ex. **A: Nani o tabemashō ka.**
B: Tempura o tabemasen ka.
A: Ee, sō shimashō.

1. A: Nani o nomimashō ka .... (nomimasu)

B: Wain o nomimasen ka .... (wain, nomimasu)

A: Ee, sō shimashō ....

2. A: Nani o kaimashō ka .... (kaimasu)

B: Kabin o kaimasenka .... (kabin, kaimasu)

A: Ee, sō shimasho. ....

B. *Decide when to do something.*

ex. **A: Itsu aimashō ka.**
B: Ashita no 3-ji wa dō desu ka.
A: Ee, sō shimashō.

1. A: Itsu purezento o kaimasu ka .... (purezento o kaimasu)

B: Do-yōbi wa dō desu ka .... (do-yōbi)

A: Ee, sō shimashō ....

2. A: Itsu gorufu o shimasu ka .... (gorufu o shimasu)

B: raigetsu wa dō desu ka .... (raigetsu)

A: Ee, sō shimasho. ....

C. *Decide where to do something.*

　　ex. **A: Doko de aimashō ka.**
　　　B: Eki no mae ni kōban ga arimasu kara, kōban no mae de aimasen ka.
　　　A: Ee, sō shimashō.

　1.　A: .... (tabemasu)

　　　B: ....
　　　　(ABC biru ni ii resutoran ga takusan arimasu, ABC biru de tabemasu)

　　　A: ....

　2.　A: .... (hanashi o shimasu)

　　　B: ....
　　　　(kono chikaku ni kōen ga arimasu, kōen de hanashi o shimasu)

　　　A: ....

IV. Make up sentences following the patterns of the examples and based on the information in the illustrations.

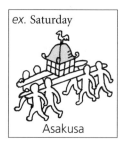

ex. Saturday — Asakusa
1. next month — Sapporo
2. tomorrow — EMBASSY
3. Tuesday — Yokohama

A. *State when and where an event will take place.*

　　ex. **Do-yōbi ni Asakusa de o-matsuri ga arimasu.**

　1. ....

　2. ....

　3. ....

B. *Invite someone to an event and accept one's invitation.*

   ex. **A: Do-yōbi ni Asakusa de o-matsuri ga arimasu. Issho ni ikimasen ka.**
       B: Ii desu ne. Ikimashō.

    1. A: ....

        B: ....

    2. A: ....

        B: ....

    3. A: ....

        B: ....

V. *Invite someone to an event and decide on a meeting place.* Make up dialogues following the pattern of the example. Substitute the underlined parts with the alternatives given.

   ex. **Sumisu:**   **Asatte Odaiba de hanabi-taikai ga arimasu. Issho ni ikimasen ka.**
       Nakamura: Ii desu ne. Ikimashō.
       Sumisu: **Doko de aimashō ka.**
       Nakamura: Shimbashi Eki no kitaguchi de aimasen ka.
       Sumisu: **Ee, sō shimashō.**

    1. Sumisu: .... (taishikan, pātī)

        Nakamura: ....

        Sumisu: ....

        Nakamura: .... (Shinjuku Eki no nishiguchi)

        Sumisu: ....

    2. Sumisu: .... (Tōkyō Hōru, konsāto)

        Nakamura: ....

        Sumisu: ....

        Nakamura: .... (Tōkyō Eki no minamiguchi)

        Sumisu: ....

VOCABULARY			
ii desu ne	that sounds good	**Shinjuku Eki**	Shinjuku Station
Shimbashi Eki	Shimbashi Station	**Shinjuku**	Shinjuku (district in Tokyo)
Shimbashi	Shimbashi (district in Tokyo)	**Tōkyō Hōru**	Tokyo Hall (fictitious building name)
		hōru	(concert) hall

VI. *Invite someone out to eat.* Make up a dialogue based on the information in the illustrations.

1. Suzuki: ....

2. Chan: ....

3. Suzuki: ....

4. Chan: ....

5. Suzuki: ....

6. Suzuki: ....

7. Chan: ....

8. Suzuki: ....

9. Suzuki: Ja, do-yōbi ni.

10. Chan: Ja, mata.

VII. Listen to the CD and fill in the blanks based on the information you hear.

TRACK 58

Sumisu-san wa .... de .... ni Nikkō ni ikimasu.

SHORT DIALOGUES

TRACK 59

I. **Nakamura: Raishū Sumisu-san to tenisu o shimasu. Chan-san mo issho ni shimasen ka.**
Chan: Arigatō gozaimasu. Zehi.

Nakamura: I'm going to be playing tennis with Mr. Smith next week. Won't you join us, Ms. Chan?
Chan: Thank you, I'd love to.

VOCABULARY

zehi   by all means, certainly

II. **Takahashi: Sumisu-san, konshū no nichi-yōbi ni uchi de pātī o shimasu. Kimasen ka.**
Sumisu: Arigatō gozaimasu. Zehi.

Takahashi: Mr. Smith, I'm having a party at my house this Sunday. Won't you come?
Smith: Thank you. I certainly will.

VOCABULARY

pātī o shimasu   have a party

NOTES

1. **(Nichi-yōbi ni uchi ni) kimasen ka.**
When inviting someone to your own home, use the phrase **kimasen ka**. Appropriate replies are **ee/hai, arigatō gozaimasu** ("yes, thank you") or, to decline the offer, **zannen desu ga, tsugō ga warui desu** ("I'm sorry, I'm afraid it wouldn't be convenient [for me]").

Invite a friend to an event.

PARTICIPATING IN A FESTIVAL

TARGET DIALOGUE

Mr. Smith meets Mr. Suzuki, who is wearing a *happi* coat, and calls out to him.

かとう：あ、スミスさん、あそこに　すずきさんが　いますよ。

スミス：ほんとうですね。すずきさん。

すずき：あ、スミスさん。スミスさんも　いっしょに　おみこしを
　　　　かつぎませんか。

スミス：でも、はっぴが　ありません。

すずき：わたしのを　かしましょうか。

スミス：いいんですか。

すずき：ええ、わたしは　２まい　ありますから。

スミス：ありがとうございます。じゃ、おねがいします。

■スミスさんは　あさくさで　すずきさんに　あいました。いっしょ
　に　おみこしを　かつぎます。

　　Katō: A, Sumisu-san, asoko ni Suzuki-san ga imasu yo.
Sumisu: Hontō desu ne. Suzuki-san.
　Suzuki: A, Sumisu-san. Sumisu-san mo issho ni o-mikoshi o katsugimasen ka.
Sumisu: Demo, happi ga arimasen.
　Suzuki: Watashi no o kashimashō ka.
Sumisu: Ii n desu ka.
　Suzuki: Ee, watashi wa 2-mai arimasu kara.
Sumisu: Arigatō gozaimasu. Ja, onegaishimasu.

■ Sumisu-san wa Asakusa de Suzuki-san ni aimashita. Issho ni o-mikoshi o katsugimasu.

　　Kato: Oh, Mr. Smith, there's Mr. Suzuki over there.
　Smith: You're right. Mr. Suzuki!
　Suzuki: Oh, Mr. Smith. Would you like to carry the *o-mikoshi* with us?
　Smith: But I don't have a *happi* coat.
　Suzuki: Shall I lend you mine?
　Smith: Is it all right with you?
　Suzuki: Yes, I have two.
　Smith: Thank you. I'll ask you to do that, then.

■ Mr. Smith has met Mr. Suzuki in Asakusa. They will carry the *o-mikoshi* together.

VOCABULARY

ほんとう	**hontō**	true
おみこし	**o-mikoshi**	portable shrine (carried during festivals)
かつぎます	**katsugimasu**	carry (on one's shoulders)
でも	**demo**	but
はっぴ	**happi**	*happi* coat
わたしの	**watashi no**	mine
かしましょうか	**kashimashō ka**	shall I lend you?
かします	**kashimasu**	lend
いいんですか	**ii n desu ka**	is it all right? (expressing reserve)
あります	**arimasu**	have (see Note 1 below)

NOTES

1. (Watashi wa) happi ga arimasen.
Arimasu can also be used in the sense of "have" or "own."

PRACTICE

WORD POWER

I. Verbs:

1. **kashimasu**

2. **tsukemasu**

3. **keshimasu**

4. **mochimasu**

5. **akemasu**

6. **shimemasu**

7. **(shashin o) torimasu**

tetsudaimasu
てつだいます

VOCABULARY				
kashimasu	lend	**akemasu**	open	
tsukemasu	turn on	**shimemasu**	close, shut	
keshimasu	turn off	**(shashin o) torimasu**	take (a photograph)	
mochimasu	carry, hold	**shashin**	photograph	151

II. Words that can be used with **arimasu** ("to have"):

1. **jikan**

2. **kuruma**

3. **yasumi**

4. **Nihon-go no jugyō**

KEY SENTENCES

1. **Chizu o kakimashō ka.**
2. **Sumisu-san wa eiga no kippu ga 2-mai arimasu.**

1. Shall I draw a map?
2. Mr. Smith has two movie tickets.

EXERCISES

I. *Offer to do something.* Make up sentences as in the example.

ex. **shashin o torimasu** → **Shashin o torimashō ka.**

1. chizu o kakimasu → <u>Chizu o Kakimashō Ka</u>

2. kono hon o kashimasu → <u>Kono hon o Kashimashō ka</u>

II. *Offer to do something and accept or reject one's offer.* Make up dialogues following the pattern of the example and based on the information in the illustrations.

ex. **Sumisu:**   **Nimotsu o mochimashō ka.**
   Nakamura: Ee, onegaishimasu.
   Suzuki: **Iie, kekkō desu.**

1. Sumisu: ....

   Nakamura: ....

2. Sumisu: ....

   Suzuki: ....

3. Sumisu: ....

   Nakamura: ....

4. Sumisu: ....

   Suzuki: ....

VOCABULARY	**nimotsu**	luggage, baggage
	doa	door
	mado	window
	eakon	air conditioner

153

III. *State what one has.* Make up sentences following the pattern of the example. Substitute the underlined word with the words suggested by the illustration.

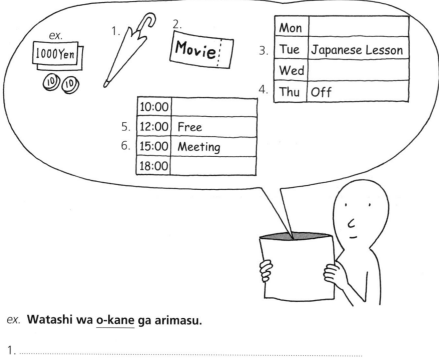

ex. **Watashi wa <u>o-kane</u> ga arimasu.**

1. ....

2. ....

3. ....

4. ....

5. ....

6. ....

IV. Make up dialogues following the patterns of the examples. Substitute the underlined parts with the alternatives given, using the same grammatical forms as in the examples.

A. *Offer to lend someone something, giving a reason for doing so, and accept one's offer.*

ex. **A: (Watashi wa) <u>kasa</u> ga <u>2-hon</u> arimasu kara, kashimashō ka.**
B: Hai, onegaishimasu.

1. A: .... (pen, 2-hon)

   B: ....

2. A: .... (happi, 2-mai)

   B: ....

B. *Invite someone to do something, giving a reason for doing so, and accept one's invitation.*

    ex. **A: (Watashi wa) kuruma ga arimasu kara, issho ni Nikkō ni ikimasen ka.**
    B: Ee, zehi.

    1. A: .... (omoshiroi DVD, mimasu)

        B: ....

    2. A: .... (eiga no kippu, ikimasu)

        B: ....

V. Make up dialogues following the patterns of the examples. Substitute the underlined parts with the alternatives given, using the same grammatical forms as in the examples.

A. *Refuse an invitation by stating one's situation.*

    ex. **Suzuki: Eiga no kippu ga 2-mai arimasu. Chan-san, komban issho ni ikimasen ka.**
    Chan: Sumimasen, komban jikan ga arimasen.
    Suzuki: Sō desu ka. Ja, mata kondo.

    1. Suzuki: ....

        Chan: .... (kaigi ga arimasu)

        Suzuki: ....

    2. Suzuki: ....

        Chan: .... (Nihon-go no jugyō ga arimasu)

        Suzuki: ....

B. *Invite someone to do something.*

    ex. **Sumisu: Suzuki-san, raishū issho ni gorufu o shimasen ka.**
    Suzuki: Demo, kurabu ga arimasen.
    Sumisu: Watashi no o kashimashō ka.
    Suzuki: Arigatō gozaimasu. Onegaishimasu.

    1. Sumisu: .... (sukī)

        Suzuki: .... (dōgu)

        Sumisu: ....

        Suzuki: ....

    2. Sumisu: .... (tenisu)

        Suzuki: .... (raketto)

        Sumisu: ....

        Suzuki: ....

VOCABULARY			
komban	this evening	**raketto**	racket
mata kondo	next time		
kurabu	golf club		
dōgu	tool, equipment		

VI. *Offer to help someone.* Make up a dialogue based on the information in the illustrations.

1. Suzuki: ....

2. Sumisu: ....

3. Suzuki: ....

4. Sumisu: ....

VII. Listen to the CD and answer the question based on the information you hear.

....

SHORT DIALOGUES

TRACK 63

I. At the festival site, Mr. Smith accidentally steps on someone's foot.

onna no hito: A, itai.
Sumisu: A, sumimasen. Daijōbu desu ka.
onna no hito: Ee, daijōbu desu.
Sumisu: Dōmo sumimasendeshita.

woman: Oh, ouch!
Smith: Oh, I'm sorry. Are you all right?
woman: Yes, I'm fine.
Smith: I'm really sorry.

VOCABULARY

itai	painful, ouch!
daijōbu desu ka	are you all right?
sumimasendeshita	I'm sorry (for what I did a while ago)

II. Mr. Kato calls out to Mr. Smith, who appears to be ill.

Katō: Daijōbu desu ka.
Sumisu: Chotto kibun ga warui n desu.
Katō: Asoko ni benchi ga arimasu kara, chotto yasumimashō.
Sumisu: Hai.

Kato: Are you all right?
Smith: I'm feeling a bit out of sorts.
Kato: There's a bench over there, so let's take a little break.
Smith: All right.

VOCABULARY

kibun ga warui n desu	I feel out of sorts; I don't feel well
benchi	bench
yasumimasu	rest, relax, take time off

Active Communication

You have two tickets for an event. Invite someone to that event.

Quiz 3 (Units 6–7)

I Fill in the blank(s) in each sentence with the appropriate particle. Where a particle is not needed, write in an *X*.

1. Chan-san wa Takahashi-san (   ) hana o moraimashita.

2. Watashi wa tanjōbi ni haha ni sukāfu (ni) agemashita.

3. Do-yōbi ni Asakusa de o-matsuri (ga) arimasu.

4. Watashi wa kuruma (   ) arimasu.

5. Watashi wa eiga no kippu (   ) 2-mai (   ) arimasu.

II Complete each question by filling in the blank with the appropriate word.

1. Tōkyō Resutoran wa (   ) resutoran desu ka.
   Kireina resutoran desu.

2. Sumisu-san wa (   ) ni eiga no kippu o moraimashita ka.
   Tomodachi ni moraimashita.

3. Kinō no konsāto wa (   ) deshita ka.
   Totemo yokatta desu.

4. Nichi-yōbi ni (   ) de bāgen-sēru ga arimasu ka.
   Tōkyō Depāto de arimasu.

III Change the word in parentheses to the form that is appropriate in the context of the sentence.

1. Tōkyō Hoteru wa (   ) hoteru desu. (kirei desu)

2. Kore wa (   ) kēki desu. (oishii desu)

3. Ano resutoran wa amari (   ). (shizuka desu)

4. Kinō no pātī wa totemo (   ). (nigiyaka desu)

5. Kinō no eiga wa amari (   ). (omoshiroi desu)

IV Change the words in parentheses to the forms that are appropriate in the context of the dialogue.

1. A: Shūmatsu ni issho ni eiga o (   ). (mimasu)
   B: Ee, mimashō.
   A: Doko de (   ). (aimasu)
   B: Tōkyō Eki wa dō desu ka.

2. A: Eakon o (   ). (tsukemasu)
   B: Iie, kekkō desu.
   A: Dewa, mado o (   ). (akemasu)
   B: Hai, onegaishimasu.

158

ON BUSINESS OUTSIDE TOKYO

Looking at Japan from a satellite, one would be surprised to see how mountainous the country is. In fact, about 73 percent of the land is mountain terrain. Another notable point is that because the country stretches more than 3,000 kilometers from northeast to southwest, its climate varies considerably according to latitude; and this in turn has given rise to differences in ways of life and a variety of local dialects. The city of Sapporo on the island of Hokkaido in northern Japan (see photo above) is both a tourist and a business destination. Other such cities include Osaka, Niigata, Nagoya, and Fukuoka. (See map on front end paper.)

UNIT
8 GRAMMAR

The -Te Form

■ Japanese verbs have several forms

Japanese verbs have several conjugated forms. All the verbs presented so far have been in, or derived from, the **-masu** form. Now we'll look at a new form, the **-te** form.

■ How to form the **-te** form

Japanese verbs are divided into three classes according to their conjugations: Regular I, Regular II and Irregular. The **-te** forms of Regular II and Irregular verbs always end with **-te**: the **-masu** comes off and **-te** is added to the stem. The **-te** forms of Regular I verbs vary, as shown in the following chart.

REGULAR I			REGULAR II		
buy	**kai-masu**	**katte**	eat	**tabe-masu**	**tabete**
wait	**machi-masu**	**matte**	open	**ake-masu**	**akete**
return, go home	**kaeri-masu**	**kaette**	see	**mi-masu**	**mite**
listen	**kiki-masu**	**kiite**	IRREGULAR		
write	**kaki-masu**	**kaite**	come	**ki-masu**	**kite**
read	**yomi-masu**	**yonde**	do	**shi-masu**	**shite**
drink	**nomi-masu**	**nonde**			
turn off	**keshi-masu**	**keshite**			

NOTE: A more detailed explanation of the grouping of Japanese verbs is given in Unit 9 Grammar, p. 178.

■ How the **-te** form is used

The **-te** form occurs in the middle of a sentence
   ex. **Gurei-san wa Sapporo-shisha ni itte, Satō-san ni aimasu.**
     "Mr. Grey will go to the Sapporo branch office and meet Mr. Sato."

or is combined with **kudasai** to form a polite imperative.
   ex. **Katarogu o okutte kudasai.** "Please send a catalog."

When one action is followed by another, the first clause is terminated by a verb in the **-te** form. In this type of sentence, the subject of the first and second clause must be the same. The **-te** form can be used to link up to three clauses, in which case the verbs of the first two end in the **-te** form. The **-te** form cannot be used if the moods and tenses of the clauses it combines are not the same. For example, the following two sentences cannot be connected using the **-te** form:
1. Statement: **Watashi wa kippu ga 2-mai arimasu.** "I have two tickets."
2. Suggestion: **Ashita issho ni eiga o mimasen ka.**
        "What do you say to seeing a movie together tomorrow?"
Furthermore, if the first clause contains a motion verb like **ikimasu**, **kimasu**, or **kaerimasu**, the verb in the second clause must express an action that occurs in the location to which the subject went in the first clause. For example, **Kinō Ginza ni itte, hiru-gohan o tabemashita** ("Yesterday I went to Ginza and ate lunch [there]") is correct, but **Kinō Ginza ni itte, Shibuya de hiru-gohan o tabemashita** ("Yesterday I went to Ginza and ate lunch in Shibuya") is incorrect, since the act of eating took place in Shibuya, not Ginza.

TALKING ABOUT PLANS

 TARGET DIALOGUE

Ms. Chan is talking with Ms. Sasaki about her sudden business trip.

チャン：ささきさん、ちょっと　よろしいですか。

ささき：はい。

チャン：あした　ほっかいどうで　はんばいかいぎが　ありますから、
　　　　さっぽろに　いきます。

ささき：かいぎは　なんじからですか。

チャン：ごぜん　10じから　ごご　3じまでです。かいぎの　あと
　　　　で　さっぽろししゃに　いって、さとうさんに　あいます。
　　　　あさって　はこだての　チョコレートこうじょうを　みて、
　　　　1じの　ひこうきで　とうきょうに　かえります。

ささき：わかりました。では、きを　つけて。

■チャンさんは　あした　さっぽろに　いきます。あさって　チョコ
　レートこうじょうを　みて、とうきょうに　かえります。

　Chan: **Sasaki-san, chotto yoroshii desu ka.**
Sasaki: **Hai.**
　Chan: **Ashita Hokkaidō de hambai-kaigi ga arimasu kara, Sapporo ni ikimasu.**
Sasaki: **Kaigi wa nan-ji kara desu ka.**
　Chan: **Gozen 10-ji kara gogo 3-ji made desu. Kaigi no ato de Sapporo-shisha ni itte,
　　　　Satō-san ni aimasu. Asatte Hakodate no chokorēto-kōjō o mite, 1-ji no hikōki de
　　　　Tōkyō ni kaerimasu.**
Sasaki: **Wakarimashita. Dewa, ki o tsukete.**

■ **Chan-san wa ashita Sapporo ni ikimasu. Asatte chokorēto kōjō o mite, Tōkyō ni kaeri-
　masu.**

　Chan: Ms. Sasaki, do you have a moment?
Sasaki: Yes, please (tell me what you want to talk about).
　Chan: There's a sales meeting in Hokkaido tomorrow, so I'm going to Sapporo.
Sasaki: What time does the meeting start?
　Chan: It's from 10:00 a.m. to 3:00 p.m. After the meeting, I'll go to the Sapporo branch office
　　　　and meet Mr. Sato. The day after tomorrow, I'll see the chocolate factory in Hakodate
　　　　and fly back to Tokyo on a 1:00 (p.m.) flight.
Sasaki: I see. Well then, take care.

■ Ms. Chan is going to Sapporo tomorrow. The day after tomorrow she will see a chocolate fac-
　tory and return to Tokyo.

VOCABULARY

ちょっと よろしいですか	**chotto yoroshii desu ka**	do you have a moment?
よろしい	**yoroshii**	good, all right (polite form of **ii**; used in interrogative sentences)
ほっかいどう	**Hokkaidō**	Hokkaido (the northernmost of the main islands of Japan)
はんばい	**hambai**	sales, marketing
～の あとで	**no ato de**	after
さとう	**Satō**	Sato (surname)
はこだて	**Hakodate**	Hakodate (city in southern Hokkaido)
こうじょう	**kōjō**	factory, manufacturing plant
きを つけて	**ki o tsukete**	take care

NOTES

1. Chotto yoroshii desu ka.

This expression is used to get the attention of someone who is in the midst of something.

PRACTICE

WORD POWER

The **-te** form:

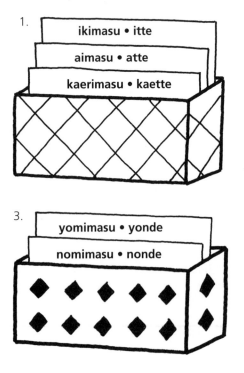

1.
- ikimasu • itte
- aimasu • atte
- kaerimasu • kaette

2.
- kakimasu • kaite
- kikimasu • kiite

3.
- yomimasu • yonde
- nomimasu • nonde

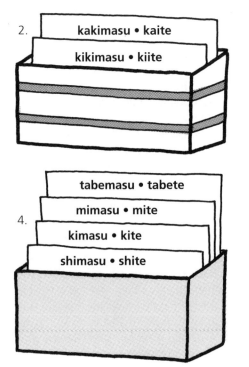

4.
- tabemasu • tabete
- mimasu • mite
- kimasu • kite
- shimasu • shite

KEY SENTENCES

> 1. **Sumisu-san wa kinō hon-ya ni itte, jisho o kaimashita.**
> 2. **Sumisu-san wa kaigi no mae ni kopī o shimasu.**
> 3. **Sumisu-san wa kinō pātī no ato de takushī de uchi ni kaerimashita.**
>
> 1. Mr. Smith went to a bookstore yesterday and bought a dictionary.
> 2. Mr. Smith will make copies before the meeting.
> 3. Mr. Smith went home by taxi after yesterday's party.

EXERCISES

 I. *Practice conjugating verbs.* Repeat the verbs below and memorize their **-te** forms.

	-MASU FORM	**-TE** FORM		**-MASU** FORM	**-TE** FORM
buy	**kaimasu**	**katte**	turn off	**keshimasu**	**keshite**
meet	**aimasu**	**atte**	eat	**tabemasu**	**tabete**
return, go home	**kaerimasu**	**kaette**	open	**akemasu**	**akete**
go	**ikimasu**	***itte**	close	**shimemasu**	**shimete**
write	**kakimasu**	**kaite**	turn on	**tsukemasu**	**tsukete**
listen (to), ask	**kikimasu**	**kiite**	see	**mimasu**	**mite**
drink	**nomimasu**	**nonde**	come	**kimasu**	**kite**
read	**yomimasu**	**yonde**	do	**shimasu**	**shite**

*irregular inflection

 II. *Practice the -te form.* Change the following verbs to their **-te** forms.

ex. **tabemasu** → **tabete**

1. kimasu → kite
2. nomimasu → nonde
3. kakimasu → kaite
4. aimasu → atte
5. kaerimasu → kaette

6. yomimasu → yonde
7. mimasu → mite
8. kikimasu → kiite
9. shimasu → shite
10. ikimasu → itte

VOCABULARY   **no mae ni**   before

163

III. *Express a sequence of actions.* Combine the sentences below as in the example.

> ex. **Mēru o kakimasu. Okurimasu.**
> → **Mēru o kaite, okurimasu.**

1. Denki o tsukemasu. Doa o shimemasu.

   → Denki o tsukete, Doa o shimemasu

2. Denwa-bangō o kikimasu. Denwa o shimasu.

   → Denwa-bangō o kiite, Denwa o shimasu

3. Uchi de hon o yomimasu. Repōto o kakimasu.

   → Uchi de hon o yonde, Repōto o kakimasu

 IV. *Ask and answer what one will do. In answering, express a sequence of actions.* Make up dialogues following the pattern of the example. Substitute the underlined parts with the appropriate forms of the alternatives given.

> ex. **A: Ashita nani o shimasu ka.**
> **B: Hon-ya ni itte, jisho o kaimasu.**

1. A: Ashita nani o shimasu ka

   B: Ginza de kaimono o shite, eiga o mimasu
   (Ginza de kaimono o shimasu, eiga o mimasu)

2. A: Ashita nani o shimasu ka

   B: Resutoran de hiru-gohan o tabete, bijutsukan ni ikimasu
   (resutoran de hiru-gohan o tabemasu, bijutsukan ni ikimasu)

 V. *Express a sequence of actions.* Combine the sentences below as in the example.

> ex. **Uchi ni kimasen ka. Hiru-gohan o tabemasen ka.**
> → **Uchi ni kite, hiru-gohan o tabemasen ka.**

1. Sumisu-san ni aimashita. Issho ni tenisu o shimashita.

   → Sumisu-san ni atte, Issho ni tenisu o shimashita

2. Doa o akemashō ka. Denki o tsukemashō ka.

   → Doa o akete, Denki o tsukemashō ka

VOCABULARY		
	denki	(electric) light
	repōto	report
	bijutsukan	art museum

VI. *Ask and answer what one did. In answering, express a sequence of actions.* Make up dialogues following the pattern of the example. Substitute the underlined parts with the appropriate forms of the alternatives given.

ex. **A: Kinō nani o shimashita ka.**
B: Depāto de kēki o katte, tomodachi no uchi ni ikimashita.

1. A: Kinō nani o shimashita ka

   B: Roppongi ni itte, shokuji o shimashita
   _____ (Roppongi ni ikimasu, shokuji o shimasu)

2. A: Kinō nani o shimashita ka

   B: Tomodachi ni atte, issho ni (Tomodachi ni aimasu, issho ni sumō o mimasu)
   sumō o mimashita.

VII. *State what someone will do before or after a given event.* Make up sentences following the patterns of the examples. Use the information in the illustration as a guide and substitute the underlined parts in each example with the alternatives given.

ex. 1. **Gogo 7-ji kara kaigi ga arimasu. Kaigi no mae ni shokuji o shimasu.**

1. _____ (kaigi, kopī o shimasu)

2. _____ (pātī, wain o kaimasu)

ex. 2. **Gogo 7-ji kara pātī ga arimasu. Pātī no ato de takushī de uchi ni kaerimasu.**

3. _____ (kaigi, repōto o kakimasu)

4. _____ (kaigi, Yamamoto-san ni aimasu)

VIII. *Ask and answer what one did after work. In answering, express a sequence of actions* Make up dialogues following the pattern of the example and based on the information in the illustrations.

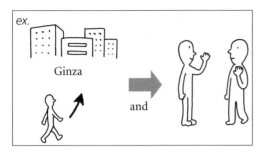

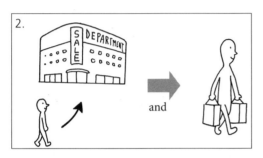

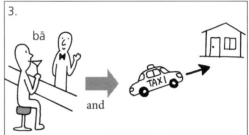

ex. **A: Kinō shigoto no ato de nani o shimashita ka.**
B: Ginza ni itte, tomodachi ni aimashita.

1. A: kinō shigoto no ato de nani o shimashita ka
   B: Tomodachi ni atte, eiga o mimashita

2. A: kinō shigoto no ato de nani o shimashita ka
   B:

3. A: kinō shigoto no ato de nani o shimashita ka
   B: Bā o tabete, uchi ni kaerimashita.

IX. *Describe a schedule.* Look at the schedule of Mr. Smith's business trip and make up sentences following the pattern of the example.

ex.	Thursday	Osaka	Meeting	→ Call Mr. Green
1.	Friday	Kobe	Golf	→ Go to a friend's house
2.	Saturday	Kyoto	Have a meal with Mr. Yamamoto	→ See old temples and gardens

ex. **Sumisu-san wa moku-yōbi ni Ōsaka ni itte, kaigi o shimasu. Kaigi no ato de Gurīn-san ni denwa o shimasu.**

1. ....

2. ....

 X. *Talk about a plan.* Make up dialogues on the pattern of the example. Substitute the underlined parts with the alternatives given.

ex. **Sasaki: Chan-san, kaigi no ato de doko ni ikimasu ka.**
Chan: Hakodate ni itte, chokorēto-kōjō o mimasu.
Sasaki: Sō desu ka.

1. Sasaki: ....

   Chan: .... (Otaru, sushi o tabemasu)

   Sasaki: ....

2. Sasaki: ....

   Chan: .... (depāto, Hokkaidō no o-miyage o kaimasu)

   Sasaki: ....

XI. Listen to the CD and choose the correct answer to the question asked.

TRACK
66

a)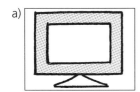

b)

c)

SHORT DIALOGUES

I. Mrs. Green is planning a party. She calls up Mrs. Matsui to invite her.

Gurin: **Nihon-jin no tomodachi ni Kyōto no yūmeina o-sake o moraimashita. Nichi-yōbi ni tomodachi o yonde, pātī o shimasu. Matsui-san mo kimasen ka.**
Matsui: Arigatō gozaimasu. Zehi.

Green: I've received some famous sake from Kyoto from a Japanese friend. On Sunday I'm getting some friends together to have a party. Won't you come, Mrs. Matsui?
Matsui: Thank you. I'll be there.

VOCABULARY

yonde	(**-te** form of **yobimasu**)
yobimasu	call, invite

II. Ms. Nakamura asks Ms. Chan if she plans to attend Mrs. Green's party.

Nakamura: Ashita no pātī ni ikimasu ka.
Chan: **Iie, ikimasen.**
Nakamura: Dōshite desu ka.
Chan: **Honkon kara haha ga kimasu kara.**

Nakamura: Will you go to the party tomorrow?
Chan: No, I will not.
Nakamura: Why (not)?
Chan: Because my mother is visiting (*lit.*, "will come") from Hong Kong.

VOCABULARY

dōshite	why
ni	(particle indicating a purpose)

Active Communication

Tell someone what you did yesterday. Then talk about your plans for the coming weekend.

MAKING A REQUEST

 TARGET DIALOGUE

Ms. Chan has come to Sapporo to attend a sales meeting.

チャン：もしもし、チャンですが、おはようございます。

すずき：あ、チャンさん、おはようございます。すずきです。

チャン：いま　さっぽろに　います。すみませんが、メールで　あたらしい　しょうひんの　カタログを　すぐ　おくってください。かいぎで　つかいますから。

すずき：はい、わかりました。

チャン：それから、サンプルの　しゃしんも　おくってください。

すずき：はい、すぐ　おくります。

チャン：じゃ、おねがいします。

■ チャンさんは　さっぽろから　ほんしゃの　すずきさんに　でんわを　しました。すずきさんは　チャンさんに　メールで　あたらしい　しょうひんの　カタログと　サンプルの　しゃしんを　おくります。

  Chan: **Moshimoshi, Chan desu ga, ohayō gozaimasu.**
Suzuki: **A, Chan-san, ohayō gozaimasu. Suzuki desu.**
  Chan: **Ima Sapporo ni imasu. Sumimasen ga, mēru de atarashii shōhin no katarogu o sugu okutte kudasai. Kaigi de tsukaimasu kara.**
Suzuki: **Hai, wakarimashita.**
  Chan: **Sorekara, sampuru no shashin mo okutte kudasai.**
Suzuki: **Hai, sugu okurimasu.**
  Chan: **Ja, onegaishimasu.**

■ **Chan-san wa Sapporo kara honsha no Suzuki-san ni denwa o shimashita. Suzuki-san wa Chan-san ni mēru de atarashii shōhin no katarogu to sampuru no shashin o okurimasu.**

  Chan: Hello, this is Chan. Good morning.
Suzuki: Oh, Ms. Chan. Good morning. This is Suzuki.
  Chan: I'm in Sapporo. I'm sorry to bother you, but could you please send me the new product catalog by e-mail right away, because I'm going to use it during the meeting.
Suzuki: Yes, all right.
  Chan: Also, please send photographs of the samples.
Suzuki: Yes, I'll send them right away.
  Chan: Thank you. Bye now.

■ Ms. Chan made a phone call from Sapporo to Mr. Suzuki at the main office. Mr. Suzuki sends Ms. Chan the new product catalog and sample photographs by e-mail.

VOCABULARY

が	**ga**	(particle; see Note 1 below)
しょうひん	**shōhin**	product, merchandise
カタログ	**katarogu**	catalog
すぐ	**sugu**	soon, right away
おくって ください	**okutte kudasai**	please send
つかいます	**tsukaimasu**	use
それから	**sorekara**	also, in addition
サンプル	**sampuru**	sample
ほんしゃ	**honsha**	main/central/head office

NOTES

1. Chan desu ga . . .

This **ga** is a conjunction that joins two clauses. It expresses a kind of courteous hesitation and indicates that the phrase before it is merely a preliminary to the principal matter.

2. Mēru de

This **de** indicates a means of telecommunication or post.

   ex. **Mēru de shiryō o okurimasu.** "I'll send the materials by e-mail."

   Takuhaibin de nimotsu o okurimasu. "I'll send the luggage by courier."

PRACTICE

WORD POWER

I. Verbs:

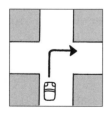 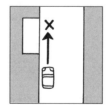  

1. **magarimasu**	2. **tomemasu**	3. **iimasu**	4. **oshiemasu**

VOCABULARY

magarimasu	turn
tomemasu	stop, park
iimasu	say
oshiemasu	teach, show, tell

5. **mottekimasu**

6. **todokemasu**

7. **machimasu**

II. Positions and directions:

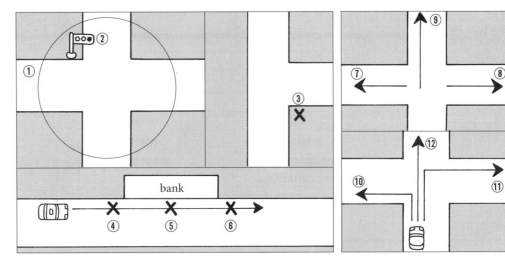

1. **kōsaten**
2. **shingō**
3. **kado**
4. **ginkō no temae**
5. **ginkō no mae**
6. **ginkō no saki**

7. **hidari**
8. **migi**
9. **massugu**
10. **kōsaten o hidari ni magarimasu**
11. **kōsaten o migi ni magarimasu**
12. **massugu ikimasu**

III. Means of communication or delivery:

1. **fakkusu**

2. **kōkūbin**

3. **funabin**

4. **takuhaibin**

KEY SENTENCES

1. **Mō ichi-do itte kudasai.**
2. **Kono nimotsu o takuhaibin de okutte kudasai.**
3. **Tsugi no shingō o migi ni magatte kudasai.**

1. Please say it again.
2. Please send this luggage by courier.
3. Turn right at the next traffic signal.

EXERCISES

I. *Practice conjugating verbs.* Repeat the verbs below and memorize their **-masu** and **-te** forms.

	-MASU FORM	**-TE** FORM
say	**iimasu**	**itte**
wait	**machimasu**	**matte**
turn	**magarimasu**	**magatte**
take	**torimasu**	**totte**
lend	**kashimasu**	**kashite**
show	**misemasu**	**misete**
stop	**tomemasu**	**tomete**
tell	**oshiemasu**	**oshiete**
deliver	**todokemasu**	**todokete**
bring	**mottekimasu**	**mottekite**

II. *Make a request.* Make up sentences as in the example.

ex. **namae o kakimasu** → **Namae o kaite kudasai.**

1. chotto machimasu → *Chotto o matte kudasai*
2. shashin o torimasu → *shashin o totte kudasai*
3. mō ichi-do iimasu → *mō ichi-do itte kudasai*
4. pen o kashimasu → *pen o kashite kudasai*
5. piza o todokemasu → *piza o todokete kudasai*

VOCABULARY	**tsugi**	next
	misemasu	show
	piza	pizza

III. Make up dialogues following the patterns of the examples. Substitute the underlined parts with the alternatives given, changing their forms as necessary.

A. *Make and accept a request.*

> *ex.* **A: Sumimasen. Ano resutoran no namae o oshiete kudasai.**
> **B: Hai.**

1. A: Sumimasen. Mēru-adoresu o kaite kudasai (mēru-adoresu, kakimasu)

   B: Hai

2. A: Sumimasen. Menyū o misete kudasai (menyū, misemasu)

   B: Hai

3. A: Sumimasen. kaigi no shiryō o mottekite (kaigi no shiryō, mottekimasu)

   B: Hai

B. *Make and accept a request to send something by a certain means.*

> *ex.* **A: Sumisu-san ni mēru de shiryō o okutte kudasai.**
> **B: Hai, wakarimashita.**

1. A: Nozomi Depāto ni fakkusu de shiryō o okutte kudasai
   (Nozomi Depāto, fakkusu, shiryō)

   B: Hai, wakarimashita

2. A: Rondon-shisha no Jonson-san ni kōkūbin de katarogu o okutte kudasai
   (Rondon-shisha no Jonson-san, kōkūbin, katarogu)

   B: Hai, wakarimashita

3. A: Yokohama-shisha no hito ni yūbin de kono nimotsu o okutte kudasai
   (Yokohama-shisha no hito, yūbin, kono nimotsu)

   B: Hai, wakarimashita

IV. *Give directions to a taxi driver.* Make up sentences following the patterns of the examples. Substitute the underlined parts with the alternatives given.

A. *ex.* **Tsugi no shingō o migi ni magatte kudasai.**

1. Tsugi no kōsaten o hidari ni magatte kudasai (tsugi no kōsaten, hidari)

2. futatsu-me no kado o migi ni magatte kudasai (futatsu-me no kado, migi)

B. *ex.* **Ginkō no mae de tomete kudasai.**

1. Byōin no temae de tomete kudasai (byōin no temae)

2. Yūbinkyoku no saki de tomete kudasai (yūbinkyoku no saki)

VOCABULARY	menyū	menu	futatsu-me	second
	shiryō	data, information, material, documents, literature	-me	(suffix that attaches to a number and turns it into an ordinal number)
	yūbin	mail, post		

V. *Give directions to a taxi driver.* Tell the driver to follow the route indicated by the arrows and to stop at the point indicated by the *X*.

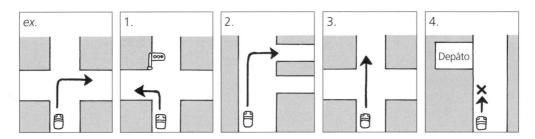

ex. **Tsugi no kōsaten o migi ni magatte kudasai.**

1. Tsugi no kōsaten o hidari ni magette kudasai

2. FU tatsu-me no ~~kado~~ *Kado* o migi ni magatte kudasai

3. massugu itte kudasai

4. Depāto no mae de tomete kudasai

VI. Make up dialogues following the patterns of the examples. Substitute the underlined parts with the alternatives given.

A. *Request that a purchase be delivered.*

ex. **Sumisu:** **Sumimasen. Uchi ni kono terebi o todokete kudasai.**
mise no hito: Hai.
Sumisu: **Ashita no gogo todokete kudasai.**
mise no hito: Hai, wakarimashita. Dewa, o-namae to go-jūsho o onegaishimasu.

1. Sumisu: Sumimasen uchi ni kono pasokon o todokete kudasai (pasokon)

   mise no hito: Hai.

   Sumisu: kin-yōbi no 2-ji made ni todokete kudasai (kin-yōbi no 2-ji made ni)

   mise no hito: Hai, wakarimashita. Dewa, o-namae to go-jūsho o onegaishimasu

2. Sumisu: sumimasen. uchi ni kono sofā o todokete kudasai (sofā)

   mise no hito: Hai

   Sumisu: nichi-yōbi ni todokete kudasai (nichi-yōbi ni)

   mise no hito: Hai, wakarimashita Dewa, o-namae to go-jūsho o onegaishimasu

VOCABULARY **go-jūsho** (another person's) address
made ni by (the time)

B. *Give directions to a taxi driver.*

ex. **Chan:** **Tōkyō Tawā no chikaku made onegaishimasu.**
  untenshu: Hai.
  Chan: (*after a while*) **Tsugi no shingō o hidari ni magatte kudasai.**
  untenshu: Hai.
  Chan: **Ano shiroi biru no mae de tomete kudasai.**
  untenshu: Hai, wakarimashita.
  untenshu: (*after a while*) **4,000-en desu.**
  Chan: **Hai.**
  untenshu: Arigatō gozaimashita.
  Chan: **Dōmo.**

1. Chan: .... (Roppongi Kōsaten)

  untenshu: ....

  Chan: .... (migi)

  untenshu: ....

  Chan: .... (kombini no temae)

  untenshu: ....

  untenshu: ....

  Chan: ....

  untenshu: ....

  Chan: ....

2. Chan: .... (Shibuya Eki)

  untenshu: ....

  Chan: .... (hidari)

  untenshu: ....

  Chan: .... (manshon no mae)

  untenshu: ....

  untenshu: ....

  Chan: ....

  untenshu: ....

  Chan: ....

VOCABULARY				
Tōkyō Tawā	Tokyo Tower		**Roppongi Kōsaten**	Roppongi Crossing
made	to, as far as (particle)		**Shibuya Eki**	Shibuya Station
shiroi	white		**manshon**	apartment (in a high-rise building), condominium
dōmo	thanks (colloquial shortening of **dōmo arigatō**)			

VII. Listen to the CD and fill in the blanks based on the information you hear.

Chan-san wa .... ni .... de kaigi no shiryō o okurimasu.

SHORT DIALOGUES

I. Ms. Chan phones room service because her room is cold.

hoteru no hito: Hai, rūmu-sābisu desu.
Chan: Sumimasen, 201 no Chan desu ga, mōfu o mottekite kudasai.
hoteru no hito: Hai, wakarimashita.

hotel employee: Yes, this is room service.
Chan: This is Ms. Chan in room 201. Please bring me a blanket.
hotel employee: Yes, will do.

― VOCABULARY

| rūmu-sābisu | room service |
| mōfu | blanket |

II. Ms. Chan is checking out of the hotel.

Chan: Sumimasen.
furonto no hito: Hai, nan deshō ka.
Chan: Kono nimotsu o 5-ji made azukatte kudasai.
furonto no hito: Hai, wakarimashita.

Chan: Excuse me.
front desk clerk: Yes, how may I help you?
Chan   Please take care of this luggage for me till 5:00 (p.m.).
front desk clerk: Yes, will do.

― VOCABULARY

nan deshō ka	how may I help you? (softer way of saying **nan desu ka**)
azukatte kudasai	please take care of
azukarimasu	take care of, be in charge of

Active Communication

If you're in Japan, try giving a taxi driver instructions in Japanese. Or, alternatively, next time you purchase a large item, ask to have it delivered to your home.

SEEING A MUSEUM

From Western art to ukiyoe, and from cutting-edge technology to ghosts and goblins, Japan is abundant in museums of all sorts. Among the many museums in the Tokyo area are the Edo-Tokyo Museum, which showcases architecture and culture from an older Japan; the Ghibli Museum, which was designed and is under the supervision of the anime genius Hayao Miyazaki; and the National Museum of Emerging Science and Innovation, where visitors can play with robots or take a ride in a spaceship module. Pictured here is the Tokyo National Museum, which houses paintings, sculptures, and other pieces from all regions of Asia.

UNIT
9 GRAMMAR

The -Nai Form

■ Classifications of Japanese verbs

As discussed briefly in Unit 8 Grammar (p. 160), Japanese verbs are divided into three classes based on their conjugations: Regular I, Regular II, and Irregular. The stems of Regular I verbs (the part just before the **-masu** ending) end with **-i**, and they change as the verbs are conjugated. The stems of Regular II verbs, on the other hand, end with either **-e** or **-i** but remain the same even as the verbs are conjugated. There are only two Irregular verbs: **shimasu** and **kimasu**. For more on verb conjugation, see Appendix E, pp. 244–46.

■ How to form the **-nai** form

For Regular I verbs, the sound before **-masu** changes as shown in the chart below, and **-nai** is added to obtain the **-nai** form. For Regular II verbs, the rule is simpler: **-masu** comes off and **-nai** is added. The Irregular verbs have irregular conjugations.

REGULAR I					
buy	**kai-masu**	**kawa-nai**	write	**kaki-masu**	**kaka-nai**
return, go home	**kaeri-masu**	**kaera-nai**	go	**iki-masu**	**ika-nai**
wait	**machi-masu**	**mata-nai**	read	**yomi-masu**	**yoma-nai**
play	**asobi-masu**	**asoba-nai**	turn off	**keshi-masu**	**kesa-nai**
REGULAR II					
eat	**tabe-masu**	**tabe-nai**	see	**mi-masu**	**mi-nai**
show	**mise-masu**	**mise-nai**	be	**i-masu**	**i-nai**
IRREGULAR					
come	**ki-masu**	**ko-nai**	do	**shi-masu**	**shi-nai**

■ How the **-nai** form is used

ex. **Koko ni kuruma o tomenaide kudasai.** "Please do not park your car here."

A negative verb used in mid-sentence usually takes the **-nai** form rather than the **-masen** form it has at the end of a sentence. For now, however, just remember the following use of the **-nai** form: verb-**naide kudasai** ("please do not . . .").

GOING TO AN ART MUSEUM

TARGET DIALOGUE

TRACK
72

Ms. Nakamura recently heard that the Sakura Art Museum is open till 8 p.m. on Fridays.

なかむら：チャンさん、あした　しごとの　あとで　さくらびじゅつ
　　　　　かんに　いきませんか。

　チャン：いいですね。いきましょう。

なかむら：なんじに　かいしゃを　でましょうか。

　チャン：ここから　さくらびじゅつかんまで　どのぐらい　かかり
　　　　　ますか。

なかむら：４０ぷんぐらい　かかります。

　チャン：じゃ、６じに　かいしゃを　でませんか。

なかむら：ええ。じゃ、あした　６じに。

■　なかむらさんと　チャンさんは　あした　しごとの　あとで　さく
　らびじゅつかんに　いきます。６じに　かいしゃを　でます。かい
　しゃから　さくらびじゅつかんまで　４０ぷんぐらい　かかります。

Nakamura: Chan-san, ashita shigoto no ato de Sakura Bijutsukan ni ikimasen ka.
　　　Chan: Ii desu ne. Ikimashō.
Nakamura: Nan-ji ni kaisha o demashō ka.
　　　Chan: Koko kara Sakura Bijutsukan made donogurai kakarimasu ka.
Nakamura: 40-pun gurai kakarimasu.
　　　Chan: Ja, 6-ji ni kaisha o demasen ka.
Nakamura: Ee. Ja, ashita 6-ji ni.

■ **Nakamura-san to Chan-san wa ashita shigoto no ato de Sakura Bijutsukan ni ikimasu. 6-ji ni kaisha o demasu. Kaisha kara Sakura Bijutsukan made 40-pun gurai kakarimasu.**

Nakamura: Ms. Chan, how about going to the Sakura Art Museum tomorrow after work?
　　　Chan: That would be nice. Let's go.
Nakamura: At what time should we leave the office?
　　　Chan: How long does it take to get from here to the Sakura Art Museum?
Nakamura: It takes about forty minutes.
　　　Chan: Well, how about leaving the office at 6:00?
Nakamura: OK. Tomorrow at 6:00, then.

■ Ms. Nakamura and Ms. Chan are going to the Sakura Art Museum tomorrow after work. They will leave the office at 6:00. It takes about forty minutes to get from the company to the Sakura Art Museum.

VOCABULARY

さくらびじゅつかん	**Sakura Bijutsukan**	Sakura Art Museum (fictitious museum name)
を	**o**	(particle; see Note 1 below)
でましょうか	**demashō ka**	shall we leave?
でます	**demasu**	leave
どのぐらい	**donogurai**	how long
かかります	**kakarimasu**	take (time)

NOTES

1. Nan-ji ni kaisha o demashō ka.

The particle **o** here indicates a point of departure.

> *ex.* **6-ji ni kaisha o demasu.** "I'll leave the office at 6:00."
>
> **Shinjuku Eki de densha o orimasu.** "I'll get off the train at Shinjuku Station."

The particle **ni**, on the other hand, indicates a point of arrival or a location toward which an action such as going, coming, entering, or boarding is directed.

> *ex.* **7-ji ni bijutsukan ni tsukimasu.** "I'll arrive at the art museum at 7:00."
>
> **Tōkyō Eki de densha ni norimasu.** "I'll board the train at Tokyo Station."

PRACTICE

WORD POWER

I. Verbs:

1. **norimasu**   2. **orimasu**   3. **demasu**   4. **tsukimasu**   5. **kakarimasu**

VOCABULARY	**norimasu**	get on (a vehicle), take	**kakarimasu**	take (time)
	orimasu	get off (a vehicle)		
	demasu	go out, leave		
	tsukimasu	arrive		

II. Periods:

	MINUTES		HOURS	DAYS
5	go-fun (kan)	1	ichi-jikan	ichi-nichi
10	juppun (kan)	2	ni-jikan	futsuka (kan)
15	jūgo-fun (kan)	3	san-jikan	mikka (kan)
20	nijuppun (kan)	4	yo-jikan	yokka (kan)
25	nijūgo-fun (kan)	5	go-jikan	itsuka (kan)
30	sanjuppun (kan)	6	roku-jikan	muika (kan)

NOTE: **san-jikan han**, three and a half hours (see also Appendix J, pp. 249–50)

	WEEKS	MONTHS	YEARS
1	isshūkan	ikkagetsu (kan)	ichi-nen (kan)
2	ni-shūkan	ni-kagetsu (kan)	ni-nen (kan)
3	san-shūkan	san-kagetsu (kan)	san-nen (kan)
4	yon-shūkan	yon-kagetsu (kan)	yo-nen (kan)
5	go-shūkan	go-kagetsu (kan)	go-nen (kan)
6	roku-shūkan	rokkagetsu (kan)	roku-nen (kan)

NOTE: **ichi-nen han**, one and a half years (see also Appendix J, pp. 249–50)

KEY SENTENCES

> 1. **Sumisu-san wa Tōkyō Eki de densha ni norimasu.**
> 2. **Sumisu-san wa Shinjuku Eki de densha o orimasu.**
> 3. **Hikōki wa 9-ji ni Tōkyō o dete, 10-ji han ni Sapporo ni tsukimasu.**
> 4. **Tōkyō kara Nikkō made densha de 1-jikan han kakarimasu.**
>
> 1. Mr. Smith will get on the train at Tokyo Station.
> 2. Mr. Smith will get off the train at Shinjuku Station.
> 3. The plane leaves Tokyo at 9:00 and arrives in Sapporo at 10:30.
> 4. It takes an hour and a half to go by train from Tokyo to Nikko.

EXERCISES

I. *Practice conjugating verbs.* Repeat the verbs below and memorize their **-te** forms.

	-MASU FORM	**-TE** FORM
get on, take	**norimasu**	**notte**
get off	**orimasu**	**orite**
go out, leave	**demasu**	**dete**
arrive	**tsukimasu**	**tsuite**
take (time)	**kakarimasu**	**kakatte**
walk	**arukimasu**	**aruite**

VOCABULARY

-fun/-pun (kan)	minute(s)	**-kagetsu**	month(s) (counter)
-jikan	hour(s)	**-nen (kan)**	year(s)
-ka/-nichi (kan)	day(s) (counter)	**arukimasu**	walk
-shūkan	week(s)		

II. Make up dialogues following the patterns of the examples. Substitute the underlined parts with the alternatives given.

A. *State where someone will get on and off a means of public transportation.*

   ex. **Sumisu-san wa Tōkyō Eki de densha ni norimasu. Shinjuku Eki de densha o orimasu.**

   1. .... (chikatetsu)

   2. .... (takushī)

   3. .... (basu)

B. *State a person's departure and arrival time.*

   ex. **Takahashi-san wa 7-ji ni uchi o demashita. 8-ji ni kaisha ni tsukimashita.**

   1. .... (10-ji ni hoteru, 11-ji ni kūkō)

   2. .... (asa Tōkyō, 1-ji goro Kyōto)

III. Make up dialogues following the patterns of the examples. Substitute the underlined words with the words suggested by the illustrations.

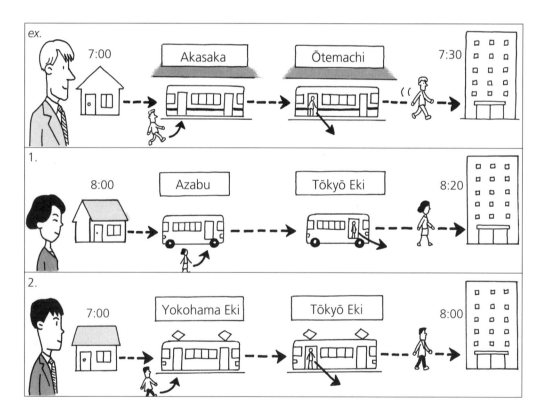

VOCABULARY	**dōyatte**	how, in what way
	Akasaka	Akasaka (district in Tokyo)
	Ōtemachi	Otemachi (district in Tokyo)
182	**Azabu**	Azabu (district in Tokyo)

A. *Ask and give the route by which one commutes to work.*

> *ex.* **Takahashi: Sumisu-san wa dōyatte kaisha ni ikimasu ka.**
> **Sumisu:** **Akasaka de chikatetsu ni notte, Ōtemachi de orimasu. Ōtemachi kara kaisha made arukimasu.**

1. Takahashi: Chan-san wa ....

   Chan: ....

2. Takahashi: Suzuki-san wa ....

   Suzuki: ....

B. *Ask and answer what time one leaves home every day and what time one arrives at the office.*

> *ex.* **Takahashi: Mainichi nan-ji ni uchi o demasu ka.**
> **Sumisu:** **7-ji ni demasu.**
> **Takahashi: Nan-ji ni kaisha ni tsukimasu ka.**
> **Sumisu:** **7-ji han ni tsukimasu.**

1. Takahashi: ....

   Chan: ....

   Takahashi: ....

   Chan: ....

2. Takahashi: ....

   Suzuki: ....

   Takahashi: ....

   Suzuki: ....

IV. *State how long one's commute to work is.* Make up sentences following the pattern of the example. Substitute the underlined words with the alternatives given.

> *ex.* **Uchi kara kaisha made chikatetsu de 40-pun kakarimasu.**

1. .... (densha, 1-jikan)

2. .... (basu, 45-fun)

V. *Ask and answer how long it takes to get somewhere.* Make up dialogues following the pattern of the example. Substitute the underlined words with the words suggested by the illustrations.

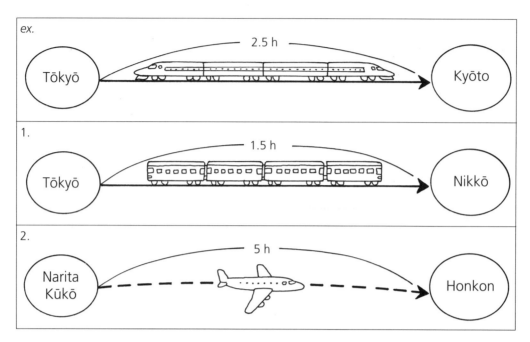

ex.
2.5 h
Tōkyō   Kyōto

1.
1.5 h
Tōkyō   Nikkō

2.
5 h
Narita Kūkō   Honkon

ex. **Sumisu:** **Tōkyō kara Kyōto made donogurai kakarimasu ka.**
Nakamura: Shinkansen de 2-jikan han kakarimasu.

1. Sumisu: ....

   Nakamura: ....

2. Nakamura: ....

   Chan: ....

VI. *Ask and answer how long one stayed in a certain place.* Make up dialogues following the pattern of the example. Substitute the underlined words with the alternatives given.

ex. **Sumisu:** **Takahashi-san wa donogurai Nyūyōku ni imashita ka.**
Takahashi: 4-ka imashita.

1. Sumisu: .... (Honkon)

   Takahashi: .... (2-shūkan)

2. Sumisu: .... (Sapporo)

   Takahashi: .... (5-kagetsu)

3. Sumisu: .... (Sanfuranshisuko)

   Takahashi: .... (3-nen)

VOCABULARY	**Narita Kūkō**	Narita Airport
	imasu	be, stay
	Nyūyōku	New York
184	**Sanfuranshisuko**	San Francisco

VII. Make up dialogues following the patterns of the examples. Substitute the underlined words with the alternatives given.

A. *Talk about a summer vacation plan.*

> *ex.* **Suzuki:** **Natsu-yasumi ni doko ni ikimasu ka.**
> **Nakamura:** **<u>Pari</u> ni itte, <u>bijutsukan</u> o mimasu.**
> **Suzuki:** **Sō desu ka. Donogurai <u>Pari</u> ni imasu ka.**
> **Nakamura:** **<u>1-shūkan</u> imasu.**
> **Suzuki:** **Ii desu ne.**

1. Suzuki: ....

   Nakamura: .... (Nyūyōku, myūjikaru)

   Suzuki: .... (Nyūyōku)

   Nakamura: .... (6-ka)

   Suzuki: ....

2. Suzuki: ....

   Nakamura: .... (Kyōto, o-tera)

   Suzuki: .... (Kyōto)

   Nakamura: .... (5-ka)

   Suzuki: ....

B. *Invite someone to an event and tell him or her what the departure time will be.*

> *ex.* **Katō:** **Ashita 11-ji kara <u>Tōkyō Hoteru</u> de o-kashi no fea ga arimasu. Chan-san mo issho ni ikimasen ka.**
> **Chan:** **Hai. Nan-ji ni kaisha o demasu ka.**
> **Katō:** **<u>Tōkyō Hoteru</u> made <u>1-jikan</u> gurai kakarimasu kara, <u>10-ji</u> ni demasu.**
> **Chan:** **Wakarimashita.**

1. Katō: .... (Odaiba)

   Chan: ....

   Katō: .... (Odaiba, 30-pun, 10-ji han)

   Chan: ....

2. Katō: .... (Yokohama)

   Chan: ....

   Katō: .... (Yokohama, 1-jikan han, 9-ji han)

   Chan: ....

VOCABULARY		
Pari	Paris	
myūjikaru	musical	
fea	fair	

VIII. *Talk about a flight itinerary.* Complete the following dialogue using the information in the illustrations as a guide.

1. Chan: ....

2. ryokō-gaisha no hito: ....

3. Chan: ....

4. ryokō-gaisha no hito: ....

5. Chan: ....

IX. Listen to the CD and fill in the blanks based on the information you hear.

TRACK 74

Kaisha kara Nozomi Depāto made .... de .... gurai kakarimasu.

SHORT DIALOGUE

TRACK
75

Mr. Green wants to go to Kamakura.

Gurīn:	**Sumimasen, kono densha wa Kamakura ni ikimasu ka.**
ekiin:	**Iie, ikimasen. Yokosuka-sen ni notte kudasai.**
Gurīn:	**Yoko— . . . nan desu ka.**
ekiin:	**Yokosuka-sen desu. Chika 1-kai no 1-bansen desu yo.**
Gurīn:	**Arigatō gozaimasu.**

Green:	Excuse me. Does this train go to Kamakura?
station employee:	No, it doesn't. Please take the Yokosuka Line.
Green:	Yoko— . . . what is that?
station employee:	The Yokosuka Line. It's platform no. 1 on the first underground floor.
Green:	Thank you.

VOCABULARY

ekiin	station employee
Yokosuka-sen	Yokosuka Line
-sen	(train) line
1-bansen	platform number one
-bansen	platform number

NOTES

1. Yoko—— . . . nan desu ka.
When you only hear one part of a word and want to ask someone to repeat it, say **nan desu ka** after the part of the word that you understood.

Active Communication

If you're in Japan, ask a station employee the route and time required to get to a place you want to go to.

AT AN ART MUSEUM

TARGET DIALOGUE

TRACK
76

Ms. Chan and Ms. Nakamura are looking at woodblock prints at the Sakura Art Museum. The two of them ask a museum employee some questions.

なかむら：きれいな　うきよえですね。

チャン：ほんとうに　きれいですね。

なかむら：すみません。うきよえの

しゃしんを　とっても　いいですか。

びじゅつかんの　ひと：はい。

なかむら：あ、ここに　えいごの

パンフレットが　ありますよ。

チャン：そうですね。すみません。この　パンフレットを

もらっても　いいですか。

びじゅつかんの　ひと：はい、どうぞ。

■チャンさんは　さくらびじゅつかんで　えいごの　パンフレットを
もらいました。

Ukiyoe

> Nakamura: Kireina ukiyoe desu ne.
> Chan: Hontō ni kirei desu ne.
> Nakamura: Sumimasen. Ukiyoe no shashin o totte mo ii desu ka.
> bijutsukan no hito: Hai.
> Nakamura: A, koko ni Eigo no panfuretto ga arimasu yo.
> Chan: Sō desu ne. Sumimasen. Kono panfuretto o moratte mo ii desu ka.
> bijutsukan no hito: Hai, dōzo.

■ **Chan-san wa Sakura Bijutsukan de Eigo no panfuretto o moraimashita.**

> Nakamura: These are lovely ukiyoe prints, aren't they?
> Chan: They really are lovely, aren't they?
> Nakamura: Excuse me. Is it all right to take pictures of the ukiyoe prints?
> museum employee: Yes.
> Nakamura: Oh, here's an English-language pamphlet.
> Chan: You're right. Excuse me, is it all right to take this pamphlet?
> museum employee: Sure, go ahead.

■ Ms. Chan received an English-language pamphlet.

VOCABULARY

うきよえ	**ukiyoe**	ukiyoe (woodblock print)
とっても　いいですか	**totte mo ii desu ka**	may I take (a photograph)?
パンフレット	**panfuretto**	pamphlet, brochure

NOTES

1. Shashin o totte mo ii desu ka.

Asking permission to do something is done using the following sentence construction: verb **-te** form + **mo ii desu ka**. To grant permission, say **hai, dōzo** ("yes, please [do]"), and to refuse permission, say **sumimasen ga, chotto . . .** ("I'm sorry, but that would be a little [difficult] . . .").

PRACTICE

WORD POWER

I. Verbs:

1. **tsukaimasu**　　2. **(tabako o) suimasu**　　3. **hairimasu**

tsukaimasu	use
(tabako o) suimasu	smoke (a cigarette)
tabako	cigarette
hairimasu	enter

II. Things available at the information counter of a museum:

1. **ehagaki**   2. **iyahōn-gaido**   3. **panfuretto**   4. **katarogu**

KEY SENTENCES

1. **Kono e no shashin o totte mo ii desu ka.**
2. **Kono pen o tsukatte mo ii desu ka.**

1. Is it all right to take a photograph of this picture?
2. Is it all right to use this pen?

EXERCISES

I. *Practice conjugating verbs.* Repeat the verbs below and memorize their **-te** forms.

	-MASU FORM	**-TE** FORM
use	**tsukaimasu**	**tsukatte**
smoke	**suimasu**	**sutte**
enter	**hairimasu**	**haitte**
rest	**yasumimasu**	**yasunde**

II. *Ask permission to do something.* Change the sentences below as in the example.

ex. **Kono katarogu o moraimasu.** → **Kono katarogu o moratte mo ii desu ka.**

1. Mado o akemasu. → ....

2. Kono iyahōn-gaido o tsukaimasu. → ....

3. Kono e no shashin o torimasu. → ....

4. Koko de tabako o suimasu. → ....

5. Ashita yasumimasu. → ....

III. *Ask and grant permission to do something.* Make up dialogues following the pattern of the example and based on the information in the illustrations.

ex. **Suzuki: Kono shiryō no kopī o shite mo ii desu ka.**
Katō: Hai, dōzo.

1. Suzuki: ....

   Katō: ....

2. Suzuki: ....

   Katō: ....

3. Suzuki: ....

   Katō: ....

IV. *Ask and refuse permission to do something.* Make up dialogues following the pattern of the example and based on the information in the illustrations.

ex. **Sumisu:** **Koko de o-kashi o tabete mo ii desu ka.**
o-tera no hito: Sumimasen ga, chotto . . . .

1. Sumisu: ....

   o-tera no hito: ....

2. Sumisu: ....

   o-tera no hito: ....

3. Sumisu: ....

   o-tera no hito: ....

V. *Get and give assistance at a store.* Make up dialogues following the pattern of the example. Substitute the underlined words with the words in parentheses.

ex. **Sumisu:** **Sumimasen, kono <u>terebi</u> no <u>katarogu</u> ga arimasu ka.**
mise no hito: Hai, kore desu.
Sumisu: **Moratte mo ii desu ka.**
mise no hito: Hai, dōzo.

1. Sumisu: .... (ryokan, panfuretto)

   mise no hito: ....

   Sumisu: ....

   mise no hito: ....

2. Sumisu: .... (resutoran, kādo)

    mise no hito: ....

    Sumisu: ....

    mise no hito: ....

 VI. **_Ask for permission to borrow a pen._** Look at the illustrations and make up a dialogue that reflects what is happening.

1. mise no hito: ....

2. Sumisu: ....

3. Sumisu: ....

4. mise no hito: ....

5. Sumisu: ....

 VII. Listen to the CD and fill in the blanks based on the information you hear.

    Sumisu-san wa .... kara .... o tsukaimasu.

VOCABULARY   **kādo**   (business) card

SHORT DIALOGUES

I. Mr. Green has gone to the hospital to visit a sick friend. He first goes to the reception desk in the visiting area.

uketsuke:	**Go-jūsho to o-namae o kaite kudasai.**
Gurin:	**Rōmaji de kaite mo ii desu ka.**
uketsuke:	**Hai.**

receptionist:	Please write your address and your name.
Green:	May I write in Roman letters?
receptionist:	Yes.

VOCABULARY

rōmaji	romanized Japanese

II. Mr. Green is visiting a friend.

Gurin:	**Koko ni nimotsu o oite mo ii desu ka.**
tomodachi:	**Hai, dōzo.**
Gurin:	(*after chatting for a while*) **Sumimasen. O-tearai o tsukatte mo ii desu ka.**
tomodachi:	**Hai, dōzo.**

Green:	May I put my luggage here?
friend:	Yes, please do.
Green:	Excuse me. May I use your bathroom?
friend:	Yes, go right ahead.

VOCABULARY

oite	(**-te** form of **okimasu**)
okimasu	put

Active Communication

If you're in Japan, go to various stores or public institutions and ask permission to do something—to take a photograph, for example.

BEING WARNED OR ADVISED

TARGET DIALOGUE

Ms. Chan and Ms. Nakamura are looking at a picture of Mt. Fuji in the art museum.

チャン：この　ふじさんの　えは　とても　きれいですね。

なかむら：そうですね。

チャン：なかむらさん、この　えの　まえで　わたしの
しゃしんを　とってください。

なかむら：はい、わかりました。とりますよ。*(takes a flash picture)*

びじゅつかんの　ひと：すみません、ここで　フラッシュを　つかわないでください。

なかむら：すみません、わかりました。

■なかむらさんは　ふじさんの　えの　まえで　チャンさんの　しゃしんを　とりました。

Chan: **Kono Fujisan no e wa totemo kirei desu ne.**
Nakamura: **Sō desu ne.**
Chan: **Nakamura-san, kono e no mae de watashi no shashin o totte kudasai.**
Nakamura: **Hai, wakarimashita. Torimasu yo.** *(takes a flash picture)*
bijutsukan no hito: **Sumimasen, koko de furasshu o tsukawanaide kudasai.**
Nakamura: **Sumimasen, wakarimashita.**

■ **Nakamura-san wa Fujisan no e no mae de Chan-san no shashin o torimashita.**

Chan: This picture of Mt. Fuji is really lovely, isn't it?
Nakamura: Yes, it is.
Chan: Ms. Nakamura, please take a photograph of me in front of this picture.
Nakamura: Okay, right. Are you ready?
museum employee: Excuse me. Please don't use a flash here.
Nakamura: I'm sorry, I understand.

■ Ms. Nakamura took a photograph of Ms. Chan in front of a picture of Mt. Fuji.

VOCABULARY

ふじさん	**Fujisan**	Mt. Fuji
とりますよ	**torimasu yo**	(said when you are about to take someone's photo)
フラッシュ	**furasshu**	flash
つかわないでください	**tsukawanaide kudasai**	please don't use

1. Koko de furasshu o tsukawanaide kudasai.

The "please do not . . ." construction is formed as follows: verb **-nai** + **de** + **kudasai**. This expression is often used by managers or officials when asking someone to refrain from doing something, although it can also be used by restaurant customers when requesting that a specific ingredient not be used.

    ex. **Satō o irenaide kudasai.** "Please don't put any sugar in it."

To make this rather strong expression sound softer, give the reason why you would like the other person to refrain from doing what they are about to do.

    ex. **Koko ni kuruma o tomenaide kudasai. Deguchi desu kara.**

      "Please do not park your car here. (This) is an exit."

PRACTICE

WORD POWER

I. The **-nai** form:

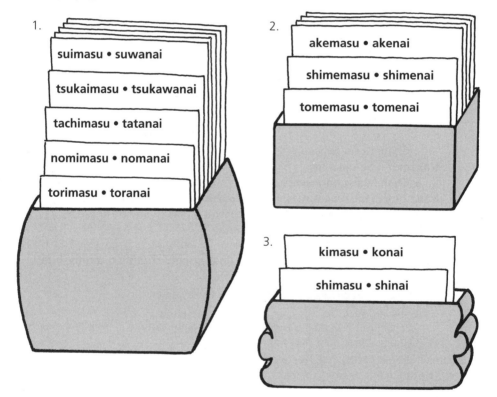

1.

    suimasu • suwanai

    tsukaimasu • tsukawanai

    tachimasu • tatanai

    nomimasu • nomanai

    torimasu • toranai

2.

    akemasu • akenai

    shimemasu • shimenai

    tomemasu • tomenai

3.

    kimasu • konai

    shimasu • shinai

VOCABULARY   **tachimasu**   stand up

II. Restrictions:

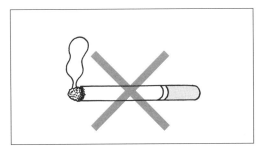

1. **kin'en**

2. **chūsha-kinshi**

KEY SENTENCES

1. **Koko wa iriguchi desu kara, kuruma o tomenaide kudasai.**
2. **Sushi ni wasabi o irenaide kudasai.**

1. This is the entrance, so please don't park your car here.
2. Please don't put any wasabi in the sushi.

EXERCISES

I. *Practice conjugating verbs.* Repeat the verbs below and memorize their **-nai** forms.

REGULAR I		REGULAR II		IRREGULAR	
-MASU FORM	**-NAI** FORM	**-MASU** FORM	**-NAI** FORM	**-MASU** FORM	**-NAI** FORM
aimasu	awanai	misemasu	misenai	kimasu	konai
kakimasu	kakanai	iremasu	irenai	shimasu	shinai
keshimasu	kesanai	tabemasu	tabenai		
tachimasu	tatanai	akemasu	akenai		
nomimasu	nomanai	shimemasu	shimenai		
kaerimasu	kaeranai	mimasu	minai		

VOCABULARY	kin'en	no smoking, nonsmoking
	chūsha-kinshi	no parking
	wasabi	wasabi, Japanese (green) horseradish
	iremasu	put in, add

II. *Practice the -nai form.* Change the following verbs to their **-nai** forms.

ex. **aimasu** → **awanai**

1. akemasu → ....

2. shimemasu → ....

3. torimasu → ....

4. kaimasu → ....

5. yomimasu → ....

6. kikimasu → ....

III. *Forbid someone to do something.* Look at the illustrations and make up sentences as in the example.

ex. **mado o akemasu** → **Mado o akenaide kudasai.**

1. shashin o torimasu → ....

2. doa o shimemasu → ....

3. denki o keshimasu → ....

4. kuruma o tomemasu → ....

IV. *Forbid someone to do something and give a reason.* Make up sentences following the pattern of the example. Substitute the underlined part with the alternatives given.

ex. **Koko wa iriguchi desu kara, kuruma o tomenaide kudasai.**

1. .... (deguchi desu)

2. .... (mise no mae desu)

3. .... (chūsha-kinshi desu)

V. Make up dialogues following the patterns of the examples. Substitute the underlined part(s) with the alternatives given.

A. *Ask someone to refrain from smoking.*

> *ex.* **Chan:** **Sumimasen, <u>kono densha wa kin'en desu</u> kara, tabako o suwanaide kudasai.**
> **otoko no hito: Hai, wakarimashita. Sumimasen.**

1. Chan: .... (kono resutoran wa kin'en desu)

   otoko no hito: ....

2. Chan: .... (akachan ga imasu)

   otoko no hito: ....

B. *Order something at a restaurant and request that a specific ingredient not be used.*

> *ex.* **Chan:** **Sumimasen, <u>hambāgā</u> o onegaishimasu.**
> **mise no hito: Hai.**
> **Chan:** **Sumimasen ga, <u>kechappu</u> o irenaide kudasai.**
> **mise no hito: Hai, wakarimashita.**

1. Chan: .... (sushi)

   mise no hito: ....

   Chan: .... (wasabi)

   mise no hito: ....

2. Chan: .... (sandoitchi)

   mise no hito: ....

   Chan: .... (mayonēzu)

   mise no hito: ....

3. Chan: .... (aisu-kōhī)

   mise no hito: ....

   Chan: .... (satō)

   mise no hito: ....

VI. Listen to the CD and fill in the blanks based on the information you hear.

TRACK 82

Gogo kara .... de .... ga arimasu.

VOCABULARY	akachan	baby		mayonēzu	mayonnaise
	hambāgā	hamburger		**aisu-kōhī**	ice coffee
	kechappu	ketchup		**satō**	sugar

SHORT DIALOGUES

I. Mr. Smith got drunk at the Sasakis' house and spilled red wine on their clean carpet. The next day, he apologizes at the office.

Sumisu: Sasaki-san, kinō wa sumimasendeshita.
Sasaki: Iie, dōzo ki ni shinaide kudasai.

Smith: Ms. Sasaki, I'm so sorry about yesterday.
Sasaki: No, please don't let it bother you.

VOCABULARY

ki ni shinaide kudasai	don't worry about it; don't let it bother you
ki ni shimasu	worry (about), be bothered (by)

II. Mr. Smith goes to the clinic with a stomachache.

isha: Kyō wa o-sake o nomanaide kudasai.
Sumisu: Hai, wakarimashita.

doctor: Don't drink any alcohol today.
Smith: Ok, I understand.

VOCABULARY

isha	(medical) doctor

Active Communication

What would you say in these situations?

1. A stranger is trying to park in front of your house.

2. The person next to you lights up a cigarette in a nonsmoking car on the Shinkansen.

Quiz 4 (Units 8–9)

I Fill in the blank(s) in each sentence with the appropriate particle. Where a particle is not needed, write in an *X*.

1. Sumisu-san wa kaigi no mae (＿＿＿) shiryō o yomimashita.

2. Futatsu-me no kado (＿＿＿) hidari (＿＿＿) magatte kudasai.

3. Depāto no saki (＿＿＿) tomete kudasai.

4. Takahashi-san wa Shibuya (＿＿＿) densha (＿＿＿) orite, basu (＿＿＿) norimasu.

5. Shibuya (＿＿＿) Asakusa (＿＿＿) chikatetsu (＿＿＿) 40-pun kakarimasu.

6. Takahashi-san wa Honkon (＿＿＿) 1-shūkan (＿＿＿) imashita.

7. Shinkansen wa 8-ji (＿＿＿) Tōkyō Eki (＿＿＿) dete, 10-ji (＿＿＿) Kyōto Eki (＿＿＿) tsukimasu.

8. Koko (＿＿＿) chūsha-kinshi desu (＿＿＿), kuruma (＿＿＿) tomenaide kudasai.

II Complete each question by filling in the blank with the appropriate word.

1. Shūmatsu ni (＿＿＿) o shimashita ka.
   Ginza ni itte, kaimono o shimashita.

2. (＿＿＿) Ōsaka-shisha ni denwa o shimashita ka.
   Kaigi no mae ni shimashita.

3. (＿＿＿) kaisha ni ikimasu ka.
   Shibuya de chikatetsu ni notte, Ginza de orimasu. Ginza kara kaisha made 10-pun arukimasu.

4. Tōkyō kara Ōsaka made hikōki de (＿＿＿) kakarimasu ka.
   1-jikan gurai kakarimasu.

III Complete the table by writing in the appropriate forms of the verbs.

	-MASU FORM	**-TE** FORM	**-NAI** FORM
ex.	tsukaimasu	tsukatte	tsukawanai
1.	kakimasu	kaite	
2.		keshite	kesanai
3.	nomimasu		nomanai
4.	torimasu	totte	
5.	shimemasu		shimenai
6.		akete	akenai
7.	mimasu		minai
8.	kimasu	kite	
9.		shite	shinai

IV Complete the sentences by filling in the blank(s) with the appropriate form of the word(s) given at the end.

1. Sumisu-san wa kinō shigoto no ato de tomodachi to eiga o (   ), ban-gohan o tabemashita. (mimasu)

2. Sumisu-san wa kinō hana o (   ), uchi ni kaerimashita. (kaimasu)

3. Oishii sushi-ya o (   ) kudasai. (oshiemasu)

4. Tsugi no kōsaten o migi ni (   ), massugu (   ) kudasai. (magarimasu, ikimasu)

5. Kono katarogu o (   ) mo ii desu ka. (moraimasu)

6. Koko wa deguchi desu kara, kuruma o (   ) kudasai. (tomemasu)

AT THE OFFICE

Walking into a traditional Japanese company, one will notice the absence of high partitions and cubicles: most Japanese offices are open, with desks facing one another so that employees can readily communicate. This arrangement is efficient because it saves on space; and in a country where land prices can be astronomical, such efficiency is important. Another feature of such offices is the conspicuous hierarchy: in one desk with a view of all others sits the office manager, and in front of him the division chief, then the section chief, and so on down to the bottom. Recently, however, Japanese companies have been modifying the traditional layout to make their offices more functional for the people who work in them, or more aesthetically pleasing to visitors.

Present Progressive and Habitual Actions

| person **wa** verb **-te imasu** |

> *ex.* **Gurei-san wa ima kaigi-shitsu de repōto o yonde imasu.**
> "Mr. Grey is reading a report in the meeting room now."
> **Gurei-san wa maishū do-yōbi ni tenisu o shite imasu.**
> "Mr. Grey plays tennis every Saturday."

A verb in the **-te** form followed by **imasu** expresses a present-progressive action ("is doing"), as in the first example above, or, when accompanied by an adverb like **maishū** ("every week") or **mainichi** ("every day"), a habitual action, as in the second example.

Current States

| person **wa** verb **-te imasu** |

> *ex.* **Gurei-san wa Yokohama ni sunde imasu.** "Mr. Grey lives in Yokohama."
> **Gurei-san wa Ginkō ni tsutomete imasu.** "Mr. Grey is employed at a bank."
> **Ano mise de terebi o utte imasu.** "At that store, (they) sell TVs."
> **Gurei-san wa Yoshida-san no jūsho o shitte imasu.** "Mr. Grey knows Mr. Yoshida's address."

The **-te imasu** form can also express a current state when the verb is one of those used in the examples above—**sumimasu**, **tsutomemasu**, **urimasu**, or **shirimasu**.

NOTE: The verb **shirimasu** ("know"), from which **shitte imasu** derives, is usually used in the **-te** form followed by **imasu**. But the form this verb takes when used in response to the question **shitte imasu ka** ("do you know?") varies, and in this way it is unlike other verbs.

> *ex.* A*a*: **Hai, shitte imasu.** "Yes, (I) know."
> A*n*: **Iie, shirimasen.** "No, (I) don't know."

BUSY AT THE MOMENT

TARGET DIALOGUE

Mr. Smith is looking for Ms. Chan. He enters the sales department office and asks Mr. Suzuki where she is.

スミス：すみません。チャンさんは　いますか。

すずき：いいえ。いま　3がいの　かいぎしつに　います。

スミス：そうですか。

すずき：いま、のぞみデパートの　たかはしさんに　あたらしい
　　　　しょうひんの　せつめいを　しています。

スミス：そうですか。わかりました。どうも。

■スミスさんは　えいぎょうぶに　いきましたが、チャンさんは
　いませんでした。

Sumisu: Sumimasen. Chan-san wa imasu ka.
Suzuki: Iie. Ima 3-gai no kaigishitsu ni imasu.
Sumisu: Sō desu ka.
Suzuki: Ima, Nozomi Depāto no Takahashi-san ni atarashii shōhin no setsumei o shite imasu.
Sumisu: Sō desu ka. Wakarimashita. Dōmo.

■ **Sumisu-san wa eigyō-bu ni ikimashita ga, Chan-san wa imasendeshita.**

Smith: Excuse me. Is Ms. Chan here?
Suzuki: No, she's in the conference room on the third floor.
Smith: Is that so?
Suzuki: Yes, she's explaining new products to Mr. Takahashi of Nozomi Department Store.
Smith: Is that so? I see. Thanks.

■ Mr. Smith went to the sales department office (to look for Ms. Chan), but Ms. Chan was not there.

VOCABULARY

せつめいを　しています	**setsumei o shite imasu**	is/are explaining
せつめいを　します	**setsumei o shimasu**	explain
えいぎょうぶ	**eigyō-bu**	sales department (office)
が	**ga**	but (see Note 1 below)

NOTES

1. Sumisu-san wa eigyō-bu ni ikimashita ga, Chan-san wa imasendeshita.
This **ga** is a conjunction that joins two clauses. It can be translated as "but."

PRACTICE

WORD POWER

I. Verbs:

1. **hanashi o shimasu**　　2. **setsumei o shimasu**　　3. **sōji o shimasu**　　4. **tsukurimasu**

II. Parts of a building:

1. **robī**　　　2. **erebētā**　　　3. **esukarētā**　　　4. **kaidan**

VOCABULARY			
hanashi o shimasu	talk	**robī**	lobby
setsumei o shimasu	explain	**erebētā**	elevator
sōji o shimasu	clean	**esukarētā**	escalator
tsukurimasu	make	**kaidan**	stairs

KEY SENTENCES

> 1. **Sumisu-san wa ima shimbun o yonde imasu.**
> 2. **Mō kaigi no repōto o kakimashita ka.**
> 3. **Sumisu-san wa Takahashi-san no uchi ni ikimashita ga, Takahashi-san wa uchi ni imasendeshita.**
>
> 1. Mr. Smith is reading a newspaper now.
> 2. Have you already written the report about the meeting?
> 3. Mr. Smith went to Mr. Takahashi's house, but Mr. Takahashi was not at home.

EXERCISES

 I. *Practice conjugating verbs.* Repeat the verbs below and memorize their **-te imasu** forms, affirmative and negative.

	-MASU FORM	**-TE IMASU** FORM	
		aff.	*neg.*
talk	**hanashi o shimasu**	**hanashi o shite imasu**	**hanashi o shite imasen**
explain	**setsumei o shimasu**	**setsumei o shite imasu**	**setsumei o shite imasen**
clean	**sōji o shimasu**	**sōji o shite imasu**	**sōji o shite imasen**
make	**tsukurimasu**	**tsukutte imasu**	**tsukutte imasen**

 II. *State what someone is doing now.* Change the following sentences as in the example.

ex. **Sumisu-san wa shimbun o yomimasu.**
→ **Sumisu-san wa shimbun o yonde imasu.**

1. Sumisu-san wa sōji o shimasu. → ....

2. Sumisu-san wa tegami o kakimasu. → ....

3. Sumisu-san wa kopī o shimasu. → ....

4. Sumisu-san wa Takahashi-san to hanashi o shimasu. → ....

5. Sumisu-san wa ryōri o tsukurimasu. → ....

III. Make up dialogues following the patterns of the examples and based on the situations depicted in the illustrations.

A. *Ask and answer what one is doing now.*

ex. 1. **A: Gurin-san wa ima nani o shite imasu ka.**
B: Denwa o shite imasu.

1. A: ....

   B: ....

2. A: ....

   B: ....

3. A: ....

   B: ....

4. A: ....

   B: ....

5. A: ....

   B: ....

6. A: ....

   B: ....

B. *Answer what one is doing now in response to a question.*

   ex. 2. **A: Katō-san wa ima repōto o kaite imasu ka.**
          B: Iie, kaigishitsu de setsumei o shite imasu.

   7. A: Sasaki-san wa ima kaigi o shite imasu ka.

      B: ....

   8. A: Nakamura-san wa ima denwa o shite imasu ka.

      B: ....

   9. A: Chan-san wa ima Sasaki-san to hanashi o shite imasu ka.

      B: ....

IV. *Ask and answer whether one has completed an action.* Make up dialogues following the pattern of the example. Substitute the underlined words with the alternatives given. Be sure to use the same grammatical form as in the example.

   ex. **A: Mō hiru-gohan o tabemashita ka.**
      B: Hai, tabemashita.

   1. A: .... (ryokō no shashin, mimasu)

      B: .... (mimasu)

   2. A: .... (kaigi no repōto, kakimasu)

      B: .... (kakimasu)

V. *Connect two clauses.* Link each pair of sentences as in the example.

   ex. **Watashi wa Takahashi-san no uchi ni ikimashita. Takahashi-san wa uchi ni imasen-deshita.**
     → Watashi wa Takahashi-san no uchi ni ikimashita ga, Takahashi-san wa uchi ni imasendeshita.

   1. Watashi wa eigyō-bu no Chan-san ni denwa o shimashita. Chan-san wa imasendeshita.

     → ....

   2. Watashi wa kinō depāto ni ikimashita. Depāto wa yasumi deshita.

     → ....

VI. Make up dialogues following the patterns of the examples. Substitute the underlined parts with the alternatives given. Be sure to use the same grammatical forms as in the examples.

A. *Explain that one is in the midst of something.*

> *ex.* **Katō:** **Mō kopī o shimashita ka.**
> **Suzuki:** **Sumimasen, ima shite imasu kara, chotto matte kudasai.**
> **Katō:** **Hai.**

1. Katō: .... (mēru, yomimasu)

   Suzuki: .... (yomimasu)

   Katō: ....

2. Katō: .... (kaigi no shiryō, tsukurimasu)

   Suzuki: .... (tsukurimasu)

   Katō: ....

B. *Respond to a cell phone call by suggesting it is inconvenient or inappropriate to talk at the moment.*

> *ex.* Mr. Smith gets a call on his cell phone from his friend Mr. Yamada. Since he is in a meeting, he answers quietly.
>
> **Yamada: Moshimoshi, Sumisu-san desu ka.**
> **Sumisu: Hai.**
> **Yamada: Yamada desu.**
> **Sumisu: Yamada-san, sumimasen ga, ima kaigi o shite imasu.**
> **Yamada: Ja, mata ato de denwa o shimasu.**
> **Sumisu: Onegaishimasu.**

1. Yamada: ....

   Sumisu: ....

   Yamada: ....

   Sumisu: .... (o-kyaku-san to hanashi o shimasu)

   Yamada: ....

   Sumisu: ....

2. Yamada: ....

   Sumisu: ....

   Yamada: ....

   Sumisu: .... (Nihon-go no gakkō de benkyō o shimasu)

   Yamada: ....

   Sumisu: ....

VOCABULARY | **mata ato de** | see you later; talk to you later

VII. Listen to the CD and choose the correct answer to the question asked.

a)  b)  c)

SHORT DIALOGUES

I. Ms. Sasaki is waiting for Ms. Chan's report on her business trip to Hokkaido.

Sasaki: Chan-san, repōto wa mō kakimashita ka.
Chan: Sumimasen, mada desu. Mō sukoshi matte kudasai.

Sasaki: Ms. Chan, have you already written the report?
Chan: I'm sorry. Not yet. Please wait a bit more.

VOCABULARY

mada	not yet
mō sukoshi	a little more

II. Mr. Suzuki is looking for an empty room.

Suzuki: Sumimasen. 3-gai no kaigishitsu o tsukatte mo ii desu ka.
Nakamura: Ee. Ima dare mo tsukatte imasen kara, dōzo.

Suzuki: Excuse me. Is it all right to use the conference room on the third floor?
Nakamura: Yes, since no one is using it now. Go right ahead.

NOTES

1. Repōto wa . . .
Although **repōto** ("report") is the object, Ms. Sasaki is singling it out as a topic for discussion, so **wa** replaces the object marker **o**.

2. Repōto wa mō kakimashita ka.
It should be noted that the verb ending **-mashita**, when used with **mō** ("already"), expresses completion in addition to indicating the past tense.

Imagine that you are in a meeting or involved in some activity that you can't break away from, and a call comes in on your cell phone. Explain in Japanese to the person on the other end of the line why it is inconvenient for you to talk at the moment.

RESPONDING TO AN INQUIRY

TARGET DIALOGUE

A customer from Nagoya has phoned to inquire about ABC Foods' new products.

チャン：はい、ABC フーズでございます。

きゃく：すみません、ABC フーズの　あたらしい　チョコレートは
　　　　どこで　うっていますか。

チャン：「ショコラショコラ」ですか。

きゃく：ええ、そうです。

チャン：とうきょうの　スーパーと　コンビニで　うっています。

きゃく：わたしは　なごやに　すんでいます。なごやでも　うっていますか。

チャン：いいえ、なごやでは　うっていません。もうしわけございません。

きゃく：そうですか。わかりました。

チャン：たいへん　もうしわけございません。

■ ABC フーズの　「ショコラショコラ」は　とうきょうの　スーパー
　　と　コンビニで　うっています。

　Chan: Hai, ABC Fūzu de gozaimasu.
kyaku: Sumimasen, ABC Fūzu no atarashii chokorēto wa doko de utte imasu ka.
　Chan: "Shokora-shokora" desu ka.
kyaku: Ee, sō desu.
　Chan: Tōkyō no sūpā to kombini de utte imasu.
kyaku: Watashi wa Nagoya ni sunde imasu. Nagoya de mo utte imasu ka.
　Chan: Iie, Nagoya de wa utte imasen. Mōshiwake gozaimasen.
kyaku: Sō desu ka. Wakarimashita.
　Chan: Taihen mōshiwake gozaimasen.

■ ABC Fūzu no "Shokora-shokora" wa Tōkyō no sūpā to kombini de utte imasu.

　Chan: Yes, this is ABC Foods.
customer: Excuse me, about ABC Foods' new chocolates—where do you sell them?
　Chan: Do you mean "Chocolat-Chocolat"?
customer: Yes, that's right.
　Chan: We sell them at supermarkets and convenience stores in Tokyo.
customer: I live in Nagoya. Do you sell them in Nagoya?
　Chan: No, we do not sell them in Nagoya. I'm sorry to have to tell you this.
customer: Is that so? I see.
　Chan: I'm really very sorry.

■ As for Chocolat-Chocolat, ABC Foods sells it in supermarkets and convenience stores in Tokyo.

うっています	**utte imasu**	sell
うります	**urimasu**	sell
ショコラショコラ	**Shokora-shokora**	Chocolat-Chocolat (fictitious product name)
なごや	**Nagoya**	Nagoya (city in central Japan)
すんでいます	**sunde imasu**	live
すみます	**sumimasu**	live
もうしわけございません	**mōshiwake gozaimasen**	I'm sorry to have to tell you this (politer way of saying **sumimasen**)
たいへん	**taihen**	very much, extremely (politer way of saying **totemo**)

NOTES

1. ABC Fūzu no atarashii chokorēto wa doko de utte imasu ka.
Although **chokorēto** is the object, here it is being singled out as the topic and therefore takes the particle **wa** instead of **o**.

2. Watashi wa Nagoya ni sunde imasu.
The particle **ni** is used to indicate the place where one lives or is employed.
   ex. **Yamada-san wa ginkō ni tsutomete imasu.** "Ms. Yamada is employed at a bank."

3. Nagoya de mo utte imasu ka.
Iie, Nagoya de wa utte imasen.
Note the positions of the particles **de** and **mo** here. In Ms. Chan's reply, she uses the topic marker **wa** after **de** to show that "Nagoya" is the topic: "As for Nagoya, (Chocolat-Chocolat) is not sold there." Note that while one particle may normally follow another, as do **mo** and **wa** after **de** in the sentences above, **mo** and **wa** never follow the particles **ga** or **o** but simply take their place. Similarly, **mo** and **wa** are never used together; one or the other is used.

PRACTICE

WORD POWER

I. Verbs:

1. **sunde imasu**

2. **tsutomete imasu**

3. **shitte imasu**

4. **utte imasu**

VOCABULARY	**sunde imasu**	live
	tsutomete imasu	be employed
	shitte imasu	know
	utte imasu	sell

213

II. Family:

	RELATED TO THE SPEAKER	RELATED TO OTHERS
child	**kodomo**	**okosan**
son	**musuko**	**musukosan**
daughter	**musume**	**ojōsan/musumesan**
older brother	**ani**	**onīsan**
older sister	**ane**	**onēsan**
younger brother	**otōto**	**otōtosan**
younger sister	**imōto**	**imōtosan**

KEY SENTENCES

1. **Takahashi-san wa Yokohama ni sunde imasu.**
2. **Sumisu-san wa ABC Fūzu ni tsutomete imasu.**
3. **Sumisu-san wa Itō-san o shitte imasu.**
4. **Kombini de konsāto no kippu o utte imasu.**

1. Mr. Takahashi lives in Yokohama.
2. Mr. Smith is employed by ABC Foods.
3. Mr. Smith knows Ms. Ito.
4. They sell concert tickets at convenience stores.

EXERCISES

I. *Practice conjugating verbs.* Repeat the verbs below and memorize their **-te imasu** forms, affirmative and negative.

	-MASU FORM	-TE IMASU FORM	
		aff.	*neg.*
live	**sumimasu**	**sunde imasu**	**sunde imasen**
be employed	**tsutomemasu**	**tsutomete imasu**	**tsutomete imasen**
know	*	**shitte imasu**	**shirimasen****
sell	**urimasu**	**utte imasu**	**utte imasen**

 * **shirimasu**—the affirmative present tense—is hardly ever used.

** The negative **-te imasu** form is **shitte imasen**, but this form is not used.

VOCABULARY **Itō** Ito (surname)

II. *State where someone lives.* Make up sentences following the pattern of the example. Substitute the underlined words with the words in parentheses.

ex. **Yamamoto-san wa Kyōto ni sunde imasu.**

1. .... (Gurīn-san, Shibuya)

2. .... (Nakamura-san, Shinjuku)

III. *Ask and answer where someone lives.* Make up dialogues following the pattern of the example. Substitute the underlined words with the words in parentheses.

ex. **A: Takahashi-san wa doko ni sunde imasu ka.**
B: Yokohama ni sunde imasu.

1. A: .... (Yamada-san)

   B: .... (Shibuya)

2. A: .... (Howaito-san)

   B: .... (Roppongi)

IV. *State where someone is employed.* Make up sentences following the pattern of the example. Substitute the underlined words with the words in parentheses.

ex. **Takahashi-san wa depāto ni tsutomete imasu.**

1. .... (Yamada-san, ginkō)

2. .... (Sumisu-san, ABC Fūzu)

V. *Ask and answer where someone is employed.* Make up dialogues following the pattern of the example. Substitute the underlined words with the words in parentheses.

ex. **Yamada: Buraun-san wa doko ni tsutomete imasu ka.**
Sumisu: Rondon Ginkō ni tsutomete imasu.

1. Yamada: .... (Howaito-san)

   Sumisu: .... (JBP Japan)

2. Yamada: .... (Suzuki-san no onīsan)

   Sumisu: .... (ryokō-gaisha)

VOCABULARY | **JBP Japan** | JBP Japan (fictitious company name)

VI. *State where someone lives and is employed.* Use the information in the table to make up sentences as in the example.

	PERSON	RESIDENCE	EMPLOYER
ex.	Andō-san	Shinagawa	JBP Japan
1.	Gurīn-san	Shibuya	ABC Fūzu
2.	Nakamura-san no imōtosan	Sapporo	ginkō
3.	Chan-san no onēsan	Honkon	depāto

ex. **Andō-san wa Shinagawa ni sunde imasu.**
Soshite, JBP Japan ni tsutomete imasu.

1. ....

....

2. ....

....

3. ....

....

VII. Make up dialogues following the patterns of the examples. Substitute the underlined words with the alternatives given.

A. *Confirm whether one knows someone or something.*

ex. **A: Sasaki-san o shitte imasu ka.**
B: Hai, shitte imasu.

1. A: .... (Buraun-san)

B: Hai, ...

2. A: .... (Takahashi-san no jūsho)

B: Hai, ...

B. *Deny that one knows someone or something.*

ex. **A: Howaito-san o shitte imasu ka.**
B: Iie, shirimasen.

1. A: .... (Chan-san no mēru-adoresu)

B: Iie, ...

2. A: .... (Suzuki-san no denwa-bangō)

B: Iie, ...

VIII. *Ask and answer whether one knows a particular address or fax number.* Use the information in the table to make up a dialogue as in the example.

	Restaurant Tokyo's fax	Restaurant Tokyo's address	Sapporo branch office's fax
Suzuki	*ex.* yes	1. yes	2. no

ex. **Sumisu: Resutoran Tōkyō no fakkusu no bangō o shitte imasu ka.**
Suzuki: Hai, shitte imasu.

1. Sumisu: ....

   Suzuki: ....

2. Sumisu: ....

   Suzuki: ....

IX. *Ask where a product is sold.* Make up dialogues following the pattern of the example. Substitute the underlined parts with the alternatives given.

ex. **A: Konsāto no kippu wa doko de utte imasu ka.**
B: Kombini de utte imasu.

1. A: .... (dejikame)

   B: .... (Nozomi Depāto)

2. A: .... (kusuri)

   B: .... (ano mise)

X. Make up dialogues following the patterns of the examples. Substitute the underlined parts with the alternatives given.

A. *Talk about a new product.*

ex. **Hofuman: ABC Fūzu no atarashii o-kashi o shitte imasu ka.**
Matsui: Ee, shitte imasu.
Hofuman: Doko de utte imasu ka.
Matsui: Ginza no depāto de utte imasu.

1. Hofuman: .... (Fuji Kompyūtā no atarashii gēmu)

   Matsui: ....

   Hofuman: ....

   Matsui: .... (Shinjuku no denki-ya)

VOCABULARY	**Resutoran Tōkyō**	Restaurant Tokyo (fictitious restaurant name)
	Fuji Kompyūtā	Fuji Computers (fictitious company name)
	denki-ya	electronics store

2. Hofuman: .... (mēpuru-shiroppu)

   Matsui: ....

   Hofuman: ....

   Matsui: .... (sūpā)

B. *Talk about a particular person.*

   ex. Mr. Smith meets various people for the first time at a party.

   Sumisu: Andō-san, o-shigoto wa nan desu ka.
   Andō: Enjinia desu. JBP Japan ni tsutomete imasu.
   Sumisu: Sō desu ka. Ja, Yokohama-shisha no Itō-san o shitte imasu ka.
   Andō: Ee, shitte imasu.

   1. Sumisu: ....

      Kojima: .... (hisho)

      Sumisu: .... (Ōsaka-shisha no Yamashita-san)

      Kojima: ....

   2. Sumisu: ....

      Kobayashi: .... (bengoshi)

      Sumisu: .... (Honkon-shisha no Wan-san)

      Kobayashi: ....

C. *Talk about a particular person's telephone number or e-mail address.*

   ex. **Sumisu: JBP Japan no Itō-san o shitte imasu ka.**
   Nakamura: Hai, shitte imasu.
   Sumisu: Ja, Itō-san no denwa-bangō o shitte imasu ka.
   Nakamura: Iie, shirimasen.

   1. Sumisu: .... (Wan-san)

      Nakamura: ....

      Sumisu: .... (Wan-san no mēru-adoresu)

      Nakamura: ....

   2. Sumisu: .... (Andō-san)

      Nakamura: ....

      Sumisu: .... (Andō-san no keitai no bangō)

      Nakamura: ....

mēpuru-shiroppu	maple syrup	**Honkon-shisha**	Hong Kong (branch) office
Kojima	Kojima (surname)	**Wan**	Wang (surname)
Yamashita	Yamashita (surname)		
Kobayashi	Kobayashi (surname)		

XI. Listen to the CD and answer the question based on the information you hear.

....

SHORT DIALOGUE

 Mr. Smith wants to make a reservation at the sushi restaurant Sushimasa, but he doesn't know the phone number.

Sumisu: Sumimasen. Sushimasa no denwa-bangō o shitte imasu ka.
Nakamura: Sā, wakarimasen. Suzuki-san ni kiite kudasai.

Smith: Excuse me. Do you know the phone number for Sushimasa?
Nakamura: Actually, I don't. Please ask Mr. Suzuki.

VOCABULARY

Sushimasa	Sushimasa (fictitious sushi bar)
sā, wakarimasen	I don't know (NOTE: The sā here expresses the speaker's hesitation about immediately answering, "I don't know.")
sā	let me see

Active Communication

1. Next time you meet a Japanese person for the first time, tell him or her where you live and where you are employed. Then ask that person where he or she lives and is employed.

2. If you're in Japan, ask where something you are looking for is sold.

SOCIALIZING

The Japanese have an international reputation of being hardworking people, the men devoted to their work and the women to their families. But while they may be diligent, they are also social, and there are many kinds of celebrations—most season-inspired—that they participate in. From cherry blossom viewing in the spring, when friends and colleagues get together to appreciate the beauty of the ephemeral cherry blossoms, to excursions in autumn to see the changing of the colors of the leaves, to year-end and new-year parties, the Japanese have get-togethers whenever the seasons beckon them. In addition to these annual events, though, they also enjoy Western-style gatherings: drinking parties, barbecues, and even home parties.

Preference and Desire

> person **wa** noun **ga suki desu**
> 〃 **jōzu desu**
> 〃 **wakarimasu**

ex. **Gurei-san wa bīru ga suki desu.** "Mr. Grey likes beer."
Gurei-san wa tenisu ga jōzu desu. "Mr. Grey is good at tennis."
Gurei-san wa Chūgoku-go ga wakarimasu. "Mr. Grey understands/knows Chinese."

■ The particle **ga** used with **suki desu**, **jōzu desu**, **itai desu**, and **wakarimasu**

Ga is used before the adjectives **suki desu** ("like"; *lit.*, "be likable"), **jōzu desu** ("be skilled"), and **itai desu** ("be painful"), and also before the verb **wakarimasu** ("understand"), to show what one likes or is skilled at, what part of one's body hurts, or what one understands.
NOTE: With **itai desu**, the topic of the sentence is always the speaker, and the subject is a body part.

> **watashi wa** verb **-tai desu**

■ Expressing desire: verb **-tai desu**

Constructions expressing desire ("I want to . . .") can be made from the **-masu** form by dropping **-masu** and adding **-tai** as follows:
iki-masu → **iki-tai**
tabe-masu → **tabe-tai**
NOTE: **-tai** is inflected like an **-i** adjective.
ex. **Ikitai desu.** "(I) want to go."
Ikitakunai desu. "(I) don't want to go."
Ikitakatta desu. "(I) wanted to go."
Ikitakunakatta desu. "(I) didn't want to go."

■ **-Tai** expresses the speaker's desire, not a third person's

ex. **Takushī de ikitai desu.** "(I) want to go by taxi."
The particle **ka** may be added to **-tai desu** to form a question ("do you want to . . .?"), although this type of question is often considered impolite, especially when directed at a social superior. To ask if someone wants to do something, it is safest to use the **-masu** form followed by **ka**, as in **Takushī de ikimasu ka** ("Do you [want to] go by taxi?").
NOTE: The particle **ga** is sometimes used instead of **o**.
ex. **Wain o/ga nomitai desu.** "(I) want to drink wine."

BEING INTRODUCED TO SOMEONE

 TARGET DIALOGUE

The Greens are having a formal party at their house. During the party, Mr. Green introduces Mr. Smith to his friend Mr. Ogawa.

グリーン：スミスさん、こちらは　おがわさんです。

おがわ：はじめまして、おがわです。よろしく　おねがいします。

スミス：ABC フーズの　スミスです。よろしく　おねがいします。

グリーン：おがわさん、わたしは　スミスさんと　まいしゅう　どよ
　　　　　うびに　テニスを　しています。スミスさんは　テニスが
　　　　　とても　じょうずです。

おがわ：そうですか。わたしも　テニスが　すきです。

スミス：じゃ、こんしゅうの　どようびに　おがわさんも　いっしょ
　　　　　に　テニスを　しませんか。

おがわ：ありがとうございます。ぜひ。

■グリーンさんは　まいしゅう　どようびに　スミスさんと　テニスを
　しています。こんしゅうの　どようびは　おがわさんも　いっしょに
　テニスを　します。

　　Gurīn: Sumisu-san, kochira wa Ogawa-san desu.
Ogawa: Hajimemashite, Ogawa desu. Yoroshiku onegaishimasu.
Sumisu: ABC Fūzu no Sumisu desu. Yoroshiku onegaishimasu.
　　Gurīn: Ogawa-san, watashi wa Sumisu-san to maishū do-yōbi ni tenisu o shite imasu.
　　　　　Sumisu-san wa tenisu ga totemo jōzu desu.
Ogawa: Sō desu ka. Watashi mo tenisu ga suki desu.
Sumisu: Ja, konshū no do-yōbi ni Ogawa-san mo issho ni tenisu o shimasen ka.
Ogawa: Arigatō gozaimasu. Zehi.

■Gurīn-san wa maishū do-yōbi ni Sumisu-san to tenisu o shite imasu. Konshū no do-
　yōbi wa Ogawa-san mo issho ni tenisu o shimasu.

　Green: Mr. Smith, this is Mr. Ogawa.
　Ogawa: How do you do. I'm Ogawa. Pleased to meet you.
　　Smith: I'm Smith from ABC Foods. Pleased to meet you.
　Green: Mr. Ogawa, I play tennis with Mr. Smith every Saturday. He's very good at tennis.
Ogawa: Is that so? I like tennis, too.
　　Smith: Well, would you like to play tennis with us this Saturday, too?
Ogawa: Thank you. I'll definitely be there.

■Mr. Green plays tennis with Mr. Smith every Saturday. This Saturday, Mr. Ogawa will play
　tennis with them.

| テニス | **tenisu** | tennis |
| じょうずです | **jōzu desu** | be skilled, be good at (**-na** adj.) |

NOTES

1. Sumisu-san wa tenisu ga totemo jōzu desu.

The adjective **jōzu desu** ("be skilled") is applied to another person. Japanese never use this word in reference to themselves or members of their families. Therefore, one does not usually ask **. . . ga jōzu desu ka** ("are you good at . . . ?").

PRACTICE

WORD POWER

I.

1. **jōzu desu**

2. **suki desu**

3. **wakarimasu**

II. Sports:

1. **sukī**

2. **sakkā**

3. **yakyū**

4. **suiei**

jōzu desu	be skilled (**-na** adj.)	**sakkā**	soccer (see also p. 142)
suki desu	like (**-na** adj.)	**yakyū**	baseball
wakarimasu	understand	**suiei**	swimming
sukī	skiing		

KEY SENTENCES

1. **Sumisu-san wa tenisu ga jōzu desu.**
2. **Takahashi-san wa kudamono ga suki desu.**
3. **Sumisu-san wa Nihon-go ga wakarimasu.**

1. Mr. Smith is good at tennis.
2. Mr. Takahashi likes fruit.
3. Mr. Smith understands Japanese.

EXERCISES

I. *Practice conjugating verbs and adjectives.* Repeat the words below and memorize their forms—present and past, affirmative and negative.

		PRESENT FORM		PAST FORM	
		aff.	*neg.*	*aff.*	*neg.*
-NA ADJ.	be skilled	**jōzu desu**	**jōzu dewa arimasen**	**jōzu deshita**	**jōzu dewa arimasendeshita**
	like, love	**suki desu**	**suki dewa arimasen**	**suki deshita**	**suki dewa arimasendeshita**
VERB	understand	**wakarimasu**	**wakarimasen**	**wakarimashita**	**wakarimasen deshita**

II. Make up sentences following the patterns of the examples. Substitute the underlined words with the words in parentheses.

A. *State what someone is skilled at.*

   ex. **Nakamura-san wa <u>gorufu</u> ga jōzu desu.**

   1. .... (tenisu)

   2. .... (sukī)

   3. .... (Eigo)

B. *State what someone likes.*

   ex. **Nakamura-san wa <u>kudamono</u> ga suki desu.**

   1. .... (sukiyaki)

   2. .... (ryokō)

   3. .... (sakkā)

VOCABULARY   **kudamono**   fruit

C. *State what someone understands.*

    ex. **Sumisu-san wa <u>Nihon-go</u> ga wakarimasu.**

    1. .... (Furansu-go)

    2. .... (kanji)

III. Make up sentences or dialogues following the patterns of the examples and based on the information in the chart below.

VOCABULARY

kanji	kanji, Chinese character(s)	**Kankoku-go**	Korean (language)
uisukī	whiskey	**Doitsu-go**	German (language)
dansu	dancing		
Chūgoku-go	Chinese (language)		

A. *State the things someone likes, is skilled at, and understands.*

    ex. **Katō-san wa o-sake ga suki desu. Gorufu ga jōzu desu. Eigo ga wakarimasu.**

    1. ....

    2. ....

    3. ....

B. *State the things someone dislikes, is unskilled at, and does not understand.*

    ex. **Katō-san wa kōhī ga suki dewa arimasen. Tenisu ga jōzu dewa arimasen. Furansu-go ga wakarimasen.**

    1. ....

    2. ....

    3. ....

C. *Ask and answer whether someone likes or understands something.*

    ex. **Takahashi: Katō-san wa o-sake ga suki desu ka.**
        Katō: Hai, suki desu.
        Takahashi: Katō-san wa Furansu-go ga wakarimasu ka.
        Katō: Iie, wakarimasen.

    1. Takahashi: Sumisu-san wa bīru ga suki desu ka.

        Sumisu: ....

        Takahashi: Sumisu-san wa Nihon-go ga wakarimasu ka.

        Sumisu: ....

    2. Takahashi: Chan-san wa kōhī ga suki desu ka.

        Chan: ....

        Takahashi: Chan-san wa Kankoku-go ga wakarimasu ka.

        Chan: ....

    3. Takahashi: Sasaki-san wa uisukī ga suki desu ka.

        Sasaki: ....

        Takahashi: Sasaki-san wa Chūgoku-go ga wakarimasu ka.

        Sasaki: ....

D. *Ask and answer whether someone is skilled at something.*

    ex. **Takahashi: Katō-san wa gorufu ga jōzu desu ka.**
        Nakamura: Hai, jōzu desu.

    1. Takahashi: Sumisu-san wa dansu ga jōzu desu ka.

        Nakamura: ....

2. Takahashi: Chan-san wa dansu ga jōzu desu ka.

   Nakamura: ....

3. Takahashi: Sasaki-san wa gorufu ga jōzu desu ka.

   Nakamura: ....

IV. *Ask for and provide detailed information about one's likes.* Make up dialogues following the pattern of the example. Substitute the underlined words with the words in parentheses.

   ex. **Chan:** Suzuki-san wa <u>supōtsu</u> ga suki desu ka.
   Suzuki: Hai, suki desu.
   Chan: Donna <u>supōtsu</u> ga suki desu ka.
   Suzuki: <u>Sakkā</u> ga suki desu.

1. Chan: .... (kudamono)

   Suzuki: ....

   Chan: .... (kudamono)

   Suzuki: .... (ringo)

2. Chan: .... (Itaria-ryōri)

   Suzuki: ....

   Chan: .... (Itaria-ryōri)

   Suzuki: .... (piza)

3. Chan: .... (ongaku)

   Suzuki: ....

   Chan: .... (ongaku)

   Suzuki: .... (jazu)

V. *Introduce a friend and give information about his or her likes.* Complete the dialogues below following the pattern of the example and based on the information in the illustrations.

ex.

1.

2.

3.

ex. **Takahashi: Chan-san, kochira wa Kāpentā-san desu.**
Kāpentā: Hajimemashite. Kāpentā desu. Yoroshiku onegaishimasu.
Takahashi: Kāpentā-san wa ryōri ga jōzu desu. Furansu no wain ga suki desu.

1. Takahashi: Chan-san, kochira wa Ochiai-san desu.

   Ochiai: Hajimemashite. Ochiai desu. Yoroshiku onegaishimasu.

   Takahashi: ....

2. Takahashi: Chan-san, kochira wa Kojima-san desu.

   Kojima: Hajimemashite. Kojima desu. Yoroshiku onegaishimasu.

   Takahashi: ....

3. Takahashi: Chan-san, kochira wa Andō-san desu.

   Andō: Hajimemashite. Andō desu. Yoroshiku onegaishimasu.

   Takahashi: ....

VOCABULARY		
piano	piano	
umi	ocean, sea	
Kāpentā	Carpenter (surname)	
Ochiai	Ochiai (surname)	

VI. Make up dialogues following the patterns of the examples. Substitute the underlined words with the words in parentheses.

A. *Talk about a mutual interest.*

ex. **Gurīn: Do-yōbi ni <u>Hakone</u> ni itte <u>gorufu</u> o <u>shimasu</u>.**
Katō: Ii desu ne. Gurīn-san wa <u>gorufu</u> ga suki desu ka.
Gurīn: Ee, suki desu. Katō-san wa?
Katō: Watashi mo suki desu.
Gurīn: Ja, kondo issho ni ikimasen ka.
Katō: Arigatō gozaimasu. Zehi.

1. Gurīn: .... (Tōkyō Sutajiamu, yakyū, mimasu)

   Katō: .... (yakyū)

   Gurīn: ....

   Katō: ....

   Gurīn: ....

   Katō: ....

2. Gurīn: .... (Ginza, Furansu-ryōri, tabemasu)

   Katō: .... (Furansu-ryōri)

   Gurīn: ....

   Katō: ....

   Gurīn: ....

   Katō: ....

B. *Describe someone in detail.*

ex. **Suzuki: Sasaki-san, achira wa donata desu ka.**
Sasaki: JBP Japan no <u>Ochiai-san</u> desu. <u>Ochiai-san</u> wa <u>Chūgoku</u> ni sunde imashita
         kara, <u>Chūgoku-go</u> ga totemo jōzu desu.
Suzuki: Sō desu ka. Watashi wa raishū kara <u>Chūgoku-go</u> o naraimasu.
Sasaki: Ja, shōkaishimashō ka.
Suzuki: Ee, onegaishimasu.

1. Suzuki: ....

   Sasaki: .... (Kāpentā-san, Furansu, Furansu-go)

   Suzuki: .... (Furansu-go)

   Sasaki: ....

   Suzuki: ....

VOCABULARY		
Tōkyō Sutajiamu	Tokyo Stadium (fictitious building name)	**shōkaishimasu** introduce
Furansu-ryōri	French food	
achira	that person over there	
naraimasu	learn, take lessons in	

2. Suzuki: ....

   Sasaki: .... (Kojima-san, Kankoku, Kankoku-go)

   Suzuki: .... (Kankoku-go)

   Sasaki: ....

   Suzuki: ....

VII. Listen to the CD and fill in the blank based on the information you hear.

Chan-san wa .... ga jōzu desu.

SHORT DIALOGUE

Ms. Nakamura is interested in Mr. Ogawa.

Nakamura: Gurīn-san, achira wa donata desu ka.
Gurīn: A, Ogawa-san desu. Tokidoki issho ni kendō no renshū o shimasu.
Nakamura: Sō desu ka. Sutekina hito desu ne.
Gurīn: Shōkaishimashō ka.
Nakamura: Ee, onegaishimasu.

Nakamura: Mr. Green, who is that?
Green: Oh, that's Mr. Ogawa. We sometimes practice kendo together.
Nakamura: Is that so? He's a fine person, isn't he?
Green: Shall I introduce you to him?
Nakamura: Yes, please do.

VOCABULARY

kendō	kendo (a martial art in which the contestants fight with bamboo swords)
renshū o shimasu	practice
sutekina	fine, wonderful, lovely (**-na** adj.)

Active Communication

Imagine you are at a party. Introduce your friends or colleagues to one another and give details about their interests and skills.

LESSON 25 AT A PARTY

TARGET DIALOGUE

TRACK 96

Mrs. Green is serving food to Mr. Smith and Mr. Ogawa. Mr. Smith and Mr. Ogawa are eating Japanese food that Mrs. Green made.

スミス：おいしいですね。

おがわ：ほんとうに　おいしいですね。グリーンさんは　りょうりが　じょうずですね。

グリーン：ありがとうございます。まいしゅう　すいようびに　ぎんざの　クッキングスクールで　にほんりょうりを　ならっています。

スミス：わたしも　にほんりょうりを　ならいたいです。その　クッキングスクールは　どこに　ありますか。

グリーン：のぞみデパートの　となりに　あります。

■グリーンさんは　まいしゅう　すいようびに　ぎんざの　クッキングスクールで　にほんりょうりを　ならっています。

Sumisu: Oishii desu ne.
Ogawa: Hontō ni oishii desu ne. Gurīn-san wa ryōri ga jōzu desu ne.
Gurīn: Arigatō gozaimasu. Maishū sui-yōbi ni Ginza no kukkingu-sukūru de Nihon-ryōri o naratte imasu.
Sumisu: Watashi mo Nihon-ryōri o naraitai desu. Sono kukkingu-sukūru wa doko ni arimasu ka.
Gurīn: Nozomi Depāto no tonari ni arimasu.

■ **Gurīn-san wa maishū sui-yōbi ni Ginza no kukkingu-sukūru de Nihon-ryōri o naratte imasu.**

Smith: This is delicious, isn't it?
Ogawa: It really is delicious, isn't it? You are a good cook, Mrs. Green.
Green: Thank you. I take lessons in Japanese cuisine at a cooking school in Ginza every Wednesday.
Smith: I'd like to learn Japanese cuisine, too. Where is that cooking school?
Green: It's next door to Nozomi Department Store.

■ Mrs. Green takes lessons in Japanese cuisine at a cooking school in Ginza every Wednesday.

VOCABULARY

クッキングスクール	**kukkingu-sukūru**	cooking school
にほんりょうり	**Nihon-ryōri**	Japanese food
ならいたいです	**naraitai desu**	want to learn
その	**sono**	(see Note 1 below)

NOTES

1. Sono kukkingu-sukūru

Sono here is in reference to what came up just before in the conversation.

PRACTICE

WORD POWER

I. Hobbies:

1. **jūdō**   2. **ikebana**   3. **o-cha**

II. Parts of the body:

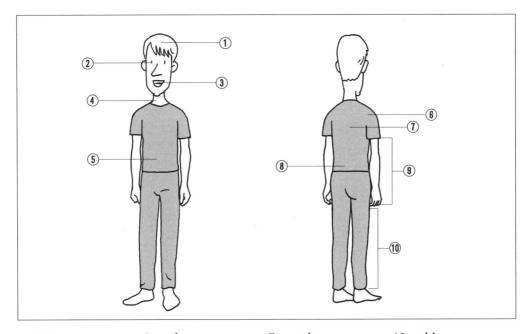

1. **atama**	4. **nodo**	7. **senaka**	10. **ashi**
2. **me**	5. **onaka**	8. **koshi**	
3. **ha**	6. **kata**	9. **te**	

VOCABULARY								
	jūdō	judo	**me**	eye	**kata**	shoulder	**ashi**	leg, foot
	ikebana	ikebana, flower arranging	**ha**	tooth	**senaka**	back		
	o-cha	tea ceremony	**nodo**	throat	**koshi**	lower back		
	atama	head	**onaka**	belly, stomach	**te**	hand, arm		

KEY SENTENCES

1. **Watashi wa onsen ni ikitai desu.**
2. **Watashi wa atama ga itai desu.**

1. I want to go to a spa.
2. I have a headache.

EXERCISES

I. *Practice conjugating verbs.* Repeat the **-tai** forms of the following verbs until you memorize them.

	PRESENT FORM		PAST FORM	
	aff.	*neg.*	*aff.*	*neg.*
want to learn	**naraitai desu**	**naraitakunai desu**	**naraitakatta desu**	**naraitakunakatta desu**
want to go	**ikitai desu**	**ikitakunai desu**	**ikitakatta desu**	**ikitakunakatta desu**

II. *State what you want to do.* Change the sentences below as in the examples.

ex. **Watashi wa onsen ni ikimasu.** → **Watashi wa onsen ni ikitai desu.**
Watashi wa onsen ni ikimasen. → **Watashi wa onsen ni ikitakunai desu.**

1. Watashi wa terebi o mimasu. → ....

2. Watashi wa Takahashi-san ni aimasen. → ....

3. Watashi wa furui kagu o kaimasu. → ....

4. Watashi wa jūdō o naraimasen. → ....

ikitai desu	want to go
itai desu	be painful, hurt
kagu	furniture

III. Make up dialogues following the patterns of the examples. Substitute the underlined parts with the alternatives given, being careful to use the correct grammatical form.

A. *Ask and answer where one wants to live.*

    ex. **A: Shōrai donna tokoro ni sumitai desu ka.**

        B: <u>Umi no chikaku</u> ni sumitai desu.

    1. A: ....

        B: .... (atatakai tokoro)

    2. A: ....

        B: .... (shizukana machi)

    3. A: ....

        B: .... (Okinawa)

B. *Ask for information.*

    ex. **A: <u>Nihon-go o naraitai desu</u>. Ii <u>gakkō</u> o shitte imasu ka.**
        B: Sumimasen, shirimasen.

    1. A: .... (onsen ni ikimasu, tokoro)

        B: ....

    2. A: .... (ikebana o naraimasu, kurasu)

        B: ....

    3. A: .... (furui kagu o kaimasu, mise)

        B: ....

IV. *State which part of your body hurts.* Make up sentences following the pattern of the example. Substitute the underlined word with the words in parentheses.

    ex. **Watashi wa <u>atama</u> ga itai desu.**

    1. .... (ha)

    2. .... (onaka)

VOCABULARY		
	shōrai	the future
	atatakai	warm
	machi	town
	kurasu	class

V. **Tell a doctor one's symptoms.** Make up dialogues following the pattern of the example and based on the information in the illustration.

ex. **isha: Dō shimashita ka.**
Chan: Kibun ga warui desu.

1. isha: ....

    Chan: ....

2. isha: ....

    Chan: ....

3. isha: ....

    Chan: ....

VI. **State what you do every week, and assuming the role of your listener, express envy and your own desire.** Make up dialogues following the pattern of the example. Substitute the underlined parts with the alternatives given. Be sure to use the same grammatical forms as in the example.

ex. **A: Watashi wa maishū Nihon-go o naratte imasu.**
B: Ii desu ne. Watashi mo naraitai desu.

1. A: .... (jogingu o shimasu)

    B: .... (shimasu)

2. A: .... (o-cha o naraimasu)

    B: .... (naraimasu)

VOCABULARY	**dō shimashita ka**	what's the matter with you?
	netsu	fever
	38-do	38 degrees (Celsius)
236	**-do**	degree

VII. Make up dialogues following the patterns of the examples. Substitute the underlined parts with the alternatives given. Be sure to use the same grammatical forms as in the examples.

A. *Give information.*

ex. **Takahashi: Nichi-yōbi ni <u>onsen ni ikimashita</u>.**
Sumisu: Ii desu ne. Watashi mo <u>ikitai desu</u>.
Takahashi: Ii <u>onsen</u> o oshiemashō ka.
Sumisu: Ee, onegaishimasu.

1. Takahashi: .... (tenisu o shimasu)

   Sumisu: .... (shimasu)

   Takahashi: .... (tenisu-kurabu)

   Sumisu: ....

2. Takahashi: ....
   (Kamakura ni itte, Nihon no furui kagu o kaimasu)

   Sumisu: .... (kaimasu)

   Takahashi: .... (mise)

   Sumisu: ....

B. *Explain why one did not go to a farewell party for a colleague.*

ex. **Katō: Kinō Howaito-san no sōbetsukai ni ikimashita ka.**
Sumisu: Iie, ikitakatta desu ga, <u>atama ga itakatta desu</u> kara, ikimasendeshita.
Katō: Sō desu ka. Zannen deshita ne.

1. Katō: ....

   Sumisu: .... (ha ga itakatta desu)

   Katō: ....

2. Katō: ....

   Sumisu: .... (netsu ga arimashita)

   Katō: ....

VIII. Listen to the CD and choose the correct answer based on the information you hear.

TRACK 98

What kind of place does Mr. Smith want to live in?

a) shizukana machi   b) ōkii machi   c) chiisai machi

SHORT DIALOGUE

The party has come to an end.

Ogawa: **Nakamura-san, kuruma de kimashita ka.**
Nakamura: Iie, densha de kimashita.
Ogawa: **Osoi desu kara, watashi no kuruma de kaerimasen ka.**
Nakamura: Arigatō gozaimasu.
Ogawa: **Sumisu-san mo issho ni ikaga desu ka.**
Sumisu: **Arigatō gozaimasu. Onegaishimasu.**

Ogawa: Ms. Nakamura, did you come by car?
Nakamura: No, I came by train.
Ogawa: It's late, so wouldn't you like to go home in my car?
Nakamura: Thank you.
Ogawa: Mr. Smith, how about going home with us?
Smith: Thank you. I'd like that.

VOCABULARY

osoi desu   be late

1. Get information about schools and teachers, or about a subject you want to take lessons in.

2. Get information about things you want to buy and places you want to visit.

Quiz 5 (Units 10–11)

I Fill in the blank in each sentence with the appropriate particle. Where a particle is not needed, write in an *X*.

1. Sumisu-san wa gorufu (　　　　) jōzu desu.

2. Takahashi-san no otōsan wa ginkō (　　　　) tsutomete imasu.

3. Konsāto no kippu wa doko (　　　　) utte imasuka.

4. Dō shimashita ka.
   Atama (　　　　) itai desu.

5. Sumisu-san no okāsan wa Sanfuranshisuko (　　　　) sunde imasu.

II Choose the word that is appropriate in the context of the sentence.

1. Sumisu-san wa ima nani o shite imasu ka.
   Kaigishitsu de Takahashi-san to hanashi o (shimasu / shite imasu).

2. Takahashi-san no denwa-bangō o (shirimasu / shitte imasu) ka.
   Iie, (shirimasen / shitte imasen).

3. Watashi wa kinō pātī ni (ikitai desu / ikitakatta desu) ga, isogashikatta desu kara, ikimasen deshita.

III Look at the illustrations and complete the dialogue by filling in the blanks with the appropriate forms of the three words given in brackets. (You may use the same word more than once.)

[shimasu, jōzu desu, suki desu]

Takahashi: Sumisu-san wa tenisu ga (1.　　　　) ka.
Sumisu:　　Ee, demo amari (2.　　　　　　　).
Takahashi: Ashita tomodachi to tenisu o (3.　　　　). Sumisu-san mo issho ni (4.　　　　) ka.
Sumisu:　　Ee, zehi.

239

APPENDIXES

			Unit	Lesson
	5. Sumisu-san wa kinō pātī no ato de takushī de kaerimashita.		8	17
	6. Katarogu o sugu mēru de okutte kudasai.		8	18
to	1. Chan-san wa kinō tomodachi to resutoran ni ikimashita.		3	6
	2. Tēburu no ue ni shimbun to hana ga arimasu.		4	8
ga	1. Dono densha ga ikimasu ka.		3	6
	2. 1-kai ni ginkō ga arimasu.		4	8
	3. Sumisu-san wa eigyō-bu ni ikimashita ga, Chan-san wa imasendeshita.		10	22
	4. Moshimoshi, Chan-desu ga, ohayō gozaimasu.		8	18
ni	1. Sumisu-san wa ashita ginkō ni/e ikimasu.		3	6
	2. Hikōki wa 10-ji han ni Sapporo ni tsukimasu.		9	19
	3. 3-gatsu 26-nichi ni Igirisu kara kimashita.		3	7
	4. Uketsuke ni onna no hito ga imasu.		4	8
	5. Sumisu-san wa ashita tomodachi ni aimasu.		5	11
	6. Sumisu-san wa tomodachi ni denwa o shimasu.		5	11
	7. Chan-san wa Sumisu-san ni hana o moraimashita.		6	13
	8. Sumisu-san wa ABC Fūzu ni tsutomete imasu.		10	23
	9. Tanaka-san wa Yokohama ni sunde imasu.		10	23
ya	1. Kaban no naka ni kagi ya hon ga arimasu.		4	8
ne	1. Kaigi wa 3-ji kara desu ne.		3	6
yo	1. Nihon no supa desu yo.		4	8
. . . wa . . . ga	1. Sumisu-san wa eiga no kippu ga 2-mai arimasu.		7	16
	2. Tanaka-san wa kudamono ga suki desu.		11	24
	3. Watashi wa atama ga itai desu.		11	25
	4. Watashi wa wain o/ga nomitai desu.		11	25

B. Interrogatives

Interrogatives	Examples	Unit	Lesson
donata	Kochira wa donata desu ka.	1	1
dare no	Kore wa dare no kasa desu ka.	1	2
dare to	Sumisu-san wa dare to Nozomi Depāto ni ikimasu ka.	3	6
dare ga	Uketsuke ni dare ga imasu ka.	4	8
dare ni	Sumisu-san wa dare ni tegami o kakimasu ka.	5	11
	Dare ni aimashita ka.	5	11*
	Dare ni eiga no kippu o moraimashita ka.	6	13
nan	Kore wa nan desu ka.	1	2
nan-ban	Tanaka-san no denwa-bangō wa nan-ban desu ka.	1	2
nan-nin	Ginkō no mae ni otoko no hito ga nan-nin imasu ka.	4	9
nan-ji	Ima nan-ji desu ka.	2	3
nan-yōbi	O-matsuri wa nan-yōbi desu ka.	3	7

*This type of sentence does not appear in the lesson's exercises.

nan-nichi	O-matsuri wa <u>nan-nichi</u> desu ka.		3	7
nan-gatsu	O-matsuri wa <u>nan-gatsu</u> desu ka.		3	7
nan de	Sumisu-san wa <u>nan de</u> Ōsaka ni ikimasu ka.		3	7
nani ga	1-kai ni <u>nani ga</u> arimasu ka.		4	8
nani o	Shūmatsu ni <u>nani o</u> shimasu ka.		5	10
itsu	Tanjōbi wa <u>itsu</u> desu ka.		3	7
	Tanaka-san wa <u>itsu</u> Ōsaka-shisha ni ikimasu ka.		3	6
ikaga	Okashi wa <u>ikaga</u> desu ka.		5	11
ikura	Sore wa <u>ikura</u> desu ka.		2	4
ikutsu	Tēburu no ue ni ringo ga <u>ikutsu</u> arimasu ka.		4	9
doko	Kōban wa <u>doko</u> desu ka.		4	9
doko no	Kore wa <u>doko no</u> pasokon desu ka.		2	5
doko ni	Sumisu-san wa ashita <u>doko ni</u> ikimasu ka.		3	6
	Sumisu-san wa <u>doko ni</u> imasu ka.		4	9
	Chūshajō wa <u>doko ni</u> arimasu ka.		4	9
	Sumisu-san wa <u>doko ni</u> tegami o kakimasu ka.		5	11
	Sumisu-san wa <u>doko ni</u> sunde imasu ka.		10	23
doko de	Katō-san wa <u>doko de</u> gorufu o shimashita ka.		5	10
dono	<u>Dono</u> basu ga ikimasu ka.		3	6
dore	Ano T-shatsu wa ikura desu ka. <u>Dore</u> desu ka.		2	5
donna	Nikkō wa <u>donna</u> tokoro desu ka.		6	12
	<u>Donna</u> supōtsu ga suki desu ka.		11	24
dō	Kinō no pātī wa <u>dō</u> deshita ka.		6	14
	<u>Dō</u> shimashita ka.		11	25
dōshite	<u>Dōshite</u> desu ka.		8	17
donogurai	Tanaka-san wa <u>donogurai</u> Nyūyōku ni imashita ka.		9	19
	<u>Donogurai</u> kakarimasu ka.		9	19
dōyatte	Sumisu-san wa <u>dōyatte</u> kaisha ni ikimasu ka.		9	19

C. Sentence Patterns

Sentence Patterns	Examples	Unit	Lesson
. . . wa . . . desu	1. (Watashi wa) Sumisu desu.	1	1
	2. Kore wa Hayashi-san no kasa desu.	1	2
	3. Shigoto wa 9-ji kara 5-ji made desu.	2	3
	4. Tanaka-san no uchi wa atarashii desu.	6	12
	5. Kore wa omoshiroi hon desu.	6	12

. . . wa . . . ga . . . desu	1. Tanaka-san wa kudamono ga suki desu.	11	24
	2. Watashi wa atama ga itai desu.	11	25
-tai desu	1. Watashi wa onsen ni ikitai desu.	11	25
. . . ni . . . ga arimasu/imasu	1. 1-kai ni ginkō ga arimasu.	4	8
	2. Uketsuke ni onna no hito ga imasu.	4	8
. . . wa . . . ni arimasu/imasu	1. Takushī-noriba wa eki no chikaku ni arimasu.	4	9
	2. Sumisu-san wa 2-kai ni imasu.	4	9
. . . o kudasai	1. Sono ringo o futatsu kudasai.	2	5
. . . ni/e -masu	1. Sumisu-san wa ashita ginkō ni/e ikimasu.	3	6
. . . de . . . o -masu	1. Sumisu-san wa kinō resutoran de ban-gohan o tabe-mashita.	5	10
. . . ni . . . o -masu	1. Chan-san wa yoku okāsan ni tegami o kakimasu.	5	11
	2. Chan-san wa Sumisu-san ni hana o moraimashita.	6	13
. . . wa . . . ga –masu	1. Sumisu-san wa eiga no kippu ga 2-mai arimasu.	7	16
	2. Sumisu-san wa Nihon-go ga wakarimasu.	11	24
. . . de . . . ga arimasu	1. Do-yōbi ni Asakusa de o-matsuri ga arimasu.	7	15
. . . ni -masu	1. Sumisu-san wa Tōkyō Eki de densha ni norimasu.	9	19
. . . o -masu	1. Sumisu-san wa Shinjuku Eki de densha o orimasu.	9	19
-masen ka	1. Shūmatsu ni issho ni eiga o mimasen ka.	7	15
	2. Nichi-yōbi ni uchi ni kimasen ka.	7	15
-mashō ka	1. Nani o tabemashō ka.	7	15
	2. Chizu o kakimashō ka.	7	15
-te, -masu	1. Sumisu-san wa kinō hon-ya ni itte, jisho o kaimashita.	8	17
-te imasu	1. Sumisu-san wa ima shimbun o yonde imasu.	10	22
	2. Tanaka-san wa Yokohama ni sunde imasu.	10	23
	3. Sumisu-san wa Satō-san o shitte imasu.	10	23
-te kudasai	1. Mō ichi-do itte kudasai.	8	18
-te mo ii desu ka	1. Kono pen o tsukatte mo ii desu ka.	9	20
-naide kudasai	1. Koko wa iriguchi desu kara, kuruma o tomenaide kudasai.	9	21

D. Adjectives

Included in the following list of adjectives are some (in gray) which do not appear in the text.

-i adjectives

abunai	dangerous	ōi	many, much
akarui	bright	oishii	delicious
amai	sweet	ōkii	big
atarashii	new, fresh	omoi	heavy
atatakai	warm	omoshiroi	interesting
atsui	hot	osoi	slow, late

243

chiisai	small	samui	cold
chikai	near	semai	narrow
furui	old	shiokarai	salty
hayai	fast, early	sukunai	few, a little
hikui	low	suppai	sour
hiroi	wide	suzushii	cool
ii	good, fine	tadashii	correct
isogashii	busy	takai	expensive, high
itai	painful	tanoshii	pleasant, enjoyable
karai	hot, spicy	tōi	far
karui	light	tsumaranai	boring
kitanai	dirty	tsumetai	cold
kurai	dark	wakai	young
mijikai	short	warui	bad
muzukashii	difficult	yasashii	easy
nagai	long	yasui	inexpensive

-na adjectives

anzenna	safe	kiraina	detestable
benrina	convenient	kireina	clean, pretty
daijina	important	nigiyakana	lively
damena	no good	shinsetsuna	kind
fubenna	inconvenient	shitsureina	rude
fushinsetsuna	unkind	shizukana	quiet
genkina	well, healthy	sukina	favorite, likable
hetana	unskillful	sutekina	fine, wonderful, lovely
himana	free	teineina	polite
iroirona	various	yūmeina	famous
jōzuna	skillful		

Color Words

Below are words for colors. Those in gray are not introduced in this text.

akai	red	kuroi	black
aoi	blue, green	midoriiro no*	green
chairoi, chairo no*	brown	murasaki no*	purple
kiiroi, kiiro no*	yellow	shiroi	white

*These words are nouns followed by the particle **no**.

E. Verb Conjugation

The conjugations of Japanese verbs fall into the following three categories:

    Regular I: Five-vowel conjugation

    Regular II: Single-vowel conjugation

    Irregular: There are only two irregular verbs: **kimasu** and **shimasu**. See Irregular Verbs, p. 246.

Regular I verbs are conjugated according to the Japanese vowel order: **a**, **i**, **u**, **e**, **o**. Regular II verbs are based on the vowels **-i** and **-e** only. From the **-nai** form it can be seen whether a verb is Regular I or Regular II. If the vowel preceding **-nai** is **-a**, the verb is Regular I. If it is **-i** or **-e**, the verb is Regular II. The chart below shows the conjugations of the verbs **kakimasu** ("write") and **tabemasu** ("eat").

	REGULAR I	REGULAR II
-nai form	**kaka-nai**	**tabe-nai**
-masu form	**kaki-masu**	**tabe-masu**
dictionary form	**kaku**	**taberu**
conditional form	**kake-ba**	**tabere-ba**
volitional form	**ka-kō**	**tabeyō**

-te form	kaite	tabete
-ta form	kaita	tabeta

Of the seven forms above, this book introduces the **-nai**, **-masu** and **-te** forms; the dictionary, conditional, volitional, and **-ta** forms are discussed in Books II and III of this series.

Note that the dictionary form—so called because it is the form listed in dictionaries—can be used at the end of a sentence instead of the **-masu** form. Likewise, the **-nai** form can be used at the end of a sentence instead of **-masen**. However, these forms are less polite than **-masu** and **-masen**.

For reference, the following are the **-masu**, **-te**, **-nai**, dictionary, and **-ta** forms of typical Regular I, Regular II, and Irregular verbs. Some of the verbs listed (in gray) are not introduced in this book.

REGULAR I VERBS					
-masu	**-te**	**-nai**	dictionary	**-ta**	meaning
aimasu	atte	awanai	au	atta	meet
arimasu	atte	nai	aru	atta	be, exist, have
arukimasu	aruite	arukanai	aruku	aruita	walk
azukarimasu	azukatte	azukaranai	azukaru	azukatta	take care of, look after
chigaimasu	chigatte	chigawanai	chigau	chigatta	be wrong
gambarimasu	gambatte	gambaranai	gambaru	gambatta	do one's best
hairimasu	haitte	hairanai	hairu	haitta	enter
iimasu	itte	iwanai	iu	itta	say
ikimasu	itte	ikanai	iku	itta	go
itadakimasu	itadaite	itadakanai	itadaku	itadaita	accept
kaerimasu	kaette	kaeranai	kaeru	kaetta	return, go home
kaimasu	katte	kawanai	kau	katta	buy
kakarimasu	kakatte	kakaranai	kakaru	kakatta	(it) takes
kakimasu	kaite	kakanai	kaku	kaita	write
kashimasu	kashite	kasanai	kasu	kashita	lend
katsugimasu	katsuide	katsuganai	katsugu	katsuida	carry (on one's shoulders)
keshimasu	keshite	kesanai	kesu	keshita	turn off
kikimasu	kiite	kikanai	kiku	kiita	listen (to), ask
komimasu	konde	komanai	komu	konda	be crowded
machimasu	matte	matanai	matsu	matta	wait
magarimasu	magatte	magaranai	magaru	magatta	turn
mochimasu	motte	motanai	motsu	motta	have, hold
moraimasu	moratte	morawanai	morau	moratta	receive
naraimasu	naratte	narawanai	narau	naratta	learn
niaimasu	niatte	niawanai	niau	niatta	suit, look good on
nomimasu	nonde	nomanai	nomu	nonda	drink
norimasu	notte	noranai	noru	notta	ride, get on
okimasu	oite	okanai	oku	oita	put, place
okurimasu	okutte	okuranai	okuru	okutta	send
oshimasu	oshite	osanai	osu	oshita	push
owarimasu	owatte	owaranai	owaru	owatta	finish
shirimasu*	shitte	shiranai	shiru	shitta	know
suimasu	sutte	suwanai	suu	sutta	smoke (cigarettes)
sumimasu	sunde	sumanai	sumu	sunda	live
tachimasu	tatte	tatanai	tatsu	tatta	stand up
torimasu	totte	toranai	toru	totta	take (a picture)
tsukaimasu	tsukatte	tsukawanai	tsukau	tsukatta	use
tsukimasu	tsuite	tsukanai	tsuku	tsuita	arrive

*This form is hardly ever used. Instead, **shitte imasu** (the **-te** form) is used.

tsukurimasu	tsukutte	tsukujranai	tsukuru	tsukutta	make
urimasu	utte	uranai	uru	utta	sell
wakarimasu	wakatte	wakaranai	wakaru	wakatta	understand
yobimasu	yonde	yobanai	yobu	yonda	invite, call, summon
yomimasu	yonde	yomanai	yomu	yonda	read

REGULAR II VERBS					
-masu	**-te**	**-nai**	dictionary	**-ta**	meaning
agemasu	agete	agenai	ageru	ageta	give
akemasu	akete	akenai	akeru	aketa	open
demasu	dete	denai	deru	deta	leave
imasu	ite	inai	iru	ita	be
iremasu	irete	irenai	ireru	ireta	put in/into
mimasu	mite	minai	miru	mita	see
misemasu	misete	misenai	miseru	miseta	show
orimasu	orite	orinai	oriru	orita	get off
oshiemasu	oshiete	oshienai	oshieru	oshieta	tell
shimemasu	shimete	shimenai	shimeru	shimeta	close
tabemasu	tabete	tabenai	taberu	tabeta	eat
todokemasu	todokete	todokenai	todokeru	todoketa	deliver
tomemasu	tomete	tomenai	tomeru	tometa	stop, park
tsukemasu	tsukete	tsukenai	tsukeru	tsuketa	turn on
(ki o) tsukemasu	tsukete	tsukenai	tsukeru	tsuketa	be careful
tsutomemasu	tsutomete	tsutomenai	tsutomeru	tsutometa	work for

IRREGULAR VERBS					
-masu	**-te**	**-nai**	dictionary	**-ta**	meaning
kimasu	kite	konai	kuru	kita	come
mottekimasu	mottekite	mottekonai	mottekuru	mottekita	bring
shimasu	shite	shinai	suru	shita	do
shitsureishimasu	shitsureishite	shitsureishinai	shitsureisuru	shitsureishita	be rude
shōkaishimasu	shōkaishite	shōkaishinai	shōkaisuru	shōkaishita	introduce

The verb **shimasu** ("do") follows various nouns, sometimes with and sometimes without the particle **o**, to express a variety of meanings. Below is a sampling of "noun **o shimasu**" combinations. The words in gray are not introduced in this text.

benkyō o shimasu	study	**sampo o shimasu**	go for a walk
denwa o shimasu	telephone	**setsumei o shimasu**	explain
doraibu o shimasu	go for a drive	**shigoto o shimasu**	work
gorufu o shimasu	play golf	**shokuji o shimasu**	have a meal
hanashi o shimasu	talk	**shutchō o shimasu**	go on a business trip
jogingu o shimasu	jog	**sōbetsukai o shimasu**	give a farewell party
kaigi o shimasu	have a meeting	**sōji o shimasu**	clean
kaimono o shimasu	shop	**sukī o shimasu**	ski
kopī o shimasu	make a copy	**supōtsu o shimasu**	play sports
pātī o shimasu	give a party	**tenisu o shimasu**	play tennis
renshū o shimasu	practice	**unten o shimasu**	drive
ryokō o shimasu	take a trip	**yoyaku o shimasu**	make a reservation

F. Ko-so-a-do Words

	ko-words	**so**-words	**a**-words	**do**-words
direction	**kochira** here, this way	**sochira** there, that way	**achira** over there	**dochira** where
people	**kochira** this person	**sochira** that person	**achira** that person over there	**donata, dare** who
thing	**kore** this	**sore** that	**are** that over there	**dore** which
place	**koko** here	**soko** there	**asoko** over there	**doko** where
demonstrative	**kono kamera** this camera	**sono kamera** that camera	**ano kamera** that camera over there	**dono kamera** which camera

G. Countries, Nationalities and Languages

	Country	Nationality	Language
Australia	**Ōsutoraria**	**Ōsutoraria-jin**	**Eigo**
Brazil	**Burajiru**	**Burajiru-jin**	**Porutogaru-go**
Canada	**Kanada**	**Kanada-jin**	**Eigo/Furansu-go**
China	**Chūgoku**	**Chūgoku-jin**	**Chūgoku-go**
Egypt	**Ejiputo**	**Ejiputo-jin**	**Arabia-go**
France	**Furansu**	**Furansu-jin**	**Furansu-go**
Germany	**Doitsu**	**Doitsu-jin**	**Doitsu-go**
Indonesia	**Indoneshia**	**Indoneshia-jin**	**Indoneshia-go**
Italy	**Itaria**	**Itaria-jin**	**Itaria-go**
Japan	**Nihon**	**Nihon-jin**	**Nihon-go**
New Zealand	**Nyūjirando**	**Nyūjirando-jin**	**Eigo**
Russia	**Roshia**	**Roshia-jin**	**Roshia-go**
Spain	**Supein**	**Supein-jin**	**Supein-go**
Switzerland	**Suisu**	**Suisu-jin**	**Doitsu-go/Furansu-go/Itaria-go**
Thailand	**Tai**	**Tai-jin**	**Tai-go**
United Kingdom	**Igirisu**	**Igirisu-jin**	**Eigo**
United States	**Amerika**	**Amerika-jin**	**Eigo**

H. Counters

The abstract numbers (**ichi**, **ni**, **san**) are given on p. 10 (0–10), p. 23 (10–30; 40, 50, . . .) and p. 30 (100, 200, . . .). (For an explanation of very large numbers, see Note 2, p. 29.) The **hitotsu, futatsu, mittsu** system is explained on p. 38 and given in full on p. 39, along with examples of two counters, **-mai** and **-hon**. Below are other counters used in this book.

Floors of a house or building: **-kai**

ikkai	1st floor	**go-kai**	5th floor	**kyū-kai**	9th floor
ni-kai	2nd floor	**rokkai**	6th floor	**jukkai**	10th floor
san-gai	3rd floor	**nana-kai**	7th floor	**jūikkai**	11th floor
yon-kai	4th floor	**hachi-kai**	8th floor	**jūni-kai**	12th floor

nan-kai/nan-gai   how many floors, which floor

Also: **chika ikkai**, (1st) basement floor (of several), **chika ni-kai**, 2nd basement floor, etc.

Liquid measure (cupful, glassful): **-hai/-bai/-pai**

ippai	1 cupful	**go-hai**	5 cupfuls	**kyū-hai**	9 cupful
ni-hai	2 cupfuls	**roppai**	6 cupfuls	**juppai**	10 cupfuls
sam-bai	3 cupfuls	**nana-hai**	7 cupfuls	**jūippai**	11 cupfuls
yon-hai	4 cupfuls	**happai**	8 cupfuls	**jūni-hai**	12 cupfuls

nan-bai   how many cups/glasses

People: **-nin**

hitori	1 person	**roku-nin**	6 people	**kyū-nin**	9 people
futari	2 people	**shichi-nin**	7 people	**ku-nin**	//
san-nin	3 people	**nana-nin**	//	**jū-nin**	10 people
yo-nin	4 people	**hachi-nin**	8 people	**jūichi-nin**	11 people
go-nin	5 people			**jūni-nin**	12 people

nan-nin   how many people

Times: **-kai, -do**

ikkai, ichi-do	once	**nana-kai, nana-do**	7 times
ni-kai, ni-do	twice	**hachi-kai, hachi-do**	8 times
san-kai, san-do	3 times	**kyū-kai, kyū-do**	9 times
yon-kai, yon-do	4 times	**jukkai, jū-do**	10 times
go-kai, go-do	5 times	**jūikkai, jūichi-do**	11 times
rokkai, roku-do	6 times	**jūni-kai, jūni-do**	12 times

nan-kai   how many times
nan-do   how many times/degrees

NOTE: Generally speaking, **-kai** and **-do** may be used interchangeably.

I. Extent, Frequency, Quantity

Extent

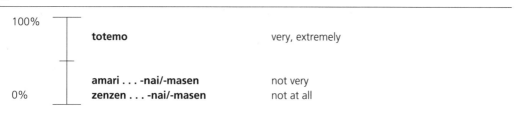

100%	**totemo**	very, extremely
	amari . . . -nai/-masen	not very
0%	**zenzen . . . -nai/-masen**	not at all

ex. **Kono nomimono wa totemo oishii desu.** "This drink is very good."
Kono nomimono wa amari oishikunai desu. "This drink is not very good."
Kono nomimono wa zenzen oishikunai desu. "This drink is not good at all."

Frequency

100%	**itsumo**	always
	yoku	often
	tokidoki	sometimes
	tamani	occasionally
	amari . . . -masen	not very often
0%	**zenzen . . . -masen**	never

ex. **Ban-gohan no ato de itsumo terebi o mimasu.** "(I) always watch TV after dinner."
Ban-gohan no ato de yoku terebi o mimasu. "(I) often watch TV after dinner."
Ban-gohan no ato de tokidoki terebi o mimasu. "(I) sometimes watch TV after dinner."
Ban-gohan no ato de tamani terebi o mimasu. "(I) occasionally watch TV after dinner."
Ban-gohan no ato de amari terebi o mimasen. "(I) don't often watch TV after dinner."
Ban-gohan no ato de zenzen terebi o mimasen. "(I) never watch TV after dinner."

Quantity

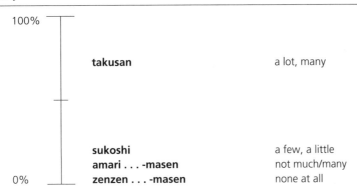

100% — takusan — a lot, many

sukoshi — a few, a little
amari . . . -masen — not much/many
0% — zenzen . . . -masen — none at all

ex. **Uchi no chikaku ni mise ga <u>takusan</u> arimasu.** "There are a lot of stores near my house."
Uchi no chikaku ni mise ga <u>sukoshi</u> arimasu. "There are a few stores near my house."
Uchi no chikaku ni mise ga <u>amari</u> ari<u>masen</u>. "There aren't many stores near my house."
Uchi no chikaku ni mise ga <u>zenzen</u> ari<u>masen</u>. "There are no stores near my house."

J. Time Expressions

Every: **mai-**

maiasa	every morning	**maishū**	every week
maiban	every evening, every night	**maitsuki/maigetsu**	every month
mainichi	every day	**mainen/maitoshi**	every year

Periods

Minutes: **-fun/-pun**

ippun (kan)	(for) 1 minute	**happun (kan)**	(for) 8 minutes
ni-fun (kan)	(for) 2 minutes	**hachi-fun (kan)**	//
sam-pun (kan)	(for) 3 minutes	**kyū-fun (kan)**	(for) 9 minutes
yom-pun (kan)	(for) 4 minutes	**juppun (kan)**	(for) 10 minutes
go-fun (kan)	(for) 5 minutes	**jūippun (kan)**	(for) 11 minutes
roppun (kan)	(for) 6 minutes	**jūni-fun (kan)**	(for) 12 minutes
nana-fun (kan)	(for) 7 minutes		
nan-pun (kan)	how many minutes		

Hours: **-jikan**

ichi-jikan	(for) 1 hour	**nana-jikan**	(for) 7 hours
ni-jikan	(for) 2 hours	**shichi-jikan**	//
san-jikan	(for) 3 hours	**hachi-jikan**	(for) 8 hours
yo-jikan	(for) 4 hours	**ku-jikan**	(for) 9 hours
go-jikan	(for) 5 hours	**jū-jikan**	(for) 10 hours
roku-jikan	(for) 6 hours	**jūichi-jikan**	(for) 11 hours
		jūni-jikan	(for) 12 hours
nan-jikan	how many hours		

Days: **-nichi (kan)**

ichi-nichi	(for) 1 day	**nanoka (kan)**	(for) 7 days
futsuka (kan)	(for) 2 days	**yōka (kan)**	(for) 8 days
mikka (kan)	(for) 3 days	**kokonoka (kan)**	(for) 9 days
yokka (kan)	(for) 4 days	**tōka (kan)**	(for) 10 days
itsuka (kan)	(for) 5 days	**jūichi-nichi (kan)**	(for) 11 days
muika (kan)	(for) 6 days	**jūni-nichi (kan)**	(for) 12 days
nan-nichi (kan)	how many days		

Weeks: -shūkan

isshūkan	(for) 1 week	**nana-shūkan**	(for) 7 weeks
ni-shūkan	(for) 2 weeks	**hasshūkan**	(for) 8 weeks
san-shūkan	(for) 3 weeks	**kyū-shūkan**	(for) 9 weeks
yon-shūkan	(for) 4 weeks	**jusshūkan**	(for) 10 weeks
go-shūkan	(for) 5 weeks	**jūisshūkan**	(for) 11 weeks
roku-shūkan	(for) 6 weeks	**jūni-shūkan**	(for) 12 weeks

nan-shūkan — how many weeks

Months: -kagetsu (kan)

ikkagetsu (kan)	(for) 1 month	**nana-kagetsu (kan)**	(for) 7 months
ni-kagetsu (kan)	(for) 2 months	**hakkagetsu (kan)**	(for) 8 months
san-kagetsu (kan)	(for) 3 months	**kyū-kagetsu (kan)**	(for) 9 months
yon-kagetsu (kan)	(for) 4 months	**jukkagetsu (kan)**	(for) 10 months
go-kagetsu (kan)	(for) 5 months	**jūikkagetsu (kan)**	(for) 11 months
rokkagetsu (kan)	(for) 6 months	**jūni-kagetsu (kan)**	(for) 12 months

nan-kagetsu (kan) — how many months

Years: -nen (kan)

ichi-nen (kan)	(for) 1 year	**shichi-nen (kan)**	(for) 7 years
ni-nen (kan)	(for) 2 years	**hachi-nen (kan)**	(for) 8 years
san-nen (kan)	(for) 3 years	**kyū-nen (kan)**	(for) 9 years
yo-nen (kan)	(for) 4 years	**jū-nen (kan)**	(for) 10 years
go-nen (kan)	(for) 5 years	**jūichi-nen (kan)**	(for) 11 years
roku-nen (kan)	(for) 6 years	**jūni-nen (kan)**	(for) 12 years
nana-nen (kan)	(for) 7 years		

nan-nen (kan) — how many years

NOTE: Except for with **-jikan** and **-shūkan**, the suffix **-kan** may be considered optional and need be added only when specificity is called for.

Relative Time

Day

ototoi	day before yesterday
kinō	yesterday
kyō	today
ashita	tomorrow
asatte	day after tomorrow

Month

sensengetsu	month before last
sengetsu	last month
kongetsu	this month
raigetsu	next month
saraigetsu	month after next

Morning

ototoi no asa	morning before last
kinō no asa	yesterday morning
kesa	this morning
ashita no asa	tomorrow morning
asatte no asa	morning of the day after tomorrow

Evening

ototoi no ban/yoru	evening/night before last
kinō no ban/yoru	yesterday evening/night
komban	this evening
ashita no ban/yoru	tomorrow evening/night
asatte no ban/yoru	evening/night of the day after tomorrow

Week

sensenshū	week before last
senshū	last week
konshū	this week
raishū	next week
saraishū	week after next

Year

ototoshi	year before last
kyonen	last year
kotoshi	this year
rainen	next year
sarainen	year after next

Seasons

haru	spring	**aki**	autumn
natsu	summer	**fuyu**	winter

ANSWERS TO SELECTED EXERCISES AND QUIZZES

Lesson 1
V.   bengoshi

Lesson 2
II.   **A.** 1. A: Kore wa hon desu ka. B: Hai, hon desu. 2. A: Kore wa kasa desu ka. B: Hai, kasa desu. 3. A: Kore wa tokei desu ka. B: Hai, tokei desu.
     B. 1. B: Iie. Kasa dewa arimasen. 2. B: Iie. Tokei dewa arimasen. 3. B: Iie. Kagi dewa arimasen.
III.   1. A: Kore wa nan desu ka. B: Kagi desu. 2. A: Kore wa nan desu ka. B: Tokei desu. 3. A: Kore wa nan desu ka. B: Keitai desu.
IV.   1. Kore wa Nakamura-san no kasa desu. 2. Kore wa Katō-san no tokei desu. 3. Kore wa Sasaki-san no kagi desu.
V.   **A.** 1. A: Kore wa Sumisu-san no hon desu ka. B: Hai, Sumisu-san no desu. 2. A: Kore wa Nakamura-san no kagi desu ka. B: Hai, Nakamura-san no desu. 3. A: Kore wa Chan-san no keitai desu ka. B: Hai, Chan-san no desu.
     B. 1. B: Iie, Sasaki-san no dewa arimasen. 2. B: Iie, Chan-san no dewa arimasen. 3. B: Iie, Sumisu-san no dewa arimasen.
     C. 1. A: Kore wa dare no hon desu ka. B: Sumisu-san no desu. 2. A: Kore wa dare no kagi desu ka. B: Nakamura-san no desu. 3. A: Kore wa dare no keitai desu ka. B: Chan-san no desu.
VI.   **A.** 1. Sasaki-san no denwa-bangō wa zero-san no san-ni-kyū-hachi no nana-nana-yon-hachi desu. 2. Taishikan no denwa-bangō wa zero-san no san-ni-ni-go no ichi-ichi-ichi-roku desu. 3. Ginkō no denwa-bangō wa zero-san no go-roku-kyū-zero no san-ichi-ichi-ichi desu. 4. Takahashi-san no denwa-bangō wa zero-san no san-yon-go-kyū no kyū-roku-ni-zero desu.
     B. 1. A: Sasaki-san no denwa-bangō wa nan-ban desu ka. B: Zero-san no san-ni-kyū-hachi no nana-nana-yon-hachi desu. 2. A: Taishikan no denwa-bangō wa nan-ban desu ka. B: Zero-san no san-ni-ni-go no ichi-ichi-ichi-roku desu. 3. A: Ginkō no denwa-bangō wa nan-ban desu ka. B: Zero-san no go-roku-kyū-zero no san-ichi-ichi-ichi desu. 4. A: Takahashi-san no denwa-bangō wa nan-ban desu ka. B: Zero-san no san-yon-go-kyū no kyū-roku-ni-zero desu.
VIII.   Zero-san no san-yon-go-kyū no kyū-roku-roku-zero.

Lesson 3
I.   1. 4-ji 2. 9-ji 3. 7-ji 15-fun 4. 10-ji 20-pun 5. 6-ji han
II.   1. A: Ima nan-ji desu ka. B: 4-ji desu. 2. A: Ima nan-ji desu ka. B: 9-ji desu. 3. A: Ima nan-ji desu ka. B: 7-ji 15-fun desu. 4. A: Ima nan-ji desu ka. B: 10-ji 20-pun desu. 5. A: Ima nan-ji desu ka. B: 6-ji han desu.
VI.   7-ji han

Lesson 4
I.   1. hachijū-en 2. hyaku-en 3. hyaku-nijū-en 4. sambyaku-en 5. happyaku-rokujū-en 6. sen-nihyaku-en 7. sanzen-en 8. yonsen-happyaku-en 9. ichiman-nanasen-en 10. samman-kyūsen-en
IV.   1. A: Sore wa ikura desu ka. 2. A: Are wa ikura desu ka. 3. A: Kore wa ikura desu ka. 4. A: Sore wa ikura desu ka. 5. A: Are wa ikura desu ka.
IX.   38,000

Lesson 5
II.   1. A: Sono kuroi kamera wa ikura desu ka. B: 20,000-en desu. 2. A: Kono aoi kamera wa ikura desu ka. B: 13,000-en desu. 3. A: Ano ōkii terebi wa ikura desu ka. B: 80,000-en desu. 4. A: Sono chiisai terebi wa ikura desu ka. B: 30,000-en desu.
V.   1. Sumisu: Sono bīru o 3-bon kudasai. 2. Sumisu: Sono ōkii ringo o yottsu kudasai. 3. Sumisu: Sono aoi T-shatsu o 2-mai kudasai. 4. Sumisu: Sono mikan o 2-kiro kudasai.
VII.   1. b) 2. a)

I.   1. wa 2. no 3. ka, ka 4. no, no 5. kara, made 6. wa, mo 7. o, X 8. no, no
II.   1. Doitsu-jin 2. nan 3. Takahashi-san, Dare 4. nan-ban 5. nan-ji, nan-ji 6. ikura 7. doko

UNIT 3

Lesson 6
VIII.   1. Sumisu-san wa raishū Sasaki-san to Ōsaka-shisha ni ikimasu. 2. Sumisu-san wa ashita dare to Honkon ni ikimasu ka. 3. Sumisu-san wa asatte uchi ni kaerimasu. 4. Sumisu-san wa kinō tomodachi to Ginza no depāto ni ikimashita. 5. Sumisu-san wa sengetsu Suzuki-san to doko ni ikimashita ka.
X.   tomodachi, depāto

Lesson 7
VII.   1. Sumisu-san wa asatte basu de depāto ni ikimasu. 2. Sumisu-san wa 2000-nen ni Takahashi-san to shinkansen de Kyōto ni ikimashita. 3. Sumisu-san wa 7-gatsu 15-nichi ni chikatetsu de taishikan ni ikimasu/ikimashita. 4. Sumisu-san wa ashita aruite tomodachi no uchi ni ikimasu.
VIII.   1. Sumisu-san wa sui-yōbi ni hitori de hikōki de Ōsaka-shisha ni ikimasu. 2. Sumisu-san wa kin-yōbi no 12-ji ni hisho to resutoran ni ikimasu. 4-ji ni Sasaki-san to Yokohama-shisha ni ikimasu. 6-ji ni Amerika Taishikan ni ikimasu. 3. Sumisu-san wa nichi-yōbi no gozen 9-ji ni tomodachi to kōen ni ikimasu. Gogo 7-ji ni Suzuki-san to tomodachi no uchi ni ikimasu.
X.   1. b) 2. c) [hikōki]

UNIT 4

Lesson 8
VI.   1. 3-gai ni resutoran ga arimasu. 2. 1-kai ni otoko no hito ga imasu. 3. 4-kai ni nani ga arimasu ka. 4. Chika 1-kai ni dare ga imasu ka. 5. Isu no ue ni kaban ga arimasu. 6. Tēburu no ue ni hana to hon ga arimasu. 7. Beddo no chikaku ni Takahashi-san ga imasu. 8. Reizōko no naka ni nani ga arimasu ka.
VIII.   1. ginkō 2. yūbinkyoku 3. resutoran

Lesson 9
V.   1. Chan: Takushī-noriba wa doko ni arimasu ka. 2. Chan: Ginkō wa doko ni arimasu ka. 3. Chan: Kāto wa doko ni arimasu ka. 4. Chan: Kusuri-ya wa doko ni arimasu ka. 5. Chan: Hon-ya wa doko ni arimasu ka. 6. Chan: O-tearai wa doko ni arimasu ka.
VII.   sūpā no tonari

UNIT 5

Lesson 10
III.   A. 1. Sumisu-san wa hon o yomimasu. 2. Sumisu-san wa kōhī o nomimasu. 3. Sumisu-san wa kitte o kaimasu. 4. Sumisu-san wa tenisu o shimasu.
       B. 1. A: Sumisu-san wa nani o yomimasu ka. B: Hon o yomimasu. 2. A: Sumisu-san wa nani o nomimasu ka. B: Kōhī o nomimasu. 3. A: Sumisu-san wa nani o kaimasu ka. B: Kitte o kaimasu. 4. A: Sumisu-san wa nani o shimasu ka. B: Tenisu o shimasu.
V.   A. 1. Sumisu-san wa toshokan de hon o yomimasu. 2. Sumisu-san wa kaisha de shigoto o shimasu. 3. Sumisu-san wa yūbinkyoku de kitte o kaimasu. 4. Sumisu-san wa supōtsu-kurabu de tenisu o shimasu.
       B. 1. A: Sumisu-san wa doko de hon o yomimasu ka. B: Toshokan de yomimasu. 2. A: Sumisu-san wa doko de shigoto o shimasu ka. B: Kaisha de shimasu. 3. A: Sumisu-san wa doko de kitte o kaimasu ka. B: Yūbinkyoku de kaimasu. 4. A: Sumisu-san wa doko de tenisu o shimasu ka. B: Supōtsu-kurabu de shimasu.
VI.   1. Katō-san wa maiasa yasai-jūsu o nomimasu. 2. Katō-san wa maiban okusan to jogingu o shimasu. 3. Katō-san wa maishū supōtsu-kurabu ni ikimasu.
VIII.   1. ōkii o-tera 2. (o-tera no) niwa de

Lesson 11
III.   A. 1. 1) Sumisu-san wa tomodachi ni tegami o kakimasu. 2) Sumisu-san wa Nozomi Depāto no shachō ni tegami o kakimasu. 3) Sumisu-san wa Ginza no hoteru ni tegami o kakimasu. 4) Sumisu-san wa Nihon-go no gakkō ni tegami o kakimasu. 2. 1) Sumisu-san wa tomodachi ni denwa o shimasu. 2) Sumisu-san wa Nozomi Depāto no shachō ni denwa o shimasu. 3) Sumisu-san wa Ginza no hoteru ni denwa o shimasu. 4) Sumisu-san wa Nihon-go no gakkō ni denwa o shimasu. 3. 1) Sumisu-san wa tomodachi ni mēru o okurimasu. 2)

Sumisu-san wa Nozomi Depāto no shachō ni mēru o okurimasu.3) Sumisu-san wa Ginza no hoteru ni mēru o okurimasu. 4) Sumisu-san wa Nihon-go no gakkō ni mēru o okurimasu.

B. 1. 1) A: Sumisu-san wa dare ni tegami o kakimasu ka. B: Tomodachi ni kakimasu. 2) A: Sumisu-san wa dare ni tegami o kakimasu ka. B: Nozomi Depāto no shachō ni kakimasu. 3) A: Sumisu-san wa doko ni tegami o kakimasu ka. B: Ginza no hoteru ni kakimasu. 4) A: Sumisu-san wa doko ni tegami o kakimasu ka. B: Nihon-go no gakkō ni kakimasu. 2. 1) A: Sumisu-san wa dare ni denwa o shimasu ka. B: Tomodachi ni shimasu. 2) A: Sumisu-san wa dare ni denwa o shimasu ka. B: Nozomi Depāto no shachō ni shimasu. 3) A: Sumisu-san wa doko ni denwa o shimasu ka. B: Ginza no hoteru ni shimasu. 4) A: Sumisu-san wa doko ni denwa o shimasu ka. B: Nihon-go no gakkō ni shimasu. 3. 1) A: Sumisu-san wa dare ni mēru o okurimasu ka. B: Tomodachi ni okurimasu. 2) A: Sumisu-san wa dare ni mēru o okurimasu ka. B: Nozomi Depāto no shachō ni okurimasu. 3) A: Sumisu-san wa doko ni mēru o okurimasu ka. B: Ginza no hoteru ni okurimasu. 4) A: Sumisu-san wa doko ni mēru o okurimasu ka. B: Nihon-go no gakkō ni okurimasu.

IV. 1. Sumisu-san wa ka-yōbi no 10-ji ni Nozomi Depāto de Takahashi-san ni aimasu. 2. Sumisu-san wa sui-yōbi no 7-ji ni Resutoran Rōma de Sasaki-san no go-shujin ni aimasu. 3. Sumisu-san wa moku-yōbi no 11-ji ni Sapporo-shisha de shisha no hito ni aimasu. 4. Sumisu-san wa kin-yōbi no 6-ji han ni hoteru no robī de Nakamura-san ni aimasu.

V. 1. Hai, tokidoki tabemasu. 2. Iie, amari shimasen. 3. Iie, zenzen mimasen.

VII. 1. Sumisu: Wain o 1-pon onegaishimasu. mise no hito: Hai. 2. Sumisu: Sarada o futatsu onegaishimasu. mise no hito: Hai. 3. Sumisu: Aisu-kurīmu o yottsu onegaishimasu. mise no hito: Hai.

IX. mēru o okuri(masu)

UNITS 3–5

I. 1. ya 2. ni, to 3. ga, ga 4. wa, ni, no 5. to, ni 6. ni 7. de, o 8. de, ni 9. X, de, o 10. X, ni 11. kara

II. 1. dare 2. doko 3. nani 4. ikutsu 5. nan-nin 6. itsu 7. Dare 8. doko 9. nan-ji 10. itsu 11. nani, dare

III. 1. arimasu 2. arimasen 3. ikimasen 4. mimasu, mimasen 5. yoku

UNIT 6

Lesson 12

IV. 1. Kore wa atarashii kuruma desu. 2. Kore wa furui biru desu. 3. Kore wa takai sētā desu. 4. Kore wa amai kēki desu. 5. Kore wa oishii ringo desu.

VIII. 1.Sumisu-san wa senshū shizukana resutoran de shokuji o shimashita. 2. Sumisu-san wa senshū kireina resutoran de shokuji o shimashita.

X. 1. Sumisu: (a) Eki kara chikai desu ne. (b) Benri desu ne. 2. Sumisu: Omoshiroi e desu ne. 3. Sumisu: Totemo furui tokei desu ne. 4. Sumisu: Kireina hana desu ne.

XII. kireina

Lesson 13

III. A. 1. A: Sumisu-san wa dare ni tokei o agemashita ka. B: Suzuki-san ni agemashita. 2. A: Sumisu-san wa dare ni Kyōto no o-miyage o agemashita ka. B: Nakamura-san ni agemashita.

B. 1. A: Suzuki-san wa dare ni tokei o moraimashita ka. B: Sumisu-san ni moraimashita. 2. A: Nakamura-san wa dare ni Kyōto no o-miyage o moraimashita ka. B: Sumisu-san ni moraimashita.

C. 1. A: Sumisu-san wa Suzuki-san ni nani o agemashita ka. B: Tokei o agemashita. 2. A: Sumisu-san wa Nakamura-san ni nani o agemashita ka. B: Kyōto no o-miyage o agemashita.

IV. A. 1. Chan-san wa Kurisumasu ni Suzuki-san ni dejikame o agemashita. Suzuki-san wa Kurisumasu ni Chan-san ni dejikame o moraimashita. 2. Suzuki-san wa Barentaindē ni Chan-san ni kireina sukāfu o agemashita. Chan-san wa Barentaindē ni Suzuki-san ni kireina sukāfu o moraimashita.

B. 1. A: Chan-san wa Kurisumasu ni Suzuki-san ni nani o agemashita ka. B: Dejikame o agemashita. 2. A: Suzuki-san wa Barentaindē ni Chan-san ni nani o agemashita ka. B: Kireina sukāfu o agemashita.

C. 1. A: Chan-san wa Kurisumasu ni dare ni dejikame o agemashita ka. B: Suzuki-san ni agemashita. 2. A: Suzuki-san wa Barentaindē ni dare ni kireina sukāfu o agemashita ka. B: Chan-san ni agemashita.

D. 1. A: Chan-san wa itsu Suzuki-san ni dejikame o agemashita ka. B: Kurisumasu ni agemashita. 2. A: Suzuki-san wa itsu Chan-san ni kireina sukāfu o agemashita ka. B: Barentaindē ni agemashita.

E. 3. A: Chan-san wa tanjōbi ni Suzuki-san ni nani o moraimashita ka. B: Hanataba o moraimashita. 4. A: Suzuki-san wa tanjōbi ni Chan-san ni nani o moraimashita ka. B: Sētā o moraimashita.

F. 3. A: Chan-san wa tanjōbi ni dare ni hanataba o moraimashita ka. B: Suzuki-san ni moraimashita. 4. A: Suzuki-san wa tanjōbi ni dare ni sētā o moraimashita ka. B: Chan-san ni moraimashita.

G. 3. A: Chan-san wa itsu Suzuki-san ni hanataba o moraimashita ka. B: Tanjōbi ni moraimashita. 4. A: Suzuki-san wa itsu Chan-san ni sētā o moraimashita ka. B: Tanjōbi ni moraimashita.

VI.   Nihon-go no hon o moraimashita.

Lesson 14

III.   A. 1. Nakamura: Kinō no pātī no ryōri wa oishikatta desu ka. Chan: Hai, oishikatta desu. Sumisu: Iie, oishikunak-atta desu. 2. Nakamura: Kinō no o-matsuri wa nigiyaka deshita ka. Chan: Hai, nigiyaka deshita. Sumisu: Iie, nigiyaka dewa arimasendeshita.

     B. 1. Katō: Kinō no konsāto wa dō deshita ka. Chan: Totemo yokatta desu. Sumisu: Amari yokunakatta desu. 2. Katō: Kinō no bāgen-sēru wa dō deshita ka. Chan: Totemo yasukatta desu. Sumisu: Amari yasukunakatta desu.

V.   nichi-yōbi, nigiyaka deshita.

UNIT 7

Lesson 15

I.   1. Kōhī o nomimasen ka. 2. Gorufu o shimasen ka.

II.   A. 1. A: Shūmatsu ni issho ni Ginza ni ikimasen ka. B: Ee, ikimashō. 2. A: Shūmatsu ni issho ni shokuji o shimasen ka. B: Ee, shimashō. 3. A: Shūmatsu ni issho ni sumō o mimasen ka. B: Ee, mimashō. 4. A: Shūmatsu ni issho ni hiru-gohan o tabemasen ka. B: Ee, tabemashō.

     B. 1. A: Shūmatsu ni issho ni Ginza ni ikimasen ka. B: Zannen desu ga, tsugō ga warui desu. 2. A: Shūmatsu ni issho ni shokuji o shimasen ka. B: Zannen desu ga, tsugō ga warui desu. 3. A: Shūmatsu ni issho ni sumō o mimasen ka. B: Zannen desu ga, tsugō ga warui desu. 4. A: Shūmatsu ni issho ni hiru-gohan o tabemasen ka. B: Zannen desu ga, tsugō ga warui desu.

IV.   A. 1. Raigetsu Sapporo de yuki-matsuri ga arimasu. 2. Ashita taishikan de pātī ga arimasu. 3. Kayō-bi ni Yoko-hama de sakkā no shiai ga arimasu.

     B. 1. A: Raigetsu Sapporo de yuki-matsuri ga arimasu. Issho ni ikimasen ka. B: Ii desu ne. Ikimashō. 2. A: Ashita taishikan de pātī ga arimasu. Issho ni ikimasen ka. B: Ii desu ne. Ikimashō. 3. A: Ka-yōbi ni Yokohama de sakkā no shiai ga arimasu. Issho ni ikimasen ka. B: Ii desu ne. Ikimashō.

VI.   1. Suzuki: Do-yōbi ni issho ni shokuji o shimasen ka. 2. Chan: Ee, shimashō. 3. Suzuki: Nani o tabemashō ka. 4. Chan: O-sushi wa dō desu ka. 5. Suzuki: ii desu ne. 6. Suzuki: Nan-ji ni aimashō ka. 7. Chan: 6-ji ni aimasen ka. 8. Suzuki: Hai, sō shimashō.

VII.   densha, nichi-yōbi

Lesson 16

I.   1. Chizu o kakimashō ka. 2 Kono hon o kashimashō ka.

II.   1. Sumisu: Doa o akemashō ka. Nakamura: Ee, onegaishimasu. 2. Sumisu: Shashin o torimashō ka. Suzuki: Iie, kekkō desu. 3. Sumisu: Mado o shimemashō ka. Nakamura: Ee, onegaishimasu. 4. Sumisu: Eakon o ke-shimashō ka. Suzuki: Iie, kekkō desu.

III.   1. Watashi wa kasa ga arimasu. 2. Watashi wa eiga no kippu ga arimasu. 3. Watashi wa Nihon-go no jugyō ga arimasu. 4. Watashi wa yasumi ga arimasu. 5. Watashi wa jikan ga arimasu. 6. Watashi wa kaigi ga ari-masu.

VI.   1. Suzuki: Kopī o shimashō ka. 2. Sumisu: Ee, onegaishimasu. 3. Suzuki: Nan-mai shimashō ka. 4. Sumisu: 3-mai onegaishimasu.

VII.   Suzuki-san ga kakimasu.

QUIZ 3   **UNITS 6–7**

I.   1. ni 2. o 3. ga 4. ga 5. ga, X

II.   1. donna 2. dare 3. dō 4. doko

III.   1. kireina 2. oishii 3. shizuka dewa arimasen 4. nigiyaka deshita 5. omoshirokunakatta desu

IV.   1. mimasen ka, aimashō ka 2. tsukemashō ka, akemashō ka

UNIT 8

Lesson 17

III.   1. Denki o tsukete, doa o shimemasu. 2. Denwa-bangō o kiite, denwa o shimasu. 3. Uchi de hon o yonde, repōto o kakimasu.

IV.   1. A: Ashita nani o shimasu ka. B: Ginza de kaimono o shite, eiga o mimasu. 2. A: Ashita nani o shimasu ka. B: Resutoran de hiru-gohan o tabete, bijutsukan ni ikimasu.

V.   1. Sumisu-san ni atte, issho ni tenisu o shimashita. 2. Doa o akete, denki o tsukemashō ka.

VI.   1. A: Kinō nani o shimashita ka. B: Roppongi ni itte, shokuji o shimashita. 2. A: Kinō nani o shimashita ka. B: Tomodachi ni atte, issho ni sumō o mimashita.

VIII.   1. A: Kinō shigoto no ato de nani o shimashita ka. B: Tomodachi ni atte, issho ni eiga o mimashita. 2. A: Kinō shigoto no ato de nani o shimashita ka. B: Depāto ni itte, kaimono o shimashita. 3. A: Kinō shigoto no ato de nani o shimashita ka. B: Bā de wain o nonde, takushī de uchi ni kaerimashita.

IX.   1. Sumisu-san wa kin-yōbi ni Kōbe ni itte, gorufu o shimasu. Gorufu no ato de tomodachi no uchi ni ikimasu. 2. Sumisu-san wa doyō-bi ni Kyōto ni itte, Yamamoto-san to shokuji o shimasu. Shokuji no ato de furui o-tera ya niwa o mimasu.

XI.   a) [terebi]

Lesson 18

II.   1. Chotto matte kudasai. 2. Shashin o totte kudasai. 3. Mō ichi-do itte kudasai. 4. Pen o kashite kudasai. 5. Piza o todokete kudasai.

III. A. 1. A: Sumimasen. Mēru-adoresu o kaite kudasai. B: Hai. 2. A: Sumimasen. Menyū o misete kudasai. B: Hai. 3. A: Sumimasen. Kaigi no shiryō o mottekite kudasai. B: Hai.

V.   1. Tsugi no shingō o hidari ni magatte kudasai. 2. Futatsu-me no kado o migi ni magatte kudasai. 3. Massugu itte kudasai. 4. Depāto no temae de tomete kudasai.

VII.   Takahashi-san, fakkusu

UNIT 9

Lesson 19

III. A. 1. Takahashi: (Chan-san wa) dōyatte kaisha ni ikimasu ka. Chan: Azabu de basu ni notte, Tōkyō Eki de orimasu. Tōkyō Eki kara kaisha made arukimasu. 2. Takahashi: (Suzuki-san wa) dōyatte kaisha ni ikimasu ka. Suzuki: Yokohama Eki de densha ni notte, Tōkyō Eki de orimasu. Tōkyō Eki kara kaisha made arukimasu.
      B. 1. Chan: 8-ji ni demasu . . . 8-ji 20-pun ni tsukimasu. 2. Suzuki: 7-ji ni demasu . . . 8-ji ni tsukimasu.

V.   1. Sumisu: Tōkyō kara Nikkō made donogurai kakarimasu ka. Nakamura: Densha de 1-jikan han kakarimasu. 2. Nakamura: Narita Kūkō kara Honkon made donogurai kakarimasu ka. Chan: Hikōki de 5-jikan kakarimasu.

VIII.   1. Chan: Hikōki wa nan-ji ni Narita o demasu ka. 2. ryokō-gaisha no hito: 11-ji ni demasu. 3. Chan: Narita kara Honoruru made donogurai kakarimasu ka. 4. ryokō-gaisha no hito: 7-jikan gurai kakarimasu. 5. Chan: Arigatō gozaimasu.

IX.   chikatetsu, 30-pun

Lesson 20

II.   1. Mado o akete mo ii desu ka. 2. Kono iyahōn-gaido o tsukatte mo ii desu ka. 3. Kono e no shashin o totte mo ii desu ka. 4. Koko de tabako o sutte mo ii desu ka. 5. Ashita yasunde mo ii desu ka.

III.   1. Suzuki: O-kyaku-san ni katarogu o misete mo ii desu ka. Katō: Hai, dōzo. 2. Suzuki: O-kyaku-san ni sampuru o okutte mo ii desu ka. Katō: Hai, dōzo. 3. Suzuki: Asatte yasunde mo ii desu ka. Katō: Hai, dōzo.

IV.   1. Sumisu: O-tera no shashin o totte mo ii desu ka. o-tera no hito: Sumimasen ga, chotto . . . 2. Sumisu: Niwa ni haitte mo ii desu ka. o-tera no hito: Sumimasen ga, chotto . . . 3. Sumisu: Koko de o-cha o nonde mo ii desu ka. o-tera no hito: Sumimasen ga, chotto . . .

VI.   1. mise no hito: Koko/Kochira ni o-namae to go-jūsho o onegaishimasu. 2. Sumisu: Sumimasen, pen ga arimasen. 3. Sumisu: Kono pen o tsukatte mo ii desu ka. 4. mise no hito: Hai, dōzo. 5. Sumisu: Arigatō.

VII.   3-ji han, kaigishitsu

Lesson 21

III.   1. Shashin o toranaide kudasai. 2. Doa o shimenaide kudasai. 3. Denki o kesanaide kudasai. 4. Kuruma o tomenaide kudasai.

IV.   1. Koko wa deguchi desu kara, kuruma o tomenaide kudasai. 2. Koko wa mise no mae desu kara, kuruma o tomenaide kudasai. 3. Koko wa chūsha-kinshi desu kara, kuruma o tomenaide kudasai.

VI.   kaigishitsu, kaigi

QUIZ 4 UNITS 8–9

I.   1. ni 2. o, ni 3. de 4. de, o, ni 5. kara, made, de 6. ni, X 7. ni, o, ni, ni 8. wa, kara, o

II.   1. nani 2. Itsu 3. Dōyatte 4. donogurai

III.   1. kakanai 2. keshimasu 3. nonde 4. toranai 5. shimete 6. akemasu 7. mite 8. konai 9. shimasu

IV.   1. mite 2. katte 3. oshiete 4. magatte, itte 5. moratte 6. tomenaide

UNIT 10

Lesson 22

III. **A.** 1. A: Chan-san wa ima nani o shite imasu ka. B: Repōto o kaite imasu. 2. A: Nakamura-san wa ima nani o shite imasu ka. B: Kopī o shite imasu. 3. A: Katō-san wa ima nani o shite imasu ka. B: Kaigishitsu de setsumei o shite imasu. 4. A: Sasaki-san wa ima nani o shite imasu ka. B: O-kyaku-san to hanashi o shite imasu. 5. A: Suzuki-san wa ima nani o shite imasu ka. B: Tabako o sutte imasu. 6. A: Takahashi-san wa ima nani o shite imasu ka. B: 1-kai de erebētā o matte imasu.

     B. 7. B: Iie, o-kyaku-san to hanashi o shite imasu. 8. B: Iie, kopī o shite imasu. 9. B: Iie, repōto o kaite imasu.

VII. c) [(Sumisu-san wa) o-kyaku-san to hanashi o shite imasu.]

Lesson 23

VI.   1. Gurīn-san wa Shibuya ni sunde imasu. Soshite, ABC Fūzu ni tsutomete imasu. 2. Nakamura-san no imō-tosan wa Sapporo ni sunde imasu. Soshite, ginkō ni tsutomete imasu. 3. Chan-san no onēsan wa Honkon ni sunde imasu. Soshite, depāto ni tsutomete imasu.

VIII. 1. Sumisu: Resutoran Tōkyō no jūsho o shitte imasu ka. Suzuki: Hai, shitte imasu. 2. Sumisu: Sapporo-shisha no fakkusu-bangō o shitte imasu ka. Suzuki: Iie, shirimasen.

XI.   03 no 3944 no 6493 desu.

UNIT 11

Lesson 24

III. **A.** 1. Sumisu-san wa bīru ga suki desu. Sukī ga jōzu desu. Nihon-go ga wakarimasu. 2. Chan-san wa kōhī ga suki desu. Dansu ga jōzu desu. Furansu-go ga wakarimasu. 3. Sasaki-san wa wain ga suki desu. Tenisu ga jōzu desu. Chūgoku-go ga wakarimasu.

     B. 1. Sumisu-san wa o-sake ga suki dewa arimasen. Dansu ga jōzu dewa arimasen. Chūgoku-go ga wakarimasen. 2. Chan-san wa bīru ga suki dewa arimasen. Sukī ga jōzu dewa arimasen. Kankoku-go ga wakarimasen. 3. Sasaki-san wa uisukī ga suki dewa arimasen. Gorufu ga jōzu dewa arimasen. Doitsu-gō ga wakarimasen.

     C. 1. Sumisu: Hai, suki desu. Sumisu: Hai, wakarimasu. 2. Chan: Hai, suki desu. Chan: Iie, wakarimasen. 3. Sasaki: Iie, suki dewa arimasen. Sasaki: Hai, wakarimasu.

     D. 1. Nakamura: Iie, jōzu dewa arimasen. 2. Nakamura: Hai, jōzu desu. 3. Nakamura: Iie, jōzu dewa arimasen.

V.   1. Takahashi: Ochiai-san wa piano ga jōzu desu. Jazu ga suki desu. 2. Takahashi: Kojima-san wa suiei ga jōzu desu. Umi ga suki desu. 3. Takahashi: Andō-san wa e ga jōzu desu. Ukiyoe ga suki desu.

VII. Furansu-go

Lesson 25

II.   1. Watashi wa terebi o mitai desu. 2. Watashi wa Takahashi-san ni aitakunai desu. 3. Watashi wa furui kagu o kaitai desu. 4. Watashi wa jūdō o naraitakunai desu.

V.   1. isha: Dō shimashita ka. Chan: Netsu ga 38-do arimasu. 2. isha: Dō shimashita ka. Chan: Nodo ga itai desu. 3. isha: Dō shimashita ka. Chan: Koshi ga itai desu.

VI.   1. A: Watashi wa maishū jogingu o shite imasu. B: Ii desu ne. Watashi mo shitai desu. 2. A: Watashi wa maishū o-cha o naratte imasu. B: Ii desu ne. Watashi mo naraitai desu.

VIII. c)

QUIZ 5 UNITS 10–11

I.   1. ga 2. ni 3. de 4. ga 5. ni

II.   1. shite imasu 2. shitte imasu, shirimasen 3. ikitakatta desu

III.   1. suki desu 2. jōzu dewa arimasen 3. shimasu 4. shimasen

CD SCRIPT FOR EXERCISES

Lesson 1, Exercise V
onna no hito: Sumisu-san wa enjinia desu ka.
Takahashi:　　Iie, bengoshi desu.

Lesson 2, Exercise VIII
onna no hito: Sumimasen. Sumisu-san no denwa-bangō wa nan-ban desu ka.
Takahashi:　　Zero-san no san-yon-go-kyū no kyū-roku-roku-zero desu.
onna no hito: Arigatō gozaimasu.

Lesson 3, Exercise VI
Sumisu:　Sumimasen. Jimu wa nan-ji kara desu ka.
Furonto: 7-ji han kara desu.
Sumisu:　Dōmo arigatō.

Lesson 4, Exercise IX
Sumisu:　　　Are wa bideo kamera desu ka.
mise no hito: Hai.
Sumisu:　　　Ikura desu ka.
mise no hito: 38,000-en desu.

Lesson 5, Exercise VII
Sumisu:　　　Sumimasen. Ano bīru wa doko no desu ka.
mise no hito: Amerika no desu.
Sumisu:　　　Are wa ikura desu ka.
mise no hito: 300-en desu.
Sumisu:　　　Ja, are o 10-pon kudasai.

Lesson 6, Exercise X
Nakamura: Sumisu-san wa asatte doko ni ikimasu ka.
Sumisu:　　Depāto ni ikimasu.
Nakamura: Dare to ikimasu ka.
Sumisu:　　Tomodachi to ikimasu.
Nakamura: Sō desu ka.

Lesson 7, Exercise X
Suzuki: Chan-san wa itsu Ōsaka-shisha ni ikimasu ka.
Chan:　Moku-yōbi ni ikimasu.
Suzuki: Nan de ikimasu ka.
Chan:　Hikōki de ikimasu.
Suzuki: Sō desu ka.

Questions:
1. Chan-san wa itsu Ōsaka-shisha ni ikimasu ka.
2. Chan-san wa nande Ōsaka-shisha ni ikimasu ka.

Lesson 8, Exercise VIII
Ms. Nakamura is talking about her building.

1. 1-kai ni ginkō ga arimasu.
2. 2-kai ni yūbinkyoku ga arimasu.
3. 3-gai ni resutoran ga arimasu.

Lesson 9, Exercise VII
Sumisu: Sumimasen. Chūshajō wa doko desu ka.
onna no hito: Sūpā no tonari desu.
Sumisu: Arigatō gozaimasu.

Lesson 10, Exercise VIII
Chan-san wa do-yōbi ni tomodachi to densha de Kamakura ni ikimashita. Kamakura de ōkii o-tera o mimashita. O-tera no niwa de hiru-gohan o tabemashita.

Lesson 11, Exercise IX
Nakamura: Chan-san wa yoku okāsan ni denwa o shimasu ka.
Chan: Iie, amari shimasen ga, yoku mēru o okurimasu. (**NOTE: Ga** means "but." See Note 1, p. 205)

Lesson 12, Exercise XII
Nakamura: Ashita tomodachi to Hakone ni ikimasu.
Sumisu: Hakone wa donna tokoro desu ka.
Nakamura: Kireina tokoro desu yo.

Lesson 13, Exercise VI
Kinō wa Sumisu-san no tanjōbi deshita. Sumisu-san wa tomodachi ni Nihon-go no hon o moraimashita.

Question: Sumisu-san wa tanjōbi ni tomodachi ni nani o moraimashita ka.

Lesson 14, Exercise V
Suzuki: Chan-san, nichi-yōbi ni nani o shimashita ka.
Chan: Asakusa de o-matsuri o mimashita.
Suzuki: Dō deshita ka.
Chan: Totemo nigiyaka deshita.

Lesson 15, Exercise VII
Suzuki: Sumisu-san, nichi-yōbi ni issho ni Nikkō ni ikimasen ka.
Sumisu: Ee, ikimashō.
Suzuki: Nan de ikimashō ka.
Sumisu: Densha wa dō desu ka.
Suzuki: Ee, sō shimashō. Ja, nichi-yōbi ni.

Lesson 16, Exercise VII
Sumisu: Suzuki-san, Furansu taishikan wa doko ni arimasu ka.
Suzuki: Hiroo desu. Chizu o kakimashō ka.
Sumisu: Ee, onegaishimasu.

Question: Dare ga chizu o kakimasu ka.

Lesson 17, Exercise XI
Nakamura: Chan-san, shūmatsu ni nani o shimasu ka.
Chan:　　Do-yōbi ni Shinjuku ni itte, terebi o kaimasu.
Nakamura: Sō desu ka.

Question: Chan-san wa do-yōbi ni nani o kaimasu ka.

Lesson 18, Exercise VII
Katō:　Chan-san, Takahashi-san ni kaigi no shiryō o fakkusu de okutte kudasai.
Chan: Hai, wakarimashita.

Lesson 19, Exercise IX
Sumisu:　　Sumimasen. Kaisha kara Nozomi Depāto made donogurai kakarimasu ka.
Nakamura: Chikatetsu de 30-pun gurai kakarimasu.
Sumisu:　　Sō desu ka. Arigatō gozaimasu.

Lesson 20, Exercise VII
Sumisu:　　Sumimasen, 3-ji han kara kaigishitsu o tsukattemo ii desu ka.
Nakamura: Hai, dōzo.
Sumisu:　　Arigatō gozaimasu.

Lesson 21, Exercise VI
Katō:　Gogo kara kaigi ga arimasu kara, kaigishitsu no eakon o kesanaide kudasai.
Chan: Hai, wakarimashita.

Lesson 22, Exercise VII
Sasaki: Sumisu-san wa doko desu ka.
Chan:　Ima 3-gai no kaigishitsu de o-kyaku-san to hanashi o shite imasu.
Sasaki: Sō desu ka.

Question: Sumisu-san wa ima nani o shite imasu ka.

Lesson 23, Exercise XI
Sumisu:　　Sumimasen. Resutoran Rōma no denwa-bangō o shitte imasu ka.
Nakamura: Hai. 03-3944-6493 desu.
Sumisu:　　Arigatō gozaimasu.

Question: Resutoran Rōma no denwa-bangō wa nan-ban desu ka.

Lesson 24, Exercise VII
Katō:　　Raishū Furansu no shisha ni ikimasu.
Sumisu: Hitori de ikimasu ka.
Katō:　　Iie, Chan-san to ikimasu. Chan-san wa Furansu-go ga jōzu desu kara.

Lesson 25, Exercise VIII
Nakamura: Sumisu-san, shōrai donna tokoro ni sumitai desu ka.
Sumisu:　　Sō desu ne. Chiisai machi ni sumitai desu.
Nakamura: Sō desu ka.

Japanese-English Glossary

a: oh, 57
ABC Fūzu: ABC Foods, 3
achira: that person over there, 230
agemasu: give, 110, 123, 124
aimasu: meet, 98, 100, 143, 162, 163, 197
aisu-kōhī: ice coffee, 199
aisu-kurīmu: ice cream, 104
akachan: baby, 199
akai (desu): red, 38
Akasaka: Akasaka (district), 182
akemasu: open, 151, 160, 163, 196, 197
amai (desu): sweet, 113, 115
amari . . . -masen: not much, 99, 248–49
Amerika: the United States, 4
Amerika-jin: American (person), 4
anata: you, 3, 7
anata no: your, 10
Andō: Ando (surname), 216
ane: older sister, 214
ani: older brother, 214
ano: that over there (used before a noun), 20, 37
aoi (desu): blue, 37, 38
are: that one over there, 20, 31
arigatō: thank you, 10 → *dōmo*
arimasu: be, exist, 68, 69, 73, 79; have, own, 151; there is/are going to be, 142
aruite: by foot, by walking, 60, 63
arukimasu: walk, 181
asa: morning, 26
asa-gohan: breakfast, 26, 90
Asakusa: Asakusa (district), 118
Asakusa Eki: Asakusa Station, 142
asatte: the day after tomorrow, 52
ashi: leg, foot, 233
ashita: tomorrow, 49, 50, 51
asoko: over there, 78
atama: head, 233
atarashii (desu): new, fresh, 113, 115
atatakai (desu): warm, 235
atsui (desu): hot (of temperature), 113, 115, 133
Azabu: Azabu (district), 182
azukarimasu: take care of, be in charge of, 176; *azukatte kudasai*: please take care of, 176

bā: bar, 93
bāgen-sēru: clearance sale, 132
-bai: cupful, glassful, 112
ban: evening, 26
-ban: number . . ., 58
bangō: number, 10
ban-gohan: dinner, 26, 90
-bansen: platform number, 187
bara: rose, 123
Barentaindē: Valentine's Day, 126
basu: bus, 58
basu-noriba: bus terminal, 79
basutei: bus stop, 85
beddo: bed, 72
benchi: bench, 157
bengoshi: attorney, lawyer, 3, 5
benkyō o shimasu: study, 91
benri desu or *benrina*: convenient, 114, 116
Berurin Mōtāzu: Berlin Motors, 7

bideo: video, 30
bideo-kamera: video camera, 30
bijutsukan: art museum, 164
bīru: beer, 38
bōrupen: ballpoint pen, 35
bōshi: hat, cap, 124
bun: part, 29
Buraun: Brown (surname), 5
burausu: blouse, 124
byōin: hospital, clinic, 79

CD (=shīdī): CD, 30
CD-purēyā: CD player, 30
Chan: Chan (surname), xiii
chekkuin-kauntā: check-in counter, 84
chichi: (my) father, 99
Chichi no hi: Father's Day, 128
chiisai (desu): small, little, 38, 113, 114
chika: basement, 71
chikai (desu): near, 113, 115
chika ikkai: first basement floor, 71
chikaku: vicinity, nearby, 72
chikatetsu: subway, 59, 61
chizu: map, 152
chō: trillion, 29
chokorēto: chocolate, 126
chotto: a little bit, 121; *chotto matte kudasai*: please wait a minute, 121; *chotto o-machi kudasai*: please wait a minute, 136; *chotto yoroshii desu ka*: do you have a moment?, 162
Chūgoku: China, 4
Chūgoku-go: Chinese (language), 226
Chūgoku-jin: Chinese (person), 4
chūrippu: tulip, 123
chūshajō: parking lot, 71
chūsha-kinshi: no parking, 197

daigaku: university, college, 7
daijōbu desu ka: are you all right?, 157
dansu: dancing, 226
dare: who, 8, 14
dare mo . . . -masen: no one, 73
de: by means of, 59; (indicating location), 90, 142; (indicating means of telecommunication or post), 170
de gozaimasu: (humble form of *desu*), 96
deguchi: exit, 198
dejikame: digital camera, 30
demashō ka: shall we leave?, 180; *demasu*: leave, 180, 181
demo: but, 151
demo ii desu ka: is . . . all right?, 36
denki: (electric) light, 164
denki-ya: electronics store, 217
densha: train, 61
denshi-jisho: electronic dictionary, 126
denwa: telephone, 10
denwa-bangō: telephone number, 10
denwa o shimasu: telephone, 88, 98, 100
depāto: department store, 3, 22
deshita: was/were, 2
desu: be, 2, 3, 79
dewa: well then, in any case, 29, 50
dewa/ja arimasen: is/are not, 2, 11
dewa/ja arimasendeshita: was/were not, 2

dō: how, 135; *dō deshita ka*: how was . . . ?, 135; *dō desu ka*: how is . . . ?, 142
-do: degree, 236
doa: door, 153
dōgu: tool, equipment, 155
dō itashimashite: you're welcome, 22
Doitsu: Germany, 4
Doitsu-go: German (language), 226
Doitsu-jin: German (person), 4
doko: where, which place, 41
dōmo: thanks, 175; *dōmo arigatō*: thank you, 10, 26; *dōmo arigatō gozaimashita*: thank you very much, 129; *dōmo arigatō gozaimasu*: thank you very much, 9
donata: who, 8
donna: what kind of, 118
dono: which (used before a noun), 58
donogurai: how long, 180
dore: which (one), 37, 58
dō shimashita ka: what's the matter with you?, 236
dōshite: why, 168
dōyatte: how, in what way, 182
do-yōbi: Saturday, 60
dōzo: please, if you please, 9, 112; *dōzo kochira e*: come right this way, 59
DVD (=dībuidī): DVD, 35

e: painting, picture, 119
e: to, 48
eakon: air conditioner, 153
ee: yes, 9, 140, 149
ehagaki: postcard, 190
eiga: movie, 23
Eigo: English (language), 35
eigyō-bu: sales department, 205
eki: station, 51
ekiin: station employee, 187
empitsu: pencil, 80
-en: yen, 29, 31
enjinia: engineer, 5
erebētā: elevator, 206
esukarētā: escalator, 206

fairu: file, 80
fakkusu: fax, 171
fea: fair, 185
Fuji Kompyūtā: Fuji Computers, 217
Fujisan: Mt. Fuji, 195
-fun (kan): minute(s), 22, 23, 181
funabin: surface mail, 171
Furansu: France, 35
Furansu-go: French (language), 35
Furansu-ryōri: French food, 230
furasshu: flash, 195
furui (desu): old, 113, 115
furonto: the front desk, 26
futari: two people, 80
futatsu: two, 39
futatsu-me: second, 173
futsuka: the second (of the month), 61

ga: (as subject marker), 68; but (conjunctive usage), 170, 205; (instead of *wa*), 58; (used with *suki desu, jōzu desu, itai desu*, etc.), 222

263

English-Japanese Glossary

Note: Idiomatic expressions have been omitted, as have counters, particles that do not translate into English, certain proper nouns, and some of the words listed in the Appendixes of this book.

The following abbreviations are used in this glossary:
adj. adjective
n. noun
v. verb

about: (of time) *goro*, 86; (of period, price, amount, etc.) *gurai*, 120
above: *ue*, 72
add: *iremasu*, 197
address: *go-jūsho*, 174; *jūsho*, 10
after: *no ato de*, 162
afternoon: *hiru*, 23
again: *mata*, 132
ahead: *saki*, 171
air conditioner: *eakon*, 153
airmail: *kōkūbin*, 171
airplane: *hikōki*, 61
airport: *kūkō*, 51
all right: *kekkō desu*, 36; *yoroshii (desu)*, 162
alone: *hitori de*, 50
already: *mō*, 207, 211
also: *mo* (particle), 29; *sorekara*, 170
a.m.: *gozen*, 23
and: *soshite*, 216; *ya* (particle), 70
anniversary: *kinembi*, 128
apartment: *manshon*, 175
approximately: *gurai*, 120
April: *shi-gatsu*, 61
arm: *te*, 233
arrive: *tsukimasu*, 180, 181
art museum: *bijutsukan*, 164
ask: *kikimasu*, 98, 162, 163
at: *ni* (particle), 59, 68
attorney: *bengoshi*, 3, 5
August: *hachi-gatsu*, 61

baby: *akachan*, 199
back: (of body) *senaka*, 233; (indicating position) *ushiro*, 72
bad: *warui (desu)*, 132, 133
baggage: *nimotsu*, 153
bakery: *pan-ya*, 79
ballpoint pen: *bōrupen*, 35
bank: *ginkō*, 7, 22
bar: *bā*, 93
baseball: *yakyū*, 224
basement: *chika*, 71
be: *arimasu*, 68, 69, 73, 79, 142, *desu*, 2, 3, 79; *imasu*, 68, 73, 178; *irasshaimasu*, 136
because: *kara* (particle), 98, 142
bed: *beddo*, 72
before: *mae*, 72, 171; *no mae ni*, 163
behind: *ushiro*, 72
belly: *onaka*, 233
below: *shita*, 72
bench: *benchi*, 157
beverage: *o-nomimono*, 105
big: *ōkii (desu)*, 38, 110, 113, 114
bill: *o-kanjō*, 106
billion: *jū-oku*, 29
birthday: *tanjōbi*, 62
black: *kuroi (desu)*, 38
blanket: *mōfu*, 176

blouse: *burausu*, 124
blue: *aoi (desu)*, 37, 38
book: *hon*, 11
bookstore: *hon-ya*, 79
boring: *tsumaranai (desu)*, 132, 133
bottom: *shita*, 72
bouquet: *hanataba*, 123
boy: *otoko no ko*, 81
branch office: *shisha*, 51
bread: *pan*, 79
break: *yasumi*, 23
breakfast: *asa-gohan*, 26, 90
briefcase: *kaban*, 72
bring: *mottekimasu*, 171, 172
brochure: *panfuretto*, 189
brother: *ani, onīsan, otōto, otōtosan*, 214
buckwheat noodle shop: *soba-ya*, 77
bus: *basu*, 58
business card: *kādo*, 193; *meishi*, 9
business trip: *shutchō*, 57
bus stop: *basutei*, 85
bus terminal: *basu-noriba*, 79
busy: *isogashii (desu)*, 113, 115
but: *demo*, 151; *ga* (particle), 170, 205
buy: *kaimasu*, 88, 91, 92, 160, 163, 178
by: *de* (particle), 59, 170; by (the time): *made ni*, 174
by all means: *zehi*, 140, 149
by what means: *nan de*, 60

cake: *kēki*, 115
call: *yobimasu*, 168
cap: *bōshi*, 124
car: *kuruma*, 41, 61
carnation: *kānēshon*, 123
carry: (on one's shoulders) *katsugimasu*, 151; (in one's hands) *mochimasu*, 151
cart: *kāto*, 84
catalog: *katarogu*, 170, 190
CD: *CD (=shīdī)*, 30
CD player: *CD-purēyā*, 30
cell phone: *keitai*, 11
certainly: *zehi*, 140, 149
chair: *isu*, 72
check: *o-kanjō*, 106
check-in counter: *chekkuin-kauntā*, 84
child: *ko*, 81; *kodomo*, 214; *okosan*, 214
chocolate: *chokorēto*, 126
class: *jugyō*, 152; *kurasu*, 235
clean: (adj.) *kirei desu* or *kireina*, 110, 112, 114, 116, 133; (v.) *sōji o shimasu*, 206, 207
clearance sale: *bāgen-sēru*, 132
client: *o-kyaku-san*, 191
clinic: *byōin*, 79
clock: *tokei*, 11
close: *shimemasu*, 151, 163, 196, 197
coat: *kōto*, 124
coffee: *kōhī*, 43, 90

coffee cup: *kōhī-kappu*, 43
cold: *samui (desu)*, 113, 115, 133
college: *daigaku*, 7
color: *iro*, 122
come: *kimasu*, 48, 50, 51, 52, 160, 162, 163, 178, 196, 197
company: *kaisha*, 9
computer: *pasokon*, 30
concert: *konsāto*, 132
concert hall: *hōru*, 147
condominium: *manshon*, 175
conference: *kaigi*, 23
conference room: *kaigishitsu*, 83
convenience store: *kombini*, 78
convenient: *benri desu* or *benrina*, 114, 116
cooking: *ryōri*, 105
cooking school: *kukkingu-sukūru*, 232
corner: *kado*, 171
country, my: *kuni*, 105
courier service: *takuhaibin*, 171
cream puff: *shūkurīmu*, 44
credit card: *kādo*, 36
cuisine: *ryōri*, 105
cup: *kappu*, 43
curry: *karē*, 115
customer: *o-kyaku-san*, 191

dancing: *dansu*, 226
data: *shiryō*, 173
datebook: *techō*, 17
daughter: *musume, musumesan*, 214
day: (period of) *-ka (kan), -nichi (kan)*, 181; (of the month) *-nichi*, 61; (of the week) *-yōbi*, 60
day after tomorrow, the: *asatte*, 52
December: *jūni-gatsu*, 61
decimal point: *ten*, 29
degree: *-do*, 236
delicious: *oishii (desu)*, 98, 113, 115, 133
deliver: *todokemasu*, 171, 172
department store: *depāto*, 3, 22
dictionary: *jisho*, 35
difficult: *muzukashii (desu)*, 113, 115
digital camera: *dejikame*, 30
dinner: *ban-gohan*, 26, 90
do: *shimasu*, 89, 92, 143, 160, 162, 163, 178, 196, 197
doctor: *isha*, 200
dog: *inu*, 95
door: *doa*, 153
draft beer: *nama-bīru*, 105
drawer: *hikidashi*, 75
drink: *nomimasu*, 88, 91, 92, 160, 162, 163, 196, 197
driver: *untenshu*, 58
drugstore: *kusuri-ya*, 79
DVD: *DVD (=dībuidī)*, 35

make: *tsukurimasu*, 206, 207
make a photocopy: *kopī o shimasu*, 156
male: *otoko*, 73
man: *otoko*, *otoko no hito*, 73
many: *takusan*, 81
map: *chizu*, 152
maple syrup: *mēpuru-shiroppu*, 218
March: *san-gatsu*, 61
marketing: *hambai*, 162
marriage: *kekkon*, 128
match: *shiai*, 142
May: *go-gatsu*, 61
mayonnaise: *mayonēzu*, 199
meal: *gohan*, 26
mechanical pencil: *shāpupenshiru*, 35
medicine: *kusuri*, 79
meet: *aimasu*, 98, 100, 143, 162, 163, 197
meeting: *kaigi*, 23
menu: *menyū*, 173
merchandise: *shōhin*, 170
middle: *naka*, 72
milk: *miruku*, 90
million: *hyaku-man*, 29
mine: *watashi no*, 151
minute(s): *-fun/-pun (kan)*, 22, 181
mobile phone: *keitai*, 11
Monday: *getsu-yōbi*, 60
money: *o-kane*, 154
month: *-gatsu*, 61; (period of) *-kagetsu*, 181
more: *mō*, 17
morning: *asa*, 26
mother: *haha*, *okāsan,,* 99
movie: *eiga*, 23
Mr., Mrs., Ms., Miss: *-san*, 3
Mt. Fuji: *Fujisan*, 195
much: *takusan*, 81
music: *ongaku*, 92
musical: *myūjikaru*, 185
my: *watashi no*, 9

name: *namae*, 9; *o-namae*, 96
near: *chikai (desu)*, 113, 115
nearby: *chikaku*, 72
necklace: *nekkuresu*, 124
necktie: *nekutai*, 124
new: *atarashii (desu)*, 113, 115
newspaper: *shimbun*, 11
next: *tsugi*, 172
next month: *raigetsu*, 51
next to: *tonari*, 72
next week: *raishū*, 51
next year: *rainen*, 51
nine: *kokonotsu*, 39; *ku*, *kyū*, 10
ninety: *kyūjū*, 23
ninth, the: (of the month) *kokonoka*, 61
no: *iie*, 2, 6, 48, 204
no one: *dare mo . . . -masen*, 73
no parking: *chūsha-kinshi*, 197
north exit: *kitaguchi*, 143
no smoking: *kin'en*, 197
notebook: *techō*, 17
no thank you: *kekkō desu*, 112
nothing: *nani mo . . . -masen*, 73
not much: *amari . . . -masen*, 99, 248–49
not yet: *mada*, 211
November: *jūichi-gatsu*, 61

now: *ima*, 21
number: *bangō*, 10

ocean: *umi*, 229
October: *jū-gatsu*, 61
of: *no* (particle), 3, 4, 9
office, the: *kaisha*, 9
old: *furui (desu)*, 113, 115
on: *ni* (particle), 59, 68
one: *hitotsu*, 38, 39; *ichi*, 10
one more time: *mō ichi-do*, 17
one person: *hitori*, 80
one time: *ichi-do*, 17
open: *akemasu*, 151, 160, 163, 196, 197
over there: *asoko*, 78
own: *arimasu*, 151

painful: *itai (desu)*, 222, 234
painting: *e*, 119
pamphlet: *panfuretto*, 189
park: (n.) *kōen*, 51; (v.) *tomemasu*, 170, 172, 196
parking lot: *chūshajō*, 71
part: *bun*, 29
party: *pātī*, 23
peach: *momo*, 130
pen: *pen*, 74
pencil: *empitsu*, 80
person: *hito*, 22 → *-jin*
person over there, that: *achira*, 230
photograph: *shashin*, 151
piano: *piano*, 229
pizza: *piza*, 172
place: *tokoro*, 118
planner: *techō*, 17
platform: *hōmu*, 143
play golf: *gorufu o shimasu*, 95
please: *dōzo*, 9, 112; (get me . . .) *onegaishimasu*, 8, 96
p.m.: *gogo*, 22
pocket: *poketto*, 75
police box: *kōban*, 79
pool: *pūru*, 26
portable shrine: *o-mikoshi*, 151
post: *yūbin*, 173
postcard: *ehagaki*, 190; *hagaki*, 38
post office: *yūbinkyoku*, 22
practice: *renshū o shimasu*, 231
present: *purezento*, 128
president: (of a company) *shachō*, 101
pretty: *kirei desu* or *kireina*, 110, 112, 114, 116, 133
product: *shōhin*, 170
put: *okimasu*, 194
put in: *iremasu*, 197

quiet: *shizuka desu* or *shizukana*, 114, 116, 133

racket: *raketto*, 155
radio: *rajio*, 30
read: *yomimasu*, 88, 91, 92, 160, 162, 163, 178
really: *hontō ni*, 120
receipt: *ryōshūsho*, 106
receive: *moraimasu*, 110, 122, 123, 124
reception desk: *uketsuke*, 8, 71
recorded guide: *iyahōn-gaido*, 190

red: *akai (desu)*, 38
refrigerator: *reizōko*, 72
relax: *yasumimasu*, 157, 190
report: *repōto*, 164
reservation: *yoyaku*, 96
rest: (n.) *yasumi*, 23; (v.) *yasumimasu*, 157, 190
restaurant: *mise*, 28; *resutoran*, 22
restroom: *o-tearai*, 71
return: *kaerimasu*, 48, 51, 52, 160, 162, 163, 178, 197
right: *migi*, 171
right?: *ne* (particle), 50
right away: *sugu*, 170
ring: *yubiwa*, 124
romanized Japanese: *rōmaji*, 194
room service: *rūmu-sābisu*, 176
rose: *bara*, 123

sake: *sake*, 90
salad: *sarada*, 90
sales: *hambai*, 162
sales department: *eigyō-bu*, 205
sample: *sampuru*, 170
sandwich: *sandoitchi*, 90
Saturday: *do-yōbi*, 60
say: *iimasu*, 170, 172
scarf: *sukāfu*, 124
school: *gakkō*, 101
scissors: *hasami*, 80
Scotch tape: *sero-tēpu*, 80
sea: *umi*, 229
second: *futatsu-me*, 173
second, the: (of the month) *futsuka*, 61
secretary: *hisho*, 5
see: *mimasu*, 88, 89, 91, 92, 143, 160, 162, 163, 178, 197
sell: *urimasu*, 204, 213, 214; *utte imasu*, 204, 213, 214
send: *okurimasu*, 98, 100
September: *ku-gatsu*, 61
seven: *nana*, *shichi*, 10; *nanatsu*, 39
seventh, the: (of the month) *nanoka*, 61
seventy: *nanajū*, 23
Shinto shrine: *jinja*, 70
shop: (v.) *kaimono o shimasu*, 91; (n.) *mise*, 28; (n.) *-ya*, 77
shoulder: *kata*, 233
show: (v.) *misemasu*, 172, 178, 197; (v.) *oshiemasu*, 170, 172; (n.) *shō*, 132
sister: *ane*, *onēsan*, *imōto*, *imōtosan*, 214
six: *muttsu*, 39; *roku*, 10
sixth, the: (of the month) *muika*, 61
sixty: *rokujū*, 23
skiing: *sukī*, 224
skilled, be: *jōzu desu*, 222, 224, 225
small: *chiisai (desu)*, 38, 113, 114
smoke (a cigarette): (*tabako o*) *suimasu*, 189, 190, 196
snow: *yuki*, 142
snow festival: *yuki-matsuri*, 142
soccer: *sakkā*, 142, 224
sofa: *sofā*, 72
sometimes: *tokidoki*, 98
son: *musuko*, *musukosan*, 214
soon: *sugu*, 170
soup: *sūpu*, 90
south exit: *minamiguchi*, 143

souvenir: *o-miyage*, 124
spa: *supa*, 70
sport(s): *supōtsu*, 94
stairs: *kaidan*, 206
stand up: *tachimasu*, 196, 197
stapler: *hotchikisu*, 80
station: *eki*, 51
station employee: *ekiin*, 187
steak: *sutēki*, 93
stomach: *onaka*, 233
stop: *tomemasu*, 170, 172, 196
store: *mise*, 28
straight ahead: *massugu*, 171
student: *gakusei*, 5
subway: *chikatetsu*, 59, 61
sugar: *satō*, 199
suit: *niaimasu*, 129
summer: *natsu*, 62
summer vacation: *natsu-yasumi*, 62
sumo wrestling: *sumō*, 144
Sunday: *nichi-yōbi*, 60
supermarket: *sūpā*, 22
surface mail: *funabin*, 171
sushi restaurant: *sushi-ya*, 103
sweater: *sētā*, 75
sweet: *amai* (*desu*), 113, 115
sweets: *o-kashi*, 112
swimming: *suiei*, 224

table: *tēburu*, 72
take: (time) *kakarimasu*, 180, 181; (a photograph) (*shashin o*) *torimasu*, 151, 172, 196
take care: *ki o tsukete*, 162
take care of: *azukarimasu*, 176
talk: *hanashi o shimasu*, 146, 206, 207
tangerine: *mikan*, 42
tasty: *oishii* (*desu*), 98, 113, 115, 133
taxi: *takushī*, 61
taxi stand: *takushī-noriba*, 79
tea: *kōcha*, 90
tea ceremony: *o-cha*, 233
teach: *oshiemasu*, 170, 172
tedious: *tsumaranai* (*desu*), 132, 133
telephone: (n.) *denwa*, 10; (v.) *denwa o shimasu*, 88, 98, 100
telephone number: *denwa-bangō*, 10
television: *terebi*, 30
tell: *oshiemasu*, 170, 172
temple: *o-tera*, 69
ten: *jū*, 23; *tō*, 38, 39
ten billion: *hyaku-oku*, 29
ten million: *sen-man*, 29
tennis: *tenisu*, 224
tennis court: *tenisu-kōto*, 95
tenth, the: (of the month) *tōka*, 61
ten thousand: *ichi-man, man*, 29, 30
thank you: (thanks) *dōmo*, 175; (thank you) *dōmo arigatō*, 10, 26; (thank you very much) *dōmo arigatō* (*gozaimasu/ gozaimashita*), 9, 129
that: *sono*, 20, 37, 232–33
that one: *sore*, 20, 28
that one over there: *are*, 20, 31
that over there: *ano*, 20, 37
there: *sochira*, 49
third, the: (of the month) *mikka*, 61
thirty: *sanjū*, 23

this: *kono*, 20, 39
this coming: *kondo*, 105
this evening: *komban*, 155
this month: *kongetsu*, 51
this one: *kochira*, 3; *kore*, 9, 20
this week: *konshū*, 51
this year: *kotoshi*, 51
thousand: *sen*, 29, 30
three: *mittsu*, 38, 39; *san*, 10, 38
three people: *san-nin*, 80
throat: *nodo*, 233
Thursday: *moku-yōbi*, 60
ticket: *kippu*, 124
ticket gate: *kaisatsuguchi*, 142
time: *jikan*, 152
to: *e* (particle), 48; *made* (particle), 175; *ni* (particle), 48, 50, 88, 180
today: *kyō*, 51
together: *issho ni*, 50
together with: *to* (particle), 50
tomorrow: *ashita*, 49, 50, 51
too: *mo*, 29
tool: *dōgu*, 155
tooth: *ha*, 233
top: *ue*, 72
tote bag: *kaban*, 72
towel: *taoru*, 43
town: *machi*, 235
traffic signal: *shingō*, 171
train: *densha*, 61
train line: *-sen*, 187
travel: *ryokō*, 62
travel agency: *ryokō-gaisha*, 186
trillion: *chō, it-chō*, 29
trip: *ryokō*, 62
true: *hontō*, 151
T-shirt: *T-shatsu*, 37, 38
Tuesday: *ka-yōbi*, 60
tulip: *chūrippu*, 123
turn: *magarimasu*, 170, 172
turn off: *keshimasu*, 151, 160, 163, 178, 197
turn on: *tsukemasu*, 151, 163
twentieth, the: (of the month) *hatsuka*, 61
twenty: *nijū*, 23
twenty-fourth, the: (of the month) *nijūyokka*, 61
two: *futatsu*, 39; *ni*, 10
two people: *futari*, 80

ukiyoe: *ukiyoe*, 189
umbrella: *kasa*, 11
under: *shita*, 72
understand: *wakarimasu*, 96, 222, 224, 225
university: *daigaku*, 7
until: *made*, 22
use: *tsukaimasu*, 170, 189, 190, 196

vase: *kabin*, 122
vegetable: *yasai*, 95
vegetable juice: *yasai-jūsu*, 95
very: *totemo*, 112
very much: *taihen*, 213
vicinity: *chikaku*, 72
video: *bideo*, 30
video camera: *bideo-kamera*, 30

wait: *machimasu*, 160, 171, 172, 178

walk: *arukimasu*, 181
wallet: *saifu*, 74
warm: *atatakai* (*desu*), 235
wasabi: *wasabi*, 197
was/were: *deshita*, 2
was/were not: *dewa/ja arimasen deshita*, 2
watch: *tokei*, 11
water: *mizu*, 75
waterfall: *taki*, 77
we: *watashitachi*, 132
weather: *tenki*, 120
wedding anniversary: *kekkon-kinembi*, 128
Wednesday: *sui-yōbi*, 60
weekend: *shūmatsu*, 89
week(s): *-shūkan*, 181
well: *yoku*, 129
well then: *dewa*, 29, 50; *ja*, 29
west exit: *nishiguchi*, 143
what: *nan*, 13; *nani*, 69
what day: (of the month) *nan-nichi*, 62; (of the week) *nan-yōbi*, 62
what kind of: *donna*, 118
what month: *nan-gatsu*, 62
what number: *nan-ban*, 15
what time: *nan-ji*, 22
when: *itsu*, 54
where: *doko*, 41
which: *dono*, 58; *dore*, 37, 58
whiskey: *uisukī*, 226
white: *shiroi* (*desu*), 175
who: *donata*, 8; *dare*, 8, 14
why: *dōshite*, 168
wife: *kanai, tsuma*, 99; *okusan*, 95, 99
window: *mado*, 153
wine: *wain*, 43
with: *to* (particle), 50
woman: *onna, onna no hito*, 22
wonderful: *sutekina*, 231
work: (n.) *shigoto*, 23; (v.) *shigoto o shimasu*, 91
worry: *ki ni shimasu*, 200
write: *kakimasu*, 98, 100, 160, 162, 163, 178, 197

year: *-nen*, 60; (period of) *-nen* (*kan*), 181
yen: *-en*, 29, 31
yes: *ee*, 9, 140, 149; *hai*, 2, 6, 48, 140, 149, 204
yesterday: *kinō*, 51
you: *anata*, 3, 7
your: *anata no*, 10

zero: *rei, zero*, 10

Index

（改訂第3版）コミュニケーションのための日本語 第1巻 ローマ字版テキスト
JAPANESE FOR BUSY PEOPLE I: Revised 3rd Edition, Romanized Version

2006年 6 月　第 1 刷発行
2008年12月　第 5 刷発行

著　者　　社団法人 国際日本語普及協会
挿　画　　角 愼作
発行者　　富田 充
発行所　　講談社インターナショナル株式会社
　　　　　〒112-8652 東京都文京区音羽 1-17-14
　　　　　電話　03-3944-6493（編集部）
　　　　　　　　03-3944-6492（営業部・業務部）
　　　　　ホームページ　www.kodansha-intl.com
印刷・製本所　大日本印刷株式会社

落丁本・乱丁本は購入書店名を明記のうえ、講談社インターナショナル業務部宛にお送りください。
送料小社負担にてお取替えします。なお、この本についてのお問い合わせは、編集部宛にお願いいた
します。本書の無断複写（コピー）、転載は著作権法の例外を除き、禁じられています。

定価はカバーに表示してあります。

© 社団法人 国際日本語普及協会 2006
Printed in Japan
ISBN 978-4-7700-3008-5